WHEN THE MONEY RUNS OUT

WHEN THE MONEY RUNS OUT

THE END OF WESTERN AFFLUENCE

STEPHEN D. KING

YALE UNIVERSITY PRESS
NEW HAVEN AND LONDON

For information about this and other Yale University Press publications, please contact:
U.S. Office: sales.press@yale.edu   yalebooks.com
Europe Office: sales@yaleup.co.uk   www.yalebooks.co.uk

Set in Minion by IDSUK (DataConnection) Ltd
Printed in the United States of America

Library of Congress Control Number 2013935708

ISBN 978-0-300-19052-6

A catalogue record for this book is available from the British Library.

10 9 8 7 6 5 4 3 2
2017 2016 2015 2014 2013

CONTENTS

To Yvonne, Helena, Olivia and Sophie

ACKNOWLEDGEMENTS

Thanks must go first and foremost to those who provided detailed comments on the manuscript. I am particularly grateful to John Llewellyn, Peter Hennessy (or, to give him his full title, Baron Hennessy of Nympsfield), Chris Brown-Humes and Karen Ward for their extraordinary generosity in reading drafts of the entire book, in the process saving me from otherwise inevitable logical or factual embarrassment. Diane Coyle was a source of inspiration when the book was in its planning stages. Later, as she launched her own quest into the usefulness of economics, she encouraged me to think more deeply about the relationship between economics and history (her edited book *What's the Use of Economics?* is essential reading for anyone wondering how to rebuild the reputation of our profession).

Colleagues and friends have been important sources of support throughout. In particular, my conversations with David Bloom, Richard Cookson, William Keegan, Sir Richard Lambert, John Lipsky, Rachel Lomax, Gerard Lyons, Stephen Macklow-Smith, George Magnus, Robbie Millen, Peter Oppenheimer, Alec Russell and Anne Spackman have been inspiring and entertaining in equal measure. I have benefited from many hundreds of meetings with HSBC clients who have, at all times, kept me on my toes. I should also mention the dozens of policy-makers who have offered me candid views on the economic challenges ahead but who, perhaps, would prefer not to be named!

My economic thinking has been honed thanks to my involvement with fellow economists in a variety of different spheres, including regular meetings at the Bank for International Settlements in Basel, the Oesterreichische Kontrollbank AG (OeKB) in Vienna and the Accumulation Society in London. Although we have rather different views, I'm grateful to Richard Layard (Baron Layard of Highgate) for having invited me to join a panel debate on 'Stimulus versus Austerity' at the Houses of Parliament, chaired by Evan Davis. The other members of the panel – Paul Krugman, Jonathan Portes and Bridget Rosewell – helped clarify some of the thinking contained in chapter 5.

As with my last book, I owe a huge debt of gratitude to Phoebe Clapham at Yale University Press, a truly brilliant editor who is never afraid to tell me when something just doesn't work. I am also, as ever, enormously grateful to Heather Nathan and Katie Harris.

At HSBC, Stuart Gulliver and Samir Assaf were, again, incredibly supportive of my book-writing ambitions, encouraging me to take time off to pursue my quest. I offer thanks to Stuart Parkinson and Michelle Nash for organizing my sabbatical with the minimum of fuss. Once again, my economics team has performed in exemplary fashion: special thanks go to Janet Henry and Madhur Jha, who contributed to an incredibly high standard of economic analysis in my absence. I also acknowledge the help and support of Pierre Goad, Charles Naylor, Jezz Farr, Lisa Baitup and Fiona McClymont. Nic Mason and Debbie Falcus have kept me sane throughout, while the superb University of Bath students have provided me with much-needed statistical assistance.

Acknowledgements

Finally, and most importantly, I am hugely grateful for the amazing support provided by my wonderful family. My wife, Yvonne, and my three daughters, Helena, Olivia and Sophie, have at all times offered understanding, patience and love. For my children's sake, I can only hope that the recommendations at the end of this book are heeded.

The best laid schemes o' Mice an' Men,
Gang aft agley,
An' lea'e us nought but grief an' pain,
For promis'd joy!

Robert Burns, 'To a Mouse' (1785)

WHATEVER HAPPENED TO THE DECADES OF PLENTY?

I count myself as one of the last of the so-called baby boomer generation. We were the lucky ones. Over the years, we enjoyed extraordinary increases in living standards. Born in 1963, I am sadly a bit too young to have experienced at first hand the Beatles, Jimi Hendrix and the Summer of Love but, economically, my birth couldn't have been better timed. In the first ten years of my life, per capita incomes in the United Kingdom – adjusted for inflationary distortions – rose around 37 per cent. By the time I reached my twenties, per capita incomes had risen a further 13 per cent. Over the following ten years, incomes went up another 29 per cent. And, as I settled down to celebrate my fortieth birthday, incomes had risen a further 36 per cent. All told, in the first four decades of my existence, per capita incomes in the UK almost tripled.[1]

As I approach my fiftieth birthday, however, something seems to have gone horribly wrong. Over the last decade, per capita incomes in the UK have risen a mere 4 per cent. Other developed countries find themselves in more or less the same boat. Some, including the United States, have done a bit better. Others, notably those in southern Europe, have fared a lot worse. Most, however, have performed poorly relative to their own histories. The economic dynamism that provided the backdrop to my formative years has gone, replaced by what increasingly appears to be an enduring – and distinctly unappealing – era of stagnation. Even as China, India and other parts of the emerging world continue to press ahead, the West has lost its way: indeed, it is now in danger of entering its second 'lost decade'. For my children – and for the children of millions of other baby boomers – it is hardly an encouraging picture.[2]

This is no ordinary period of economic setback. The recessions of my childhood and my early adulthood were extraordinarily painful affairs both for nations as a whole and, on a personal level, for my own family: in Thatcherism's darkest days, my father was unemployed for many months. Even during the deepest recessions, however, there was always the hope of subsequent recovery. Long-term economic growth was supposedly God-given. Recessions were merely annoying interruptions, blamed variously on policy-making incompetence, excessive union power, short-sighted financial institutions, lazy managers and nasty oil shocks.

Our modern era of economic stagnation is a fundamentally different proposition. Many of the factors that led to such scintillating rates of economic expansion in the Western world in earlier decades are no longer working their magic: the forces of globalization are in retreat, the boomers are ageing, women are thankfully better represented in the workforce,[3] wages are being squeezed as competition from the emerging superpowers hots up and, as those superpowers demand a bigger share of the world's scarce resources, Westerners are forced to pay more for food and energy.

In the 1990s, it looked for a while as though new technologies might overcome these constraints. We hoped our economies would still be able to expand thanks to the impact of technology on productivity. The story didn't last. The technology bubble burst in 2000. Fearing the onset of a Japanese-style stagnation, Western policy-makers pulled out all the stops: interest rates plunged, taxes were cut and public spending was boosted. Yet, even before the onset of the subprime crisis in 2007, it looked as though these policies had led only to a serious misallocation of resources: too much money was pouring into housing and financial services (and, particularly across Europe, into public spending) and not enough into productive investment. The underlying rate of economic growth began to slow.

Following the failure of Lehman Brothers in September 2008, Western economies seemed to be heading for a repeat of the 1930s Great Depression. In response, policy-makers offered even more stimulus. Alongside interest rate cuts and fiscal support to an ailing financial sector, they even began to pursue so-called 'unconventional' monetary policies. Thankfully, with one or two unfortunate exceptions in the eurozone, there has been no repeat – at least, not yet – of the total economic and financial collapse of the 1930s.

Yet, for all the stimulus on offer, the growth rates of old are now no more than a distant memory. By the standards of past recoveries, economic growth remains pitifully weak. Credit systems are partially frozen. Levels of economic activity in the major Western economies are between 7 and 15 per cent lower than forecast before the onset of the financial crisis. The West appears to be suffering a structural deterioration in economic performance. Economists, politicians and the media insist, however, in analysing the problem in old-fashioned cyclical terms, primarily through the 'stimulus versus austerity' debate.

Oddly, the protagonists on both sides believe in much the same thing, namely that the appropriate macroeconomic policies will ultimately deliver a return to the growth rates of old. It just so happens – as is often the case in the economics profession – that the two sides fundamentally disagree over the necessary policies.

Those in favour of stimulus believe that, without a sizeable shot in the arm through a loosening of fiscal policy, households and companies will continue to repay debt, hoard cash and save rather than spend, condemning economies to years of contraction. Those in favour of austerity fear that, in the absence of appropriate and credible fiscal consolidation, high and rising levels of government debt will eventually spark a financial crisis, leading to interest rate spikes, currency wobbles and stock-market meltdowns. Both sides believe in economic recovery. Each happens to think that the opposing view is totally wrong.

What, however, if *both* sides are wrong? What if both sides suffer from what I call an 'optimism bias'? Thanks to Reinhart and Rogoff, we know that, in the aftermath of major financial crises, the subsequent recovery can be long and arduous.[4] This, however, is a financial crisis without parallel. Never before have we seen so many economies so weak at the same time[5] and never before have we seen a global financial system so badly damaged.

Some are beginning to ask whether the West will ever regain its former poise. In 2012, Robert J. Gordon, an American economist, asked a very simple question: 'Is US Economic Growth Over?'[6] Even with continued innovation – which was by no means a certainty – Gordon concluded that 'the US faces six headwinds that are in the process of dragging long-term growth to half or less of the 1.9 percent annual rate experienced between 1860 and 2007. These include demography, education, inequality, globalization, energy/environment, and the overhang of consumer and government debt.' And it's not just those whose crystal balls claim to offer very long-run predictions who are having doubts about the underlying rate of economic growth. In a November 2012 speech, Ben Bernanke, the Chairman of the Federal Reserve, noted that 'the accumulating evidence does appear consistent with the financial crisis and the associated recession having reduced the potential growth rate of our economy somewhat during the past few years.'[7] Pimco, a major California-based financial company, raised the possibility in 2009 of a 'new normal', a persistent period of lower 'trend' growth than we've experienced before.[8]

Of course, these can all be readily dismissed as no more than Cassandra-like predictions of a less bountiful future. Who, after all, knows what sort of technological innovation might materialize in coming decades? Our disturbing early twenty-first century reality of continuing stagnation cannot, however, be so easily ignored. Yet we haven't even begun to think about the consequences for society of a world in which levels of activity are persistently much lower than we all-too-casually used to assume.

Without reasonable growth, we cannot meet the entitlements we created for ourselves during the years of plenty. We have promised ourselves no end of riches, from pensions through to health care, and from education through to big stock-market gains. These promises can only be met, however, if our economies continue to expand at a rate we've become accustomed to. Stagnation chips away at our entitlements, bit by bit.

Meanwhile, we are now far removed from the 'push button' economic policies that governed the Western world before the onset of the financial crisis, when a tweak in interest rates in one direction or the other would be good enough to keep an economy on an even keel. Economic policy is no longer for the technocrats. It has become inherently political. To understand the consequences of this change, I have gone back through history, uncovering periods when monetary decisions were politically charged, when economic shocks upset the political applecart, when a desire to stick to the conventional thinking of the time led to acts of rebellion and when nations simply ran out of money.

There is much to be gained from economic and political history: it is such a shame that so little of it is taught to budding economists working their way through their university degrees. History may not repeat itself but it is a brilliant way of highlighting issues that modern-day economists have, foolishly, brushed to one side. And it offers a sobering reminder of the risks associated with enduring economic disappointment: inequality, nationalism, racism, revolution and warfare are, it seems, the 'default' settings when economies persistently fail to deliver the goods.

Put simply, our societies are not geared for a world of very low growth. Our attachment to the Enlightenment idea of ongoing progress – a reflection of persistent post-war economic success – has left us with little knowledge or understanding of worlds in which rising prosperity is no longer guaranteed.

We have arrogantly ignored the experiences of countries like Argentina and Japan, nations that have suffered from persistent economic stagnation, arguing that they are, somehow, special cases, the economic equivalent of genetic mutations that have no relevance for ourselves. Yet the gathering evidence suggests that, like those two once-successful economic powerhouses, the West has lost the ability to grow.

Without growth, social and political strains will surely emerge. Already, there are more than enough battles taking place in response to weak fiscal positions. The southern states within the eurozone appear to be on the road to perdition, the UK has failed to deliver on its fiscal promises, Republicans and Democrats in the US cannot agree on the appropriate budgetary model and Japanese government debt appears to be spiralling out of control.

None of this is surprising. It is rare for governments to plan on the basis of anything other than an extrapolation of past trends. Economic performance in the 1980s and, with the exception of Japan, the 1990s gave rise to a mixture of commitments – low taxes, generous welfare benefits and large increases in public spending – that could be afforded only so long as the economic goose kept laying golden eggs. Unfortunately, at the beginning of the twenty-first century, the goose became, at best, menopausal.

These issues, however, only scratch the surface. With ten years already of weaker than expected growth, the claims we all make on increasingly limited resources simply do not add up. Tensions that already exist between the world's creditor and debtor nations thanks to, for example, the Greek financial crisis will only escalate in the years ahead. Those who want their money back will only push harder to be repaid. Those who have borrowed will increasingly struggle to keep their creditors happy. Strains between the generations will surely increase. With the baby boomers heading into retirement fully expecting a combination of reasonable living standards and generous medical support, the young may struggle to make ends meet, faced with a mixture of higher education costs, more expensive housing and higher indebtedness. And, after thirty years of dramatic increases in income inequality in the Western world, economic stagnation threatens to destabilize an already tense relationship between rich and poor.

With stagnation comes a breakdown of trust. One person's gain is another's loss. The cooperative arrangements that typically characterize a period of economic expansion begin to fall by the wayside, threatening to lock in stagnation for the long run.

Policy-makers are understandably focused on avoiding the next disaster – no one, after all, wants another financial crisis – but they are in danger of losing sight of the need for growth. As part of the process of 'disaster-avoidance', each country is intent on minimizing its own losses even though, collectively, such actions increase the risks to the economic system as a whole. An unseemly cocktail of short-sighted policies, risk minimization and politically convenient scapegoating threatens to lock in persistently low economic growth, increasing the danger of political and social disaster.

The title of this book should be taken for what it is: a turn of phrase, not the literal truth. As those who've manned the printing presses for countries succumbing to hyperinflation know only too well, paper money never actually runs out. Money can always be created and, if necessary, dropped from the sky out of helicopters or other suitable flying machines. It's increasingly clear, however, that no amount of policy stimulus has returned Western economic growth to the rates enjoyed by my generation in decades past. While most of the debate regarding our current economic challenges focuses on the best cyclical measures to kick-start economic growth, this book offers something different: an analysis of what happens if the recovery simply fails to materialize or is substantially weaker than those seen in the past. Its mixture of economics, politics and history is deliberate. Without an understanding of the political and historical context, economics on its own threatens to become increasingly irrelevant. Armed with the requisite knowledge, however, it's just about possible to tease out the kinds of structural reforms that may ultimately be needed to enable us to escape from the stagnation trap.

First of all, though, it's time to go back to the dreams of my youth, dreams that took us to the moon and led us to thoughts of life on Mars.

CHAPTER ONE

TAKING PROGRESS FOR GRANTED

One of my earliest childhood memories was waking up at some ridiculously early hour of the morning to watch the late Neil Armstrong step out of the Eagle – Apollo 11's lunar module – and utter his now famous 'one small step' mini-speech. In the years that followed – alongside millions of other young boys – I became obsessed with space travel. I read articles and books which predicted – with considerable confidence, I might add – that lunar colonies would soon be established and that humans would be heading to Mars before the end of the twentieth century. I hoped to become the next Captain Kirk.

As it turned out, this was all wishful thinking: more science fantasy than science fiction. Mankind may since have travelled remotely to the outer reaches of the solar system and beyond but man himself has, of course, still got no further than our nearest celestial neighbour. The Apollo missions were scrapped in the light of the financial and economic upheavals of the mid-1970s. Since then, we've had the Shuttle and Soyuz, the International Space Station and the Hubble Space Telescope, but nothing has quite grabbed the imagination like the first moon landings. Even those momentous events are now fading from our collective memories: for younger generations, Buzz Lightyear is more familiar than Buzz Aldrin. Meanwhile, the next man on the lunar surface, if Beijing has its way, is likely to be Chinese, not American.

Yet the sentiments that led to overly optimistic expectations about space travel have proved to be correct in so many other ways. Back in 1969, the year in which Neil Armstrong's boot first touched the dusty lunar surface, my parents' television was a small black and white device hiding in the corner. There were only two channels (BBC1 and ITV; newfangled TVs offered BBC2 but we couldn't afford the upgrade). Our television used valve technology – which meant the set took around five minutes to warm up – and the valves frequently broke, leaving us all-too-often without television altogether. The images were grainy at best. To change channels – or to alter the volume – we used human, rather than remote, control.

Today, we can tune in to hundreds of channels. We watch programmes on our televisions, our computers, our iPads and all sorts of other devices. Thanks to HD, the pictures are crystal clear and, thanks to 3D, the images can seemingly come to life. The sound is impressive (sometimes overly impressive: viewers at home can now actually hear the chants sung at soccer matches). We can record programmes for later viewing, enabling us to skip the ad breaks. Or we can download programmes from the internet thanks to iPlayer and other equivalent systems. Our ability to observe the world around us – and to act upon those observations, for good or bad – is simply extraordinary.

We may not have progressed beyond the moon but here on earth – at least within the Western industrialized world – progress is hard-wired into our collective psyche. We have come to expect continuous technological advance. And, by inference, we hope to become ever richer. We may no longer have the enthusiasm to put a man on the moon – or send a manned mission to Mars – but we nevertheless believe that technological progress will deliver a pace of economic expansion that will steadily and – for the most part – predictably make us better off over time.

These beliefs are ultimately rooted in the eighteenth-century Enlightenment. Back then, the outpouring of ideas that subsequently became mainstream Western thinking – the persistence of scientific progress, the benefits of pure reason, the rights of man – helped capture the underlying idea of inevitable human advance.

Even Enlightenment thinkers, however, would surely have been amazed by the West's progress in the second half of the twentieth century, a period during which living standards in Western Europe quadrupled and in the US went up threefold. Scientific advance in the eighteenth and nineteenth centuries was certainly remarkable but only in the second half of the twentieth century did technological progress translate into such extraordinary increases in living standards. And this wasn't just about money. Life expectancy rose, diseases were eradicated and quality of life went up.

Yet while technological progress was important, it wasn't the only factor driving Western economies onwards. After half a century of on-and-off conflict, the outbreak of peace in 1945 re-established cross-border business relationships that had been trampled under the jackboots of war. With world trade and international financial relationships nurtured by newly created international institutions, the protectionism and isolationism of the interwar years became but a distant memory: economic activity in the industrialized world thus began to flourish thanks to the unleashing of huge trade multipliers, with exports from Japan to the US, for example, rising at an annual rate of approaching 20 per cent throughout the 1950s and 1960s. Financial innovations that had first appeared in the 1920s – most obviously, the arrival of consumer credit – began to spread far and wide, allowing consumers to spend today and pay tomorrow. US household debt rose from less than 40 per cent of household income at the beginning of the 1950s to almost 140 per cent of household income before the onset of the financial crisis. The resulting increase in consumer demand encouraged industry to deliver substantial economies of scale, with mass production becoming ever more commonplace. Social security systems designed to prevent a repeat of the terrible impoverishment of the 1930s became increasingly widespread, reducing the need for households to stuff cash under the mattress for unforeseen emergencies: they could thus spend more freely. With the reforms initiated by Deng Xiaoping at the end of the 1970s and the fall of the Berlin Wall in 1989, countries that had been trapped in the economic equivalent of a deep-freeze were able to come in from the cold, creating new opportunities for trade and investment: trade between China and the US, for example, expanded massively. Women, sorely underrepresented in the workforce through lack of opportunity and lack of pay, suddenly found themselves in gainful employment thanks to sex discrimination legislation. In the early 1960s, fewer than 40 per cent of US women of working age were either in work or actively looking for work: by the end of the twentieth century, approaching 70 per cent were involved. The quality of education improved, with more and more school leavers going to university before venturing into the real world: in 1950, only 15 per cent of American men and 4 per cent of American women between the ages of 20 and 24 were enrolled in college: at the beginning of the twenty-first century, the numbers for both sexes had risen to over 30 per cent. And back-breaking housework, once the preserve of servants and housewives, headed off into the sunset. Westerners instead began to rely on washing machines, tumble driers, dishwashers, takeaways and heat-up meals, freeing up time for more productive endeavours and, for many, greater investment in health and fitness.

DON'T CRY FOR ME . . .

The second half of the twentieth century was, thus, an unusual period replete with economic bounty. Many of the factors behind this persistent increase in Western living standards appear, however, to have been one-offs: we can only have one reopening of world trade, one substantial increase in consumer credit, one fall in the Berlin Wall. Yet we don't like to think in those terms. Our belief in ever rising prosperity is sacrosanct. It may also, unfortunately, be seriously misguided. We take for granted our future prosperity, counting our economic chickens long before they've hatched. We expect our pensions to be paid in full, even though we save very little. We expect easy access to medical care, no matter how expensive it might prove to be. Our governments make their budgetary arithmetic add up only by having faith in continuous rapid economic expansion. Our banks believe their assets have value only because they assume economic growth will prevent good loans from turning bad. We regard any economic setback as cyclical, not structural. Economies are always assumed to bounce back from adversity.

Yet it hasn't always been so. Economies can suddenly – and unexpectedly – hit a brick wall. The financial, political and social consequences can be immense.

A hundred years ago, the inhabitants of Argentina and Germany were similarly well off: their per capita incomes were more or less the same. Argentina, however, had made by far the more impressive progress in the preceding decades. In 1870, for example, its per capita incomes were only seven-tenths of Germany's. Anyone opting to extrapolate the trends of the late nineteenth century into the twentieth century would surely have concluded that Argentina would have ended up far richer than Germany. And anyone who invested on that basis would presumably have decided that Buenos Aires was a better bet than Berlin.

During the early decades of the twentieth century, the bet would have paid off. Argentine living standards remained mostly higher than those in Germany. Following the First World War and Germany's subsequent hyperinflation-related economic collapse, German living standards fell further behind those of their Argentine counterparts. It wasn't until 1934 that parity was restored. Germany then temporarily moved ahead: the Nazis were a decidedly unpleasant bunch but rearmament, autobahn construction and the arrival of the Volkswagen Beetle provided an economic shot in the arm. In the chaos that followed the Second World War, Germany fell behind again. Only in the early 1950s did (West) Germany finally overtake Argentina. Germany then moved into the economic fast lane. By 2008, German living standards – even with the costs associated with reunification – were double those in Argentina.[1]

Of these two remarkably divergent experiences, it is Argentina's that is distinctly odd. Germany's story should be familiar to anyone brought up in the developed world in the second half of the twentieth century. Other Western European countries, after all, had similar post-war economic renaissances. Japan and, later on, Taiwan and South Korea eventually caught up with Europe. The US went one better: its population enjoyed average per capita incomes by the beginning of the twenty-first century fully 50 per cent higher than those in Germany and three times higher than those in Argentina.

What accounts for Argentina's spectacular fall from grace?

Argentina was a major outperformer between 1870 and the outbreak of the First World War, thanks largely to the free-trade instincts of the late nineteenth-century British Empire, new scientific advances and the mass migration of people in the late nineteenth century. It may have been a long way away from Europe and the US but Argentina was able to take full advantage of the Royal Navy's commitment to keep international sea lanes open. New refrigerator technologies – and faster ships – meant its beef could be exported to destinations many thousands of miles away. Its working age population grew rapidly, a reflection of the Belle Époque mass migration from Europe – particularly from southern Europe – that led to equally dramatic demographic changes in the US, Canada and Australia. The growth of international financial markets, meanwhile, led to huge improvements in Argentina's capital stock.

After the First World War, Argentina, alongside Australia and Canada, lost out. Impoverished Britain could no longer easily keep its empire afloat. War had destroyed the international financial system via inflation and a temporary suspension of the pre-war Gold Standard. And the politics of isolationism and protectionism began to dominate. Argentina, unusually dependent for its economic success on its – distant – connections with the rest of the world, was suddenly vulnerable. Its relatively youthful population didn't help: its young families – with lots of hungry children – inevitably saved little. As a result, growth in capital spending was unusually dependent on access to international capital markets that, post war, no longer had the capacity to supply Argentina with the necessary funds.[2]

Underneath all this were systemic weaknesses. At the end of the nineteenth century, both Buenos Aires and Chicago were both heavily dependent on their agricultural hinterlands. However, while Chicago's citizens were, by that stage, mostly well educated with high levels of literacy, 20 per cent of Buenos Aires' population was illiterate, not helped by the economy's reliance on poorly educated itinerant agricultural workers from southern Europe.[3] Chicago was able to diversify away from the agricultural industries that had been the mainstay of its economic success at the end of the nineteenth century. Buenos Aires, in contrast, was trapped, unable to move on: agriculture alone does not allow a nation to flourish economically.

Worse was to follow. In an attempt to reduce Argentina's high dependency on developments – both good and bad – elsewhere in the world economy, Argentine politicians in the 1930s moved rapidly to push through their version of economic autarky. Rejecting international linkages – which were increasingly blamed for Argentina's woes – Buenos Aires tried to develop its own manufacturing capacity behind closed doors, an approach ruled out by both the Canadians and Australians thanks to their privileged access to the markets of the British Empire and, indeed, to Britain's own influence on their behaviour.[4]

To do this, a labyrinthine arrangement of tariffs and capital controls was developed, leading in turn to huge distortions in the allocation of resources. With domestic activity aimed primarily at satisfying immediate demands for higher consumption, Argentina increasingly became a 'hand to mouth' economy. Short of domestic savings and absent a sensible export strategy, Argentina was simply unable to afford the capital goods that might have led to faster long-term growth.

After the Second World War, Argentina's political destiny was shaped by Juan Perón and his wife Eva, the ultimate political populists (how many other political lives have been turned into an internationally successful musical?[5]). In a bid to divert resources to the working classes following Perón's rise to power in 1945, the new government managed to increase the price of capital goods still further relative to consumer goods, again through the copious use of import tariffs. Argentine industry as a result became increasingly uncompetitive. The Argentine economy stagnated, losing ground against all its major industrialized competitors: it had simply failed to meet its late nineteenth-century promise.

Perón modelled himself on Mussolini's brand of fascism (it's not surprising, then, that both Adolf Eichmann and Josef Mengele, two of history's real charmers, chose to hide in Argentina after the Second World War). He gained huge support from the unions (by extending workers' benefits, he successfully wooed the union leaders in the immediate aftermath of the 1943 coup while working at the Department of Labour). Later, he was happy to stamp out dissent where and when necessary.

For a while, the model seemed to work, thanks largely to higher world food prices reflecting tremendous shortages in war-torn Europe. In the early 1950s, however, everything changed. With a return to relative peace, food prices slowly declined and Perón's Argentina was no longer economically viable: a huge welfare state – the ultimate populist expression – could no longer be supported. Ousted in another coup in 1955, Perón eventually fled to General Franco's Spain. The military took over and, as the years went by, life became ever more unpleasant. The generals' job – as they saw it – was to keep populist Peronism at bay for as long as possible.

From Spain, Perón's response was opportunistic in the extreme. He offered support to the Montoneros, a group of Marxist guerrillas who were totally opposed to the Alianza Anticomunista Argentina, which itself now represented the views of far-right enclaves of the Peronist movement. The situation was now both impossible and impossibly violent: Perón's 1973 return prompted the Ezeiza Massacre, where at least 13 people were shot dead and many hundreds of others wounded as gunmen opened fire on left-wing elements within the crowds that had gathered to welcome Perón home. Worse followed. Another military coup took place in 1976, two years after Perón's death, leading to thousands of *los desaparecidos* (the disappeared). Democracy returned to Argentina in 1983 but, since then, the democratic choice has mostly been between different brands of Peronism. Populism and intolerance of dissent have become central to Argentina's political model.

Given these political upheavals, it's hardly surprising that, over the last century or so, Argentina went from one financial crisis to the next: from 1890 through to the beginning of the twenty-first century, Argentina had to cope with five debt defaults or restructurings[6] and

17

six stock-market crashes that led, in turn, to sustained periods of economic contraction.[7] Argentina ended the twentieth century with one of the worst financial records in history. Claims on future Argentine economic output have often ended up totally worthless.

In hindsight, it is easy to see why, in the interwar period, Argentina went down an ultimately doomed road to autarky: international financiers had seemingly let Argentina down, the crumbling British Empire no longer offered the certainties of old, the Americans preferred to invest at home rather than abroad and the slow march towards another war in Europe persuaded Argentina that self-sufficiency was best. The argument was seductive. It was also, sadly, wrong.

Self-sufficiency beckoned only because Argentina's engagement with other nations in the interwar period – nations that, themselves, were increasingly heading towards a more protectionist model – had been so damaging. Yet as the pursuit of self-sufficiency led to economic stagnation, so Argentina's political debate became increasingly introspective and violent. The poor who wanted to become richer could only do so by taking wealth away from the already rich. The rich became increasingly focused on preserving what they already had, suspicious of any reform that might threaten their claims on scare resources. The Peronists, meanwhile, were only interested in clinging to power. They had no plan to heal Argentine society's ever widening rifts. Indeed, their actions doubtless contributed to Argentina's increasing polarization.

The debate was no longer about growth but, instead, how to divide up a cake that had failed to rise. Inevitably, all sorts of tactics were tried to deal with competing claims within Argentine society. Inflation robbed savers of their savings, compelling many to take their money offshore (thereby reducing still further the funds that might have been used for investment). The Peronists benefited from the support of the poor by making commitments – labour reforms, for example – that could be met only by stealing from shareholders and other owners of capital. Successive governments dipped their fingers into pension funds, making sure that jam today would be at the expense of jam tomorrow. And, as international capital markets reopened to emerging nations in the 1980s and 1990s, Argentina borrowed heavily from foreign savers only to default in 2002.

Argentina had become a no-go area. Only with the more recent rise of China and other emerging markets – and the consequent increase in the price of raw materials – has a semblance of stability returned to the Argentine economy. It might not last.

Argentina's twentieth-century decline is a story about economic hardship, poor policy choices, pursuit of autarky, an inability to diversify, polarization of society, the pursuit of populism and, ultimately, massive political instability. It shows, above all, that economic failure can lead to poorly functioning political institutions, an ultimately acrimonious – possibly violent – debate between winners and losers, and decades of relative decline. Even as technology advanced, so Argentina's economy was unable to fulfil its early twentieth-century promise.

ARGENTINA ISN'T THE ONLY ONE

Argentina might be seen merely as a statistical quirk, a freak of economic nature with no relevance for other nations. After all, at the beginning of the twenty-first century, more and more countries are enjoying unprecedented rates of economic growth. China and India are emulating – on a much grander scale – the earlier extraordinary success of other Asian nations. Brazil has been powering ahead, having waved goodbye to the hyperinflation that so damaged its performance in the 1970s and 1980s. Even parts of Africa are growing at a rapid pace: Angola, Botswana, Ethiopia, Nigeria, Rwanda, Uganda and Tanzania have all enjoyed growth rates since 2000 once thought to be the preserve of Asia alone.

For all the excitement, however, one economy most definitely has not shared in the spoils. Japan increasingly looks like a modern-day economic – although, thankfully, not political – version of twentieth-century Argentina, offering only stagnation even as others have unlocked the secrets of continued economic expansion. From the 1950s through to the end of the 1980s, the Japanese economy was a perennial outperformer. A vast literature grew up to explain Japan's economic miracle. Other nations looked on enviously as Japanese living standards jumped from one year to the next. Policy-makers were keen to mimic the key factors regarded as critical to Japan's success: prime candidates included lifetime employment (whereby firms committed to investing in their workers, thus guaranteeing good industrial relations), long-term financing, state planning through what was then known as the Ministry for International Trade and Industry (MITI) and, at least according to the popular press, a single canteen for both managers and staff, reducing the risk of industrial strife. The Japanese salaryman ruled supreme.

By the end of the 1980s, Japan was everything the West was not. Japanese workers would rather sing the company song than go on strike. The stock market was reaching new highs, able to escape the clutches of gravity. Inflation and interest rates were remarkably low. The yen, meanwhile, went through the roof.

As the Japanese became richer, Westerners were becoming poorer, at least in relative terms. By the beginning of the 1990s, as the US succumbed to recession, Japan's per capita incomes came within a whisker of overtaking those in the US. Meanwhile, the price of a steak sandwich in the Palace Hotel in Tokyo's Marunouchi district had risen to around $50, a reflection of the dollar's late-1980s collapse. Even as Westerners found life in Japan inordinately expensive, it seemed as though the Japanese could do no wrong.

When the Japanese stock market first started to decline following its end-1989 peak, most commentators welcomed the development as a desirable removal of excessive 'froth'. People were still happily drinking sake with added gold leaf, paying through the nose for the perfect melon and coughing up a king's ransom for golf club membership fees. Admittedly, inflation was a bit of a worry but, under the leadership of Governor Yasushi Mieno, the Bank of Japan was bringing it to heel, an outcome that led *Euromoney* to name Mr Mieno its 'central bank governor of the year' in 1991.[8]

Between 1950 and 1991, Japan's per capita incomes had risen from just 20 per cent of those in the US to a peak of 85 per cent. Japan had seemingly discovered the elixir of ever rising prosperity. Since 1991, however, Japan has been in steady and seemingly irreversible relative decline. Its per capita incomes at one point dropped to a mere 72 per cent of those in the US. The stock market, meanwhile, has lost three-quarters of its value since the 1989 peak while land prices have fallen by around 60 per cent. Earlier fears of inflation have been superseded by persistent problems with deflation. In hindsight, it appears that Japan has become the economic equivalent of the Grand Old Duke of York: when it was up, it was up but now that it's down, it is most definitely down.

Japan's initial decline was regarded by many as a failure of macroeconomic policy. The Bank of Japan was slow to cut interest rates[9] and the Ministry of Finance was reluctant to offer fiscal stimulus. Persistent economic weakness led, in turn, to deflation and economic stagnation.

As time went by, however, this view seemed overly simplistic. Macroeconomic policy failure might help to explain perhaps two or three years of relative decline but it could hardly account for a 20-year fall from grace.

Ben Bernanke, in 2002 a member of the Federal Reserve's Federal Open Markets Committee (FOMC), provided a more nuanced account of Japan's difficulties, an account that, for Western policy-makers today, should be required reading:[10]

Japan's economy faces some significant barriers to growth besides deflation, including massive financial problems in the banking and corporate sectors and a large overhang of government debt. Plausibly, private-sector financial problems have muted the effects of the monetary policies that have been tried in Japan, even as the heavy overhang of government debt has made Japanese policy-makers more reluctant to use aggressive fiscal policies.

The failure to end deflation in Japan does not necessarily reflect any technical infeasibility of achieving that goal. Rather, it is a byproduct of a longstanding political debate about how best to address Japan's overall economic problems … comprehensive economic reform will likely impose large costs on many, for example, in the form of unemployment or bankruptcy. As a natural result, politicians, economists, businesspeople, and the general public in Japan have sharply disagreed about competing proposals for reform. In the resulting political deadlock, strong policy actions are discouraged, and cooperation among policy-makers is difficult to achieve.

Japan's existential problem reflected its inability to deliver on prom-ises implicitly incorporated into asset values in the late 1980s. Everyone knows the future is inherently uncertain. Nevertheless, reams of Japanese and foreign investors were happy in the late 1980s to make financial bets that, collectively, made extraordinarily high claims on Japan's future economic progress. People became wealthier but, on the back of this new-found wealth, also became more and more indebted. By the end of the 1980s, it was not unusual to find Japanese homebuyers taking out 100-year mortgages, happy, it seems, to pass the burden on to their children and even their grand-children. Creditors, meanwhile, naturally assumed the next genera-tion would repay even if, in some cases, the offspring were no more than a twinkle in their parents' eyes. Why worry? After all, land prices, it seemed, only went up.

Yet, for all Japan's post-war success, it was merely catching up with higher living standards elsewhere in the world, most notably in the US and Europe. It may have been a particularly quick learner but, once it had converged with economic 'best practice' elsewhere, it was not obvious why it should carry on growing at such an impressive pace. No one, after all, expects children to carry on growing into adulthood unless, like Robert Wadlow, the world's tallest ever man, they have the misfortune of suffering from a misbehaving pituitary gland. Yet, by the end of the 1980s, many policy-makers and investors believed Japan really could carry on growing. Sadly, Japan had merely mortgaged its future. The process isn't yet over. Even as Japanese companies carry on repaying the debts built up in the 1980s, so the Japanese government year by year continues to add to public sector debt.

Japan is caught in a trap. Private companies don't want to invest. An ageing population prefers not to spend. The resulting lack of demand inevitably puts pressure on government to spend more. Yet, too often, extra government spending, rather than kick-starting economic growth, has merely led to the construction of so-called 'bridges to nowhere', vanity projects that say more about the 'pork barrel' nature of political reality than about the strength or otherwise of the overall economy.

One good example is the town of Hamada in Shimane prefecture. With a population of around 70,000 mostly elderly people, it benefits from the Hamada Marine Bridge – largely devoid of traffic – a university, a prison, an art museum for children, a ski resort and an aquarium, all of which represent gifts from current and future Japanese taxpayers. The Marine Bridge, which cost $70 million, connects Hamada to another, sparsely populated, island – even though an existing bridge served the same purpose long before the Marine Bridge was constructed – and is, not surprisingly, regarded by locals as a *hakomono* – in other words, a white elephant. It is, perhaps, no coincidence that Noburo Takeshita, the late former Japanese Prime Minister, came from Shimane prefecture.[11]

The evidence from Japan suggests that, after a debt-fuelled boom, ever larger budget deficits provide no guarantee of lasting economic recovery. Worse, in the absence of market discipline, too many funds end up channelled into 'political' projects reeking of cronyism. With the private and social returns on such projects typically low, it's no great surprise that growth fails to lift off. For Japan, big budget deficits and higher public spending have not offered a route out of persistent stagnation.

POLITICS TRUMPS ECONOMICS

Most of the time, of course, economies rebound from adversity. But in both the Argentine and the Japanese cases, the rebound didn't materialize, at least not on a scale commensurate with a return to 'business as usual'. Recessions are typically followed by recoveries: they are no more than bumps in the road. Policy-makers are able to shift people's behaviour through, for example, cutting interest rates or lowering taxes to enable people to spend more freely and, thus, to encourage innovative behaviour.

The Argentine and Japanese economies, however, came off the road altogether. Expectations went unmet, the economies languished, and citizens scratched their heads, wondering what on earth had gone wrong. Nor did they know how to put it right. As frustration mounted, so the ability politically to fix their problems disappeared into the night.

Fortunately, modern day Japan has, so far at least, avoided the political upheavals that have plagued Argentina over the last one hundred years. At first sight, this might seem odd. Both nations have similar ethnic characteristics (Japan's population is almost entirely Japanese, while Argentina's is 97 per cent white, mostly of Italian or Spanish origin). Both are on the outer fringe of a large continent. And both nations have been governed over the last 60 years mostly by factions within one dominant political movement (the Peronists in Argentina and the Liberal Democratic Party (LDP) in Japan).

If anything, Japan might have done worse than Argentina. It has had a far more challenging demographic profile, thanks to a rapidly ageing population. It has an absence of natural resources. And whereas Argentina came through the Second World War relatively unscathed, Japan's economy was completely destroyed.

Yet while the LDP dominated Japanese politics from its formation in 1955 through to its defeat in 2009, its approach was always one of openness to the rest of the world. Its mercantilist policies may occasionally have invoked America's ire but Japan quickly reinvented itself as fully signed up member of the industrialized world in the second half of the twentieth century, becoming one of America's most important strategic allies. Peronism, in contrast, was an extension of interwar isolationist thinking.

The benefits of Japanese economic success were equally distributed. On any measure of income inequality, Japanese society is much more equal than any of its main industrial rivals: indeed, alongside Scandinavia, Japan is one of the most equal societies in the world. Argentina, in contrast, has one of the world's more unequal societies: under these circumstances, economic setback is politically likely to be a lot more challenging.

Meanwhile, Japan was able to diversify into a wide range of manufacturing industries, becoming supremely competitive in the process. Its high level of domestic savings ensured there was no shortage of funds for domestic investment. Argentina, in contrast, remained wedded to its agricultural traditions, thanks to a shortage of domestic savings and a succession of governments determined to keep workers happy at the expense of capital formation.

Ultimately, however, Argentina and Japan have both faced the same existential problem: what to do when the money runs out. For Argentina, dependent on heavy domestic and foreign borrowing, the answer has been a mixture of inflation and default. Both rob savers of their nest eggs. For Japan, as yet there has been neither inflation nor default but, after the glory years, living standards have stagnated (and investors in equity and land have made huge losses). Eleven thousand miles may separate Buenos Aires from Tokyo but, in terms of relative economic decline, Japan is now following Argentina's well-trodden path.

Will others now join them?

WHAT IT MEANS FOR THE INDUSTRIALIZED WEST

While all this economic mayhem was taking place in Argentina and, later, in Japan, Western industrialized economies sailed serenely on. It seemed the West's progress was somehow inevitable. At the beginning of the twentieth century, Max Weber took Enlightenment thinking one stage further with his attempt to explain the unique qualities that had led to such remarkable gains for northern Europe and, by implication, its offshoots in North America, Australia and New Zealand.

Weber's Protestant work ethic[12] is an idea that continues to divide north and south Europe to this day. After all, Germany's view on (largely Catholic) southern Europe's difficulties – in a nutshell, that the Spanish, Greeks and Italians are lazy, feckless, and need to work harder[13] – is one reason why a solution to the eurozone crisis that began in 2010 has proved so elusive. Others have not been afraid to follow in Weber's path. David Landes discusses both Western economic success and other nations' failure in his masterly *The Wealth and Poverty of Nations*. Niall Ferguson talks about 'six killer apps' to explain the West's enduring success, in the process invoking Weber's ideas.[14]

And it's certainly true that living standards in the Western industrialized world are mostly very high, underlining the advantages of continued economic gains over many years. For all China's recent success, its living standards are still, on average, only around a quarter or a fifth of those taken for granted in the Western world. India's per capita incomes, meanwhile, are only half those in China. It is all too easy to be seduced by the miraculous growth rates achieved by nations in the emerging world. To date, however, they've been merely catching up with best practice already established in the wealthy West. And we know from Japan's experience that, once convergence has been achieved, an economic brick wall can inconveniently pop up.

Yet despite the West's enduring success, something more recently seems to have gone badly wrong. Western nations may not have hit a brick wall but they are, nevertheless, suffering from a debilitating malaise. Like Steve Austin, the *Six Million Dollar Man*, they have started operating in slow motion. The first ten years of the new millennium were profoundly disappointing. Growth as a whole averaged just 1.5 per cent per annum, the weakest performance by far in any decade during the post-Second World War period and, even more remarkably, a lot weaker than in the first half of the twentieth century, a period when economies were ravaged by war, depression, protectionism, isolationism and various decidedly unpleasant forms of ethnic cleansing.

Per capita, the results are even more striking. On this basis, Western growth averaged just 0.9 per cent in the first decade of the twenty-first century, less than half the rate recorded in the last 20 years of the twentieth century and less than a third of the rate recorded in the so-called 'golden age' of Western economic expansion in the 1950s and 1960s. And this slowdown has happened even while the rest of the world appears to have adopted, to borrow some Star Trek terminology, warp drive. China, India and others have contributed more and more to global growth even as the US and Europe have lost their way. The West may be languishing but the world economy as a whole has gone from strength to strength. Average growth – both in aggregate and on a per capita basis – has been stronger than at any point since the 1960s and 1970s. This is a disturbing result for the West: rapid growth in the emerging world was supposed to act as an economic aphrodisiac for Western exporters, leading to higher incomes, more jobs and, ultimately, higher consumption.[15]

Just as Japan and Argentina ended up in the economic rough, the evidence since the beginning of the new millennium suggests that the Western world, too, is in trouble. Could it be that Weber's protestant ethic has gone wrong? Are the killer apps being killed off? If so, why?

Disappointment since the beginning of the twenty-first century reflects four key stories.

The first was the discovery that, despite their own enormous success, emerging nations would not provide a shot in the arm for Western economies. Even as global growth accelerated, the West's share of the spoils was declining rapidly. It wasn't just that the emerging nations were growing more quickly than Western nations: by their own standards, Western nations were underperforming. Part of their underperformance reflected the – at the time, unrecognized – negative effects of emerging success on Western growth. At the margin, companies preferred to invest in China than the West, reducing the volume of Western capital spending. Faced with heightened global competition, Western workers could no longer demand the pay increases of old. Thanks to strong emerging demand, commodity prices ended up a lot higher, a process that squeezed real spending power in the West even as it lined the pockets of commodity producers in other parts of the world.

The second, predating the financial crisis that began in 2007, was simply a loss of momentum following the exuberance associated

with the so-called 'new economy' in the 1990s. This seemingly miraculous development offered an intoxicating mix of rapid productivity
gains (particularly in the US), technological advance, strong growth,
low inflation and ever higher stock prices. The elixir of ever rising
wealth that, temporarily, had been Japan's monopoly to enjoy in the
1980s had been uncovered by the US and, in patchy fashion, by
Europe too. Technology companies with only the vaguest of business
plans found that money grew on trees, a repeat of the extraordinary
events first seen in the 1720 South Sea Bubble when, famously, a
company hoped to raise money *for carrying out an undertaking of
great advantage, but nobody to know what it is'.

Such was the enthusiasm for the new economy that *Business Week*
ran the following story at the end of January 2000 under the head-
line 'The New Economy: It works in America: Will it go global?'

It seems almost too good to be true. With the information technology sector leading the way, the U.S. has enjoyed almost 4%
growth since 1994. Unemployment has fallen from 6% to about
4%, and inflation just keeps getting lower and lower. Leaving out
food and energy, consumer inflation in 1999 was only 1.9%, the
smallest increase in 34 years.

This spectacular boom was not built on smoke and mirrors.
Rather, it reflects a willingness to undertake massive risky investments in innovative information technology, combined with a
decade of retooling U.S. financial markets, governments, and
corporations to cut costs and increase flexibility and efficiency.
The result is the so-called New Economy: faster growth and lower
inflation.

Most corporate executives and policymakers in Europe and
Asia, once skeptical about the U.S. performance, have taken
this lesson to heart. There are still widespread misgivings about
the U.S. model of free-market capitalism. But driven by a desire
for faster growth, combined with a fear of being left behind,

the rest of the world is starting to embrace the benefits of a technology-driven expansion.[16]

That story, however, went wrong only a few weeks later. Stock markets collapsed, the technology sector was no longer able to raise funds and recession threatened. Keen to avoid a repeat of Japan's ongoing stagnation, and confident that they had the tools to do so, Western policy-makers offered massive monetary and fiscal stimulus: interest rates tumbled, budget deficits rose and the threat of debt deflation – of falling prices that would increase the real value of debt – was averted. However, all was not well. With low interest rates and gossamer-thin regulation, housing markets boomed, as did the issuance of mortgage-backed securities, which offered higher returns than government bonds and, so it seemed, more safety than jittery stock markets.

Economic growth returned but millions upon millions of unsuspecting people – whether borrowers or lenders, whether Americans or foreigners – found themselves directly or indirectly owning a stake in an apparently ever rising US housing market. Constructing houses, however, tends not to be as productive as building the internet, developing mobile telephony or reorganizing working methods as a result of technological innovations. The white heat of the 1990s technological revolution was replaced by the stone cold of a housing boom. Underlying economic growth began to slow down even before the financial crisis materialized.

The third period of disappointment – disaster is, frankly, a more accurate description – was the financial crisis itself. Northern Rock, Royal Bank of Scotland and HBOS were the three highest profile bank failures in the UK. In Europe, Fortis and Dexia grabbed the headlines. And, in the US, Bear Stearns, Washington Mutual, IndyMac, Lehman and AIG dominated the newswires. The underlying situation, however, was even worse. Between 2007 and 2012, approaching 500 US banks had failed (including the aptly named Cape Fear Bank in Wilmington, North Carolina). That compared with only 24 failures in the previous six years.[17]

Capital markets ultimately are responsible for linking savers with investors. Yet the financial crisis revealed that the linkages were often tenuous – person A put her savings in pension fund B, which then purchased a bundle of pieces of paper known as collateralized debt obligations from bank C, which had assembled the bundle via investments in mortgage-backed securities – some of dubious quality – issued by banks D, E and F, which, in turn, had used the money raised to lend to homebuyers G, H and I, one or more of whom had a dubious credit history and, hence, was 'subprime'. Person A had no direct connection with the homebuyers – indeed, the saver was likely to be thousands of miles away from the ultimate borrower – but the indirect connection was there, nevertheless.

It was the financial equivalent of a daisy chain: fleeting, transitory, initially effective but ultimately doomed to fail. It all rested on three key assumptions: that US house prices only ever went upwards, that subprime customers wouldn't walk away from their homes, leaving their keys behind, and that financial alchemy worked. Certainly the ratings agencies thought so: they gave their seal of approval to the whole process.

For most of the post-war period, these assumptions held but in 2006 US house prices peaked. Six years later, they were down 35 per cent from the peak,[18] the financial system was crippled, subprime customers were leaving their homes in their droves and the ratings agencies had egg all over their faces.

As the daisy chain fell apart, breaking up into so many tiny fragments, so the capital markets that had delivered such strong growth at the end of the twentieth century were no longer able to do the job expected of them. In response to both the haemorrhaging of the credit system and the related extraordinary loss of confidence among businesses and consumers, Western economies collapsed. From the 2008 peaks, national income across the major Western nations dropped precipitously. From peak to trough, US national income was down 5.1 per cent. Others fared even worse: Germany down 6.8 per cent, the UK down 7.1 per cent and – given it made the headlines for all the wrong reasons at the time – Iceland down 10.0 per cent.

This was another Great Depression in the making, an economic collapse associated with a meltdown of the financial system. There was no alternative other than to launch an extraordinary rescue operation, a lifeboat for the financial system using every macroeconomic tool known to man. Interest rates fell to zero – or near enough to make no difference – governments allowed their borrowing to rise dramatically in an attempt to offset massive household and bank deleveraging and, eventually, central banks resorted to so-called unconventional policies – in effect, attempts to rig the financial system through printing money to tease out some much needed economic growth.

And this takes us to the fourth story. Western policy-makers had persuaded themselves they were wiser than the Japanese. They knew how to avoid stagnation. Japan's problems supposedly reflected a lack of macroeconomic imagination, an unwillingness to pull out all the stops when crisis beckoned. Western policy-makers, in contrast, were prepared to act with unprecedented aggression. Yet for all the policy stimulus on offer, the results were mostly disappointing. The deepest Western recession since the 1930s was followed by one of the weakest recoveries. The cyclical rules of the game had been torn up. In the past, deep recessions were always followed by strong recoveries. Not this time.

The combination of deep recession and shallow recovery has left Western economies terribly scarred.

In 1994, four years into Japan's first *lost decade*, its national income was up 8 per cent. Four years into the West's economic crisis, national income in the US and Germany was barely higher than it had been at the beginning of 2008: the UK, meanwhile, was down over 4 per cent. Japan's experience may have been bad but the West's, so far, has been worse.

Relative to forecasts published at the beginning of 2008, when most commentators were still fairly sanguine about the future even though the financial system was already looking distinctly rickety, subsequent economic performance was thoroughly miserable. Levels of national income by the beginning of 2012 were, on average, 10 per cent lower than expected just a handful of years earlier. Yet despite this terrible setback, economists mostly expected to see a return to 'business as usual', with growth returning to the averages of the 1980s and 1990s. It's as if the first decade of the twenty-first century was no more than a bad dream. At the end of 2010, for example, both the Bank of England and the Office for Budget Responsibility confidently predicted that the UK economy would grow at a rate close to 3 per cent by 2012 and would maintain that rate of expansion in subsequent years. Instead, the economy continued to flirt with recession.

For the US, economic performance during and since the crisis has been profoundly disappointing by its own – admittedly high – standards, far worse than any other post-war experience. Four years after the economic peak at the end of 2007, national income was only 0.8 per cent higher. The average across all previous post-war cycles was a gain of 13.7 per cent. The worst, following the 1973 quadrupling of oil prices, was 7.7 per cent, while the best, in the late 1940s, was 23.4 per cent. Nothing in the post-war period equates to the experience the US has had to endure in the first few years of the twenty-first century.

While the UK's performance was even more miserable, the early 1980s collapse provided a precedent of sorts (although, on that occasion, the recession was followed by a strong recovery, which is more than can be said for the UK's experience following the financial crisis). Even financially conservative countries succumbed to ongoing disappointment. Although Germany's decline in 2008 and early 2009 was followed by a strong trade-led recovery, the momentum didn't last: by 2012, German exporters were being hit by a collapse in demand in southern Europe as a global banking crisis evolved into a eurozone sovereign crisis.

Absent a decent recovery, the process of repaying debt – of deleveraging – has been made all the more difficult. Having thought they could grow their way out of their debt difficulties, Western policy-makers have been forced to rethink their plans. Worse, persistently low levels of economic activity have made it much more difficult to deliver on the promises made before the onset of the financial crisis. Economic stagnation brings with it a new political tension, a debate between potential winners and losers. That debate, however, is far from being resolved.

MOON LANDINGS REVISITED

The West now has the growth profile of Japan and, in some cases, levels of income inequality approaching Argentina's. For Westerners used to ever rising living standards, who have come to expect continuous improvements in their daily lives from one year to the next, this presents a major challenge.

Based on our collective belief in continuously rising living standards, we have spent the last half-century watching our financial wealth and our political and economic 'rights' accumulate at an incredible pace. We all, directly or indirectly, own pieces of paper or rely on political promises that make claims on future economic prosperity. The pieces of paper range from cash through to government bonds, from equities through to property deeds and from asset-backed securities through to collateralized debt obligations.

The language deployed may vary from the very simple to the incredibly complicated but these pieces of paper all have one thing in common: they represent claims on assumed future economic success. They are all manifestations of the same act of faith: namely that the future will be better than the present and vastly superior to the past. And we rely on political promises regarding education, health care, our treatment in old age and our national defence, all of which are based on ever rising prosperity.

What happens, however, if the future is no better? What happens if, collectively, the claims incorporated into our pieces of paper and our political promises cannot be honoured?

Back to Neil Armstrong. Imagine that, as a consequence of the moon landings, an entrepreneur had decided to sell tickets offering the gullible a chance to head off on a Martian space holiday before the end of the twentieth century: more Thomas Crook than Thomas Cook, perhaps. For extreme science fantasists, this might have been an opportunity too good to miss. Queuing up to buy their tickets, they would be exhibiting three extraordinary acts of faith: faith in technological progress, faith in the ability of humankind to harness that progress and faith in the integrity of our imaginative entrepreneur. They would eventually discover, of course, that their tickets were worthless. Those who woke up to reality early enough might have managed to sell their tickets to the even more gullible without incurring any significant financial loss (although, with eBay not properly established until 1995, finding the even more gullible might not have been particularly easy). Someone, however, would eventually have to take a loss: the tickets, after all, were claims on something destined never to materialize.

Selling tickets to Mars would have been a fraudulent act. We have plenty of laws to prevent that sort of thing happening. Bernie Madoff, the disgraced investor, sits behind bars for his own version of fraud. Fraudulent acts are acts of deliberate deception, where one party sets out to rip off others. What happens, however, if all parties share a roughly similar view of the future, which then turns out to be hopelessly wrong, a collective delusion perhaps based on an inappropriate extrapolation of past trends? What if our financial wealth has been accumulated on the back of this delusion? What if political promises – even those made in good faith – can no longer be met? How should we cope with the subsequent disappointment?

And did it have to be like this?

CHAPTER TWO

THE PAIN OF STAGNATION

While stagnation seems to present a whole host of problems, would it really be so bad? Western nations are, after all, a lot better off than they used to be and a lot richer than industrial powers in Asia, Latin America and elsewhere. Maybe, after the debt-fuelled gains pre-financial crisis, we should simply get used to living within our means. Perhaps, as the Skidelsky family would argue, we already have enough.[1] Perhaps we should accept, with equanimity, our declining influence in world economic and political affairs and, as I put it in *Losing Control*, learn to grow old gracefully.

For good or bad, plenty of sages have warned that nature imposes a natural and inevitable limit on living standards and that stagnation, or worse, is our ultimate destiny.

Thomas Malthus argued in his *Essay on the Principles of Population* (1798):

Population, when unchecked, increases in a geometrical ratio. Subsistence increases only in an arithmetic ratio ... By that law of our nature which makes food necessary to the life of man, the effects of these two unequal powers must be kept equal. This implies a strong and constantly operating check on population from the difficulty of subsistence. This difficulty must fall somewhere and must necessarily be severely felt by a large portion of mankind.[2]

As it turned out, Malthus wrote his *Essay* at just the wrong time. The nineteenth century witnessed the arrival of the Industrial Revolution, an extraordinary leap forward in economic and financial affairs. New steam-related technologies emerged to deliver enormous productivity gains. Financial innovations – the growth of the joint-stock company, the development of banks and other financial institutions – allowed savings to be channelled more effectively into the new investment opportunities. Back-breaking work slowly disappeared, the children of labourers – on the land and in the factories – became the aspirational middle classes and per capita incomes went through the roof: between 1820 and 1900, the incomes of British citizens rose 167 per cent. Industrial economies ended up producing a lot more output from any given input.

Modern-day Malthusians worry less about food and a lot more about climate change. Unlike Malthus, however, they have been sensible enough to argue that *minimizing* climate change today will *maximize* growth over the very long run (sceptics might at this point mention Keynes's aphorism that 'In the long run we are all dead'). As the Stern Review put it:

> The evidence shows that ignoring climate change will eventually damage economic growth. Our actions over the coming few decades could create risks of major disruption to economic and social activity, later in this century and the next, on a scale similar to those associated with the great wars and the economic depression of the first half of the 20th century.[3]

Both fears – a shortage of food or an excess of hot air – suggest we have a tendency to live beyond our means. Malthus took the view that, faced with a temporary increase in living standards, we'd all have far too many children, thus ensuring the next generation's living standards were brought back down to subsistence level. Stern's view is that, faced with a hotter planet, we are surely consuming today at the expense of the living standards of future generations. Either way, the good times cannot continue indefinitely. At some point, according to Malthusian arguments, either we, or our children, will have to accept, at best, a slower pace of increase in living standards and, at worst, an outright decline.

SMITH'S MELANCHOLY

One obvious problem with both of these arguments is that they casually push to one side the impact of productivity gains that allow more outputs from given inputs. Argentina may have lost its way during the twentieth century but the increase in living standards elsewhere owed a great deal to continuous invention and innovation. Argentina simply failed to harness what was rapidly becoming available elsewhere.

Yet while the denial of productivity gains may be the most readily identified Malthusian failing, there is another major problem with Malthusian views, admirably identified by Adam Smith long before Malthus put pen (or quill) to paper. We need economic growth because, without it, society is in danger of fragmenting:

> It is in the progressive state, while the society is advancing to the further acquisition, rather than when it has acquired its full complement of riches, that the condition of the labouring poor, of the great body of the people, seems to be the happiest and the most comfortable. It is hard in the stationary, and miserable in the

declining state. The progressive state is in reality the cheerful and the hearty state to all the different orders of society. The stationary state is dull: the declining melancholy.[4]

The reason is not just that the poor, understandably, would like to be better off. It is also a reflection of our fear of losing what we already have. The 'progressive state' – one in which there is positive economic growth – offers the possibility of becoming richer without anyone else becoming poorer. It is, in theory, a 'win–win' situation. The 'stationary state' – where there is no growth – is not just dull but also full of uncertainties: one person's gains must be another person's losses. And the 'declining state' is one in which the vast majority of people are likely to end up worse off, an outcome that, at the very least, is melancholy.

In a growing economy, everyone has a chance of becoming richer. In a stagnant economy, some will almost certainly become poorer. In a growing economy, citizens may choose to maximize their benefits. In a stagnant economy, they may instead seek to minimize their losses. They thus resist reforms that might be necessary to enable growth to return. Entrepreneurial spirit vanishes, replaced by a desire only to protect existing income and wealth.

This feature is not uniquely Argentine or Japanese. It is a deeply embedded psychological characteristic. It's called loss aversion. Standard economic theory suggests that individuals treat gains and losses in similar fashion. In reality, however, people dislike losses far more than they enjoy gains. An economic system that seems to offer individuals the equal possibility of gains and losses – a world of stagnation rather than growth – is one that's likely to be dominated by loss aversion. Entrepreneurial activity falls by the wayside.

What we already think we have – or we are entitled to – we'll not give up easily, even if we are much better off than previous generations. We are hard-wired from birth to think in this way and no amount of rational discussion makes 'letting go' any easier. Our minds play tricks on us, persuading us that we're making rational choices when, in fact, we are governed by in-built biases of one sort or another.

Take, for example, a simple series of choices involving sums of money.

I give you a £50 note and then ask whether you'd like to take a guaranteed further £25 or, instead, whether you'd prefer a 50:50 gamble that would give you either nothing more or an additional £50. If you're typical of the population at large, you're likely to take the guaranteed £25 and reject the gamble.

Now I give you £100 and then ask whether you'd like to take a guaranteed £25 loss or, instead, a 50:50 gamble of either no loss or, instead, a loss of £50. In this case, if you're typical of the majority of people, you'll opt for the gamble. If you have a chance of minimizing your loss, you'll probably take it.

A moment's reflection, however, will show that the two scenarios are, in fact, identical. Yet the way they're worded has a significant impact on the choices we're likely to make. Knowing you can make £50 with a guarantee of an extra £25 sounds enticing. Knowing that you can make £100 and, by taking a gamble, avoid any loss whatsoever sounds just wonderful.

This, of course, is a story about gambling. Many of us deliberately avoid heading to the nearest casino or bookmakers because we're not sure we can trust our instincts. But what about things we actually own?

Kahneman, Knetsch and Thaler[5] brilliantly showed how unreliable our instincts are by experimenting with coffee mugs. Their experiment involved Buyers, Sellers and 'Choosers' of coffee mugs. The Buyers had to spend their own money to purchase a mug, while the Choosers were offered the choice of either a mug or a sum of money. The Sellers started off with mugs but no money. In their experiments, the authors found that Sellers valued their mugs far more highly than the Choosers even though both groups were, in effect, faced with the same choice: both would go home either with a mug or some cash. The difference relates to loss aversion. We don't like to lose things we already own. The Sellers had an 'emotional' attachment to their coffee mugs.

This psychological insight is incredibly important in a world of economic stagnation or contraction, Smith's dull and melancholy states. Melancholia sets in not just because there is an absence of economic progress but, worse, because there is a fight over the spoils of economic endeavour. Some will use their power and influence – using all the tricks of bribery and corruption – to jump to the front of the queue. Some will form cartels or abuse monopoly positions to maximize their economic 'rent' – the income over and above what they'd be paid in a properly competitive marketplace. Some will go to war. In the process, many others will lose out: they'll end up with low incomes, facing unemployment or as cannon fodder.

Faced with a fight over the spoils – where nefarious techniques lead to a complete breakdown of trust – society then struggles to move back to a path consistent with continuously rising prosperity. Put simply, with persistent economic stagnation or contraction, society is in danger of becoming increasingly fragmented, leading to even more stagnation or contraction. The incentive to cheat rises and, as a result, the legal and moral anchors that underpin market behaviour become increasingly unreliable.

As Argentina and Japan have discovered, reforms intended to fix the problem – in other words, reforms designed to put an economy back on the path towards prosperity – then become increasingly difficult. In the absence of an immediate rise in prosperity, reforms will typically be regarded as mechanisms to reward some at the expense of others. Rather than binding society together, reforms can tear it apart. In a world of stagnation, those who lose out from reform may do so both relatively and absolutely, at least in the short term. As such, enthusiasm for reform will be much more limited. It's not difficult to see how a stagnant society can all too easily be associated with racism, sexism and a range of other undesirable '-isms'.

Sustained economic growth doesn't just make society richer: it also makes it easier to distribute the benefits of economic endeavour to a wide range of people, whatever their background. Stagnation removes those opportunities and leads, instead, to increasing fractures. We end up having battles over the spoils. We go back to the laws of the jungle.

Compare, for example, the situation in the West today with life in Victorian England. Back then, there were plenty of rich people. Yet average incomes were very low and the poorest of all, of course, had to put up with life in the workhouse.

> The evening arrived; the boys took their places. The master, in his cook's uniform, stationed himself at the copper; his pauper assistants ranged themselves behind him; the gruel was served out; and a long grace was said over the short commons. The gruel disappeared; the boys whispered each other, and winked at Oliver; while his next neighbours nudged him. Child as he was, he was desperate with hunger, and reckless with misery. He rose from the table; and advancing to the master, basin and spoon in hand, said: somewhat alarmed at his own temerity:
>
> 'Please, sir, I want some more.'
>
> The master was a fat, healthy man; but he turned very pale. He gazed in stupefied astonishment on the small rebel for some seconds, and then clung for support to the copper. The assistants were paralysed with wonder; the boys with fear.
>
> 'What!' said the master at length, in a faint voice.
>
> 'Please, sir,' replied Oliver, 'I want some more.'
>
> The master aimed a blow at Oliver's head with the ladle; pinioned him in his arm; and shrieked aloud for the beadle.
> (Charles Dickens, *Oliver Twist*)

Thanks to persistent economic growth, twenty-first century Britain is a very different proposition. Incomes per capita have risen twelve-fold since Dickens published *Oliver Twist* in 1838[6] and, thankfully, we no longer have workhouses. Yes, poverty still exists and vulnerable individuals are still, at times, poorly treated. Amazingly, during the Queen's Diamond Jubilee celebrations in June 2012, up to 30 unemployed people bussed in from the West Country to work as stewards in the Jubilee Thames Pageant found themselves having to sleep rough under London Bridge before performing their (unpaid) duties.[7] But, for the most part, twenty-first century Britain has a different and more enlightened attitude. It's built on the principles of the welfare state, established in the 1942 Beveridge Report,[8] and affordable only thanks to the benefits of sustained economic growth. An enthusiastic eugenicist, Sir William Beveridge was certainly a touch peculiar, but his vision of the welfare state was quite clear:

> any proposals for the future, while they should use to the full the experience gathered in the past, should not be restricted by consideration of sectional interests established in the obtaining of that experience . . .
>
> . . . organisation of social insurance should be treated as one part only of a comprehensive policy of social progress. Social insurance fully developed may provide income security; it is an attack upon Want. But Want is one only of five giants on the road of reconstruction and in some ways the easiest to attack. The others are Disease, Ignorance, Squalor and Idleness.
>
> . . . social security must be achieved by co-operation between the State and the individual. The State should offer security for service and contribution. The State in organising security should not stifle incentive, opportunity, responsibility; in establishing a national minimum, it should leave room and encouragement for voluntary action by each individual to provide more than that minimum for himself and his family.

Beveridge's principles – which gave rise to universal National Insurance and the National Health Service – offer something for all shades of the political spectrum: a guarantee of a national minimum level of financial security but, at the same time, incentives for individuals to do much better. Thanks to social insurance, latter-day Oliver Twists would no longer have to survive on gruel. The state, however, would not guarantee any income beyond a 'national minimum'. It was up to individuals to work hard, to take their responsibilities seriously, to grab opportunities whenever and wherever they materialized and to make their way in the world. Beveridge certainly wanted to avoid the creation of what might best be described as an 'entitlement culture'.

Yet we have ended up with a welfare state that looks radically different from Beveridge's original plan. What Beveridge would have thought of modern-day Britain – or, indeed, many other parts of the Western industrialized world – is not hard to guess. 'Please, sir, I want some more' has been replaced by 'I insist, sir, I am entitled to more'. We have been seduced into creating entitlements that we could afford only on the basis of continued economic expansion and, in the process, we have lost sight of Beveridge's original principles.

The sense of entitlement is reflected most obviously in developments in social spending. In Beveridge's day, public spending on health amounted to a mere 1 per cent of national income. In 1948, following the creation of the National Health Service, it had doubled. When Neil Armstrong was walking on the moon, it was approaching 4 per cent of national income. On the election of Margaret Thatcher in 1979, it had reached 5 per cent of national income. And by the time Gordon Brown was voted out of office in 2010, it had risen to 8 per cent of national income. Social health provision has jumped a long way from providing merely a 'national minimum'.

For the record, not every conceivable treatment is currently available on the National Health Service. Penis enlargement for cosmetic reasons – although not necessarily for psychological reasons – is ruled out, as is treatment for erectile dysfunction, unless related to diabetes, multiple sclerosis, Parkinson's disease or a range of other debilitating conditions. Free dental care, however, is available for pregnant women and women in the first year after childbirth (assuming, of course, that their partner's erectile dysfunction hasn't ruled out pregnancy in the first place). And, for those with an 'alternative' outlook on health care, free complementary treatments can be found up and down the nation: good news for acupuncturists, osteopaths, homoeopathists and chiropractors.[9] Is this the 'national minimum' that Beveridge had in mind?

Remarkably, despite the huge increase in health spending over the years – not just in absolute terms but also relative to overall national income – statisticians have been unable to reach agreement on how to measure health 'output'. In 2006, the Office for National Statistics came up with six different measures of health productivity.[10] Some estimates suggested a decline while others, in contrast, pointed to a rise. In part, the measured gains reflected the increased use of statins – designed to reduce the risks of high cholesterol and, thus, of heart disease – which, frankly, says more about the productivity of the pharmaceutical industry than of the health service. Nevertheless, despite all the uncertainty over how, precisely, the nation's money is being spent, few dare to question the wisdom of devoting resources to an area of expenditure that seems to be intrinsically worthy. We are 'entitled' to a high standard of health care and we'll spend any amount of our own or other people's money in the pursuit of this secular Holy Grail – whether or not we can afford it, and whether or not the money is used wisely.

Social security spending has also risen hugely during the post-war period. According to the Institute for Fiscal Studies, social security spending amounted to around 4 per cent of the UK's national income at the beginning of the 1950s but, by 2010, was close to 14 per cent of a now much higher level of national income. While some social security spending – most obviously on unemployment benefit – has a distinctly cyclical pattern, there has nevertheless been a persistent secular increase in overall expenditure, a reflection of greater generosity over the years alongside an increase in the numbers of people entitled to claim. For example, the Basic State Pension rose from around 14 per cent of average male earnings in the late 1940s to around 20 per cent of earnings by the early 1980s, while the number of eligible pensioners rose from 6.8 million to 10 million over the same period. In the early years of the twenty-first century, following a relatively fallow decade, social security expenditure reaccelerated despite the absence of any major economic setback: the biggest increases were in child tax credits and housing benefit. The benefits of the economic boom were partially redistributed to those deemed the neediest on the assumption that, with continued economic expansion, such generosity could be funded without difficulty. No one thought to ask whether these now higher benefits could be so easily afforded in the face of persistent economic setback.[11]

Understandably, most of us hope to enjoy a long and rewarding retirement (all that extra spending on health care has implications for longevity). Yet why do we believe we should be entitled to such a long 'holiday' in our later years? At the turn of the twentieth century, a typical US 20-year-old male – assuming he'd spent time digesting the contents of actuarial tables – might reasonably have expected to live until the age of 60 or thereabouts. A hundred years later – and a few generations on – average life expectancy for a young adult American male is now around 80. Despite this increase, the official retirement age of 65 has hardly budged – and many Americans hope to retire long before reaching that official milestone. Our great-grandparents worked and then died. In contrast, our generation works, retires and then puts its feet up, hoping to enjoy many years sunning itself in its dotage.[12]

Admittedly, we didn't always have that ambition. In 1965, the Who famously proclaimed that 'I hope I die before I get old'. Keith Moon, the Who's drummer, achieved this ambition in spectacular fashion: he dropped dead from an overdose of prescription drugs at the age of 32. John Entwhistle, the Who's bassist, did a lot better, although, like Moon, he didn't make it to retirement age. As I write, however, both Roger Daltrey (born 1944) – the Who's lead singer – and Pete Townshend (born 1945) – its lead guitarist and chief songwriter – are following in the footsteps of others of their generation, growing old before they, too, plan on meeting their maker. Yet we are nowhere near working out how to afford the associated 'age-related' expenditure. The European Commission, for example, estimates substantial further increases in such spending by 2060, with gains of around 3.5 per cent of GDP for France and 4 per cent for the UK to around 6 per cent for Germany and a whopping 8 per cent for the Netherlands.[13]

Nor is entitlement confined to the public sector, to health care or to the elderly. While Beveridge's principles may have been undermined through subsequent developments in the public sector, behaviour in the private sector has been no better. Executive pay has increasingly been structured to incentivize those at the top to take risks that might provide them with short-term reward even if the company's shareholders and bondholders (or, in the case of banks, a country's taxpayers) are left to pick up the pieces. Corporate executives justify their bounty on the basis of peer group comparisons but, if the peers all behave in the same way, it's hardly surprising that a gap then opens up between their compensation and their – at times underwhelming – achievements. According to one analysis, CEOs of sampled companies in the S&P500 earned, on average, 380 times more than the typical US worker in 2011, up from a multiple of only 42 in 1980.[14] Bankers justify their rewards on the basis of a comparison with their peers too, even though, following the financial crisis, it has become increasingly difficult to measure the precise contribution of their sometimes esoteric skills to economic well-being. And there are plenty of people who avoid paying their taxes, figuring that their free-riding behaviour will have little impact on the total tax take for the government. In an expanding economy, after all, a little bit of cheating is unlikely to upset the apple cart. Economic expansion masks all manner of sins, and allows us all too easily to make promises to ourselves that, in the event of sustained economic setback, simply will not be met. We can all be on the make and on the take.

THE FUTURE OF AN ILLUSION

Westerners are a lot richer today than they once were, so in that sense the promises we have made to ourselves are not unreasonable. Per capita incomes are around seven times higher today than they were at the turn of the twentieth century. Asking society to pay more for pensions, health care, education and a host of other worthy items is hardly an act of foolishness. Yet we have spent – in advance – money we have yet to earn. We have become devotees of the economics of extrapolation. It's a dangerous game.

Prior to the financial crisis, society became dependent on illusory wealth to fund personal consumption, higher tax revenues and a range of entitlements. It's not difficult to see why. Continuous increases in prosperity over many decades created the impression that we could have it all. Society, it seemed, could win a lottery jackpot each and every year.

Politicians dispensed their largesse as if they were, indeed, lottery winners. As a result, there was an extraordinary increase in public spending. Between 2000 and 2012, public spending as a share of national income jumped from 51.6 per cent to 55.9 per cent in France, from 31.2 per cent to 44.1 per cent in Ireland, from 45.9 per cent to 49.8 per cent in Italy, from 41.1 per cent to 46.9 per cent in

Portugal, from 36.5 per cent to 48.9 per cent in the UK and from 33.9 per cent to 41.1 per cent in the US.[15]

On average, around half of this increase occurred *before* the onset of the financial crisis. Some countries went a lot further: two-thirds of the UK's spending increase, for example, occurred between 2000 and 2007. It is not enough, then, to argue that the rise in the ratio of public spending to national income was simply an inevitable consequence of the crisis itself, stemming from increases in social expenditure (unemployment benefit and the like) and much lower economic activity. The fiscal rot was established much earlier and owed a lot to what might broadly be described as a triumph of wishful thinking.

Admittedly, not all countries ended up in the same boat. Germany, for example, kept its public spending constant as a share of national income. For the most part, however, governments adopted a philosophy first expounded by Viv Nicholson in 1961. She won £152,319 on the football pools and famously declared she would 'spend, spend, spend'. Five husbands and a battle with the bottle later, she faced bankruptcy. Spending is fine so long as there is income to support it. Both Ms Nicholson and a large number of the world's richest nations forgot this simple maxim.

It's very easy to increase public spending. It's a lot more difficult to cut it. And, if it has to be cut, it's typically infrastructure projects that are slashed. These projects tend to benefit future, not current, voters and, therefore, are first for the chop. Other areas of public spending are essentially 'sticky'. During the good times, they tend to rise. During the bad times, they rarely fall very far. When the bad times were short-lived, that didn't matter too much. Enduring stagnation is, however, another matter altogether. How should societies adjust to a world where economic growth is no longer guaranteed, a world in which entitlements cannot continue to expand in almost infinite fashion?

For many years, borrowers, lenders and financial go-betweens – whether in the public or private sectors – were happy to accept continued economic expansion as fact, an automatic process that would allow them to plan for the future with ease, dispensing all manner of benefits and bonuses. Yet, at the beginning of the twenty-first century, this sense of ever rising income turns out to have been no more than an illusion humming with quasi-religious fervour. Indeed, Sigmund Freud's critique of religious belief – *The Future of an Illusion* – can equally be applied to our continuous faith in economic and financial progress: 'we call a belief an illusion when wish-fulfilment is a prominent factor in its motivation, while disregarding its relations to reality, just as the illusion does.'[16]

ILLUSIONS AND DELUSIONS

The illusion can be found in almost every walk of economic life. Pension funds assume high rates of return on their assets not because their fund managers are necessarily very able but, instead, because it's the only way in which the funds' future liabilities can be met. Households assume their properties will rise in value to allow not only the repayment of any mortgage but also a few holidays in the sun and, if they're lucky, an early retirement. Banks assume a decent rate of economic growth and continued gains in house prices both to increase their loan books (and, hence, their profitability) and also to limit the number of non-performing loans.[17]

Think, for example, of the behaviour of UK banks before the onset of the financial crisis. Back then, loan-to-value ratios on UK mortgages averaged around 75 per cent. Some of the more outlandish banks – most obviously, Northern Rock – were offering loan-to-value ratios of 125 per cent, based on the foolish expectation that property prices would forever rise. In 2012, five years after the collapse of Northern Rock, average loan-to-value ratios were down to around 55 per cent and the mortgage market was barely growing. Consumer credit had stagnated while commercial real estate loans were shrinking fast. Delusional behaviour creates its own problems.

The most obvious place to see the illusion in action, however, is the public sector. The assumptions made by fiscal authorities are neatly laid out and, thus, can be given a rigorous sanity check. This can be done on both a backward-looking and forward-looking basis. In 2007, for example, the UK Treasury confidently thought that the UK's budget deficit would amount to around 1.4 per cent of national income by 2012, based on projections of continued economic growth at the prevailing rate. The actual deficit in 2012 was 9.3 per cent of national income. Meanwhile, government debt was supposed to be less than 40 per cent of national income when, in actual fact, it came close to 70 per cent of national income.

Of course, it makes perfect sense for governments to borrow more when the rest of the economy is repaying its debts. The rot sets in, however, when the hoped-for recovery fails to materialize, when stagnation becomes the new reality. At that point, the government is caught between the devil and the deep blue sea: if it borrows even more and recovery still fails to show up, the nation ends up with a parlous fiscal situation roughly in line with Japan's experience over the last 20 years; if it offers austerity, the government risks throwing an already stagnant economy back into recession.

As for the forward-looking version of the illusion, it's worth turning to the US. The Congressional Budget Office reported in June 2012 that:

> the ageing of the population and the rising cost of health care would cause spending on the major health programs and Social Security to grow from more than 10 percent of GDP today to almost 16 percent of GDP 25 years from now. That combined

increase of more than 5 percentage points for such spending as a share of the economy is equivalent to about $850bn today. (By comparison, spending on all of the federal government's programs and activities, excluding net outlays for interest, has averaged about 18.5 percent of GDP over the past 40 years.)[18]

Worrying in themselves, these numbers rest upon economic growth assumptions that look suspiciously like wishful thinking. The economic stagnation that has blighted the US economy since the onset of the subprime crisis magically vanishes, to be replaced by a growth surge between 2014 and 2017, with a peak rate of expansion of almost 5 per cent in 2015. Assumptions concerning labour productivity appear to be remarkably upbeat: having delivered average gains of 1.4 per cent per annum between 2002 and 2011, the CBO projects gains of 1.7 per cent per year between 2012 and 2022, one of the fastest rates of increase in the entire post-war period.

Why this happens is unclear: perhaps a wonderful new technology is about to be unleashed, or maybe, despite their apparent reluctance, US companies are about to rebuild the capital stock at a remarkable pace. Maybe the discovery of cheap shale oil and gas leads to an industrial renaissance. We can only hope. On the CBO's projections, America's intergenerational problem looks bad, but it will be a lot worse in the absence of a strong recovery in economic activity.

To put this into context, each 1 per cent shortfall of GDP adds between 0.3 and 0.4 percentage points to the US budget deficit (as a share of GDP), a reflection of revenue shortfalls and increases in social security spending. Assuming, for argument's sake, that US growth continues at a lacklustre pace of around 2 per cent per year until 2022, as opposed to the more optimistic CBO baseline, the budget deficit would end up almost 4 per cent larger as a share of GDP than contained within the CBO's numbers by 2022. That, in turn, would imply a persistent – and unwelcome – increase in the ratio of US government debt to national income, a polite way of saying that, if nothing else changes, the US is heading towards bankruptcy.

Other countries would be even worse off: each 1 per cent shortfall of GDP adds around 0.45 per cent to the UK budget deficit, 0.51 per cent to the German deficit and 0.53 per cent to the French and Spanish deficits, a reflection of their bigger public sectors relative to the US.[19] With poorly performing asset markets and much lower prospective economic growth, our entitlements are about to take a hammering. On current plans, only wishful thinking on economic growth stops government debt from spiralling out of control in the decades ahead. If that wishful thinking proves to be wrong, we will be in serious trouble.

Can a wave of the policy-makers' magic wand sort the problem out?

CHAPTER THREE

FIXING A BROKEN ECONOMY

We need our economies to continue expanding at the rates of old because, otherwise, we cannot easily meet the promises we've made to ourselves. We are simply not primed for a world of ongoing stagnation. We prefer to stick to our illusions. If economies are incapable of healing on their own, we put our faith in the policy-maker's magic wand.

The debate on the ability or otherwise of economies to 'self-adjust' is long and tortuous. Before the Weimar Republic's hyperinflation in the early 1920s and the Great Depression of the 1930s, there had been few recognized instances of major macroeconomic calamities. The assumption was that markets 'cleared'. A rise in unemployment would be met by a fall in wages, thereby allowing workers to price themselves back into the market. An excessive increase in consumer demand would lead to higher prices: wage earners would end up worse off in real terms, bringing demand back on track. A sudden reduction in capital spending would lead to lower interest rates – the supply of savings would now be greater than the demand for loans – thus encouraging households to spend rather than save. Demand would then stabilize. Other than as a consequence of major political upheavals – war was hardly conducive to rising living standards – economies seemed destined to stick to a path ultimately determined by a mixture of population growth, capital accumulation and advances in technology. Macroeconomics had yet to be invented.

While the Weimar Republic's experience was readily understandable – rebuilding Germany's economy after the First World War while, at the same time, paying reparations to the victorious (and vindictive) Allies led inevitably to the printing press – the Great Depression was a far bigger challenge to the prevailing orthodoxy. US wages were in free fall – in times past an indication that the labour market was 'clearing' – yet unemployment was inexorably rising. As the US economy plumbed new depths, a quarter of the male workforce found themselves out of work: no jobs, no prospects and no hope.

It was time for a rethink. Members of the Austrian school of economics – including luminaries such as Ludwig von Mises (1881–1973) and, later, Friedrich Hayek (1889–1992) – argued that the problem stemmed from a distorted cost of capital – thanks in part to misguided central banks – which, in turn, had led to an excessive expansion of credit. According to von Mises:

> Credit expansion cannot increase the supply of real goods. It merely brings about a rearrangement. It diverts capital investment away from the course prescribed by the state of economic wealth and market conditions. It causes production to pursue paths which it would not follow unless the economy were to acquire an increase in material goods. As a result, the upswing lacks a solid base. It is not real prosperity. It is illusory prosperity. It did not develop from an increase in economic wealth. Rather, it arose because the credit expansion created the illusion of such an

increase. Sooner or later it must become apparent that this economic situation is built on sand.[1]

The Depression was, thus, a natural consequence of the easy credit associated with the Roaring Twenties. People had been living beyond their means and, thanks to excessively low interest rates, resources had ended up going to the wrong areas. The solution was simple: people had to adjust to a new, at least temporarily lower, standard of living and, to do so, would have to accept substantial wage cuts. Only if wages were prevented from falling – a result, perhaps, of union power – would unemployment remain high and the economy not eventually recover.

Von Mises was certainly on to something. The Roaring Twenties were a period of easy credit, in part because the Federal Reserve kept US interest rates low to discourage financial outflows from the UK, which, having rejoined the Gold Standard, was struggling to maintain sterling's value on the foreign exchanges. In hindsight, however, von Mises's message seemed overly nihilistic, particularly from a policy-maker's perspective. If policy-makers had left credit too loose, it was presumably their fault if economic collapse subsequently beckoned. Few policy-makers were likely to buy into that theory. In any case, von Mises's prediction that falling wages would reduce unemployment was at variance with the facts.

John Maynard Keynes offered a more attractive argument, at least from the policy-maker's perspective. Like Karl Marx before him, he thought capitalism was unstable. Unlike von Mises, he didn't think markets could easily heal. Instead, he came up with the idea of 'deficient demand', whereby the private sector, left to its own devices, could settle at a level of activity woefully too low to support full employment. This provided an automatic justification for policy activism. Keynes devised the 'multiplier', where an initial monetary or fiscal stimulus would lead to a much bigger overall effect on aggregate demand. For example, an increase in government spending funded by a larger budget deficit would create new jobs that, in turn, would boost aggregate household incomes, some of which would be spent on consumer goods, boosting company profits and, hence, triggering a new wave of job creation: the process would repeat itself, with each incremental increase in demand dependent on the extent of any increase in income spent rather than saved (the so-called marginal propensity to consume). Thus there was no reason why slumps should be sustained. Wise policy-makers would recognize the demand shortfall and offer appropriate remedial action.

Even when interest rates had dropped to zero and, thus, could fall no further, the economy could still be stimulated either through conventional fiscal policy – tax cuts or public spending increases – or via what might now be termed 'unconventional' monetary policy, even if the immediate benefits of such stimulus might seem rather pointless:

> If the Treasury were to fill old bottles with banknotes, bury them at suitable depths in disused coalmines which are then filled up to the surface with town rubbish, and leave it to private enterprise on well-tried principles of laissez-faire to dig the notes up again (the right to do so being obtained, of course, by tendering for leases of the note-bearing territory), there need be no more unemployment and, with the help of the repercussions, the real income of the community, and its capital wealth also, would probably become a good deal greater than it actually is. It would, indeed, be more sensible to build houses and the like; but if there are political and practical difficulties in the way of this, the above would be better than nothing.[2]

Many doubted Keynes's logic. Keynes's *General Theory of Employment, Interest and Money* was published in February 1936, after the Great

Depression had already ended: it was too late, then, to test some of the *Theory*'s main claims. In 1943, Arthur Pigou (1877–1959) argued that, even allowing for the possibility of deficient demand, it need not persist: he suggested that, with falling prices and wages, the real value of money balances would rise and, hence, people would eventually spend more, thereby returning the economy back to full employment.[3]

Michael Kalecki (1899–1970) countered that, in a world of falling prices and wages, real debt levels would also rise, leading to wave upon wave of bankruptcies, thereby making the real balance effect largely irrelevant.[4] Others suggested that, in the real world, wages and prices were typically 'sticky' and thus couldn't fall far enough to deliver the adjustment that might otherwise have returned an economy to full employment. And, much later, Milton Friedman (1912–2006) and Anna Schwartz (born 1915) argued that the Great Depression was less a failure of the private sector but, instead, a failure on behalf of the Federal Reserve to offer enough liquidity to a system desperately short of money: Friedman's monetarism is nowadays typically associated with the painful austerity established in the early 1980s by Margaret Thatcher in the UK and Paul Volcker in the US in a bid to bring inflation back to heel. Yet it could also offer a soothing balm at times of depression associated with falling, not rising, prices.[5]

Each of these economic prophets thought they had the answer: avoid credit booms, make prices and wages flexible, offer monetary and fiscal stimulus. And each of them has, in their own way, encouraged modern-day policy-makers to believe that, with a set of simple rules and the occasional tweak of assorted policy levers, it should be easy enough to keep economies on the straight and narrow.

There is, apparently, no reason to fear the onset of depression, stagnation or inflation because, nowadays, we know how to fix such problems. Inflation targeting – an amalgamation (more accurately, a bastardization) of the views of von Mises and Friedman – supposedly reduces the likelihood of crises fuelled by excessive inflation or credit growth. Meanwhile, following the – totally unexpected – collapse in economic activity in 2008 and 2009, Keynesian policies came in from the cold after decades during which they had been banished to the free market wilderness: the financial crisis, surely, was a classic case of market failure to be solved using Keynes's own unique brand of macroeconomic medicine.

It is as if macroeconomic management requires skills more conventionally associated with pigeon fanciers and shepherds. Homing pigeons do exactly what they're supposed to do: they come home. A simple set of rules – make sure the pigeons are fed and kept safe from both disease and cats – is all that's necessary. But should the rules no longer work, the Keynesian shepherd can be called upon. Give the shepherd the ability to whistle and an intelligent dog and it's not long before the sheep end up where the shepherd wants them to be. In the economic world, policy-makers are no more than pigeon fanciers and shepherds, with their simple rules, their monetary whistles and their fiscal dogs.

Normally, things shouldn't go wrong. On the rare occasions that they do, our policy-makers will put things right. There may be bumps along the way but the path towards ever rising prosperity is nevertheless secure.

After 60 years of ever rising income, policy-makers' confidence didn't seem entirely misplaced. But after hubris came nemesis. Far from preventing the economic crisis, the pursuit of inflation targeting and a dependency on continued Keynesian-style rescue operations from policy-makers may have contributed to the West's financial downfall.

Take, for example, inflation targeting in the UK. In the early years of the new millennium, inflation had a tendency to drop too low, thanks to the deflationary effects on manufactured goods prices of low-cost producers in China and elsewhere in the emerging world. To keep inflation close to target, the Bank of England loosened monetary policy with the intention of delivering higher 'domestically generated' inflation. In other words, credit conditions domestically became excessively loose, a result that doubtless had von Mises spinning in his grave. The inflation target was hit only by allowing domestic imbalances to arise: too much consumption, too much consumer indebtedness, too much leverage within the financial system and too little policy-making wisdom.

Later in the decade, the deflationary impact of falling manufactured goods prices was swamped by rising commodity prices as China, India and others began to exert a dominant influence on demand for the world's scarce resources. In response, the Bank of England raised interest rates. For international investors, higher UK interest rates proved as attractive as a naked flame to the average moth. 'Hot money' poured into the UK, driving up the value of sterling on the foreign exchanges.

For inflation hawks at the Bank of England, this process was welcome: a higher value for sterling meant lower import costs and, hence, reduced inflationary pressures. There was, however, a catch. With the UK financial system now awash with liquidity, lending increased rapidly both within the financial system and to other parts of the economy that, frankly, didn't need any refreshing. In particular, the property sector boomed thanks to an abundance of credit and a gradual reduction in lending standards. Even as official interest rates were rising, interest rates on junk bonds were coming down.

Meanwhile, the US had become dependent on serial bailouts. Alan Greenspan, 'rescuer-in-chief', established his bailout credentials when, as the newly appointed Chairman of the Federal Reserve, he saved the US from economic oblivion following the 1987 stock-market crash – thanks to both interest rate cuts and a browbeating session with bankers to make sure that they didn't starve each other of necessary funds. More was to follow: the 1990 recession was surprisingly mild, the 1994 collapse in the US Treasury market, when bond yields rose dramatically, was shrugged off with remarkable ease, the 1997 Asian crisis hardly registered beyond the – by now tiny – US manufacturing sector, the 2000 technology-related stock-market crash was followed by only the gentlest of recessions, while the recovery that followed seemingly confirmed that American policy-makers, in their collective wisdom, knew how to avoid a Japanese-style stagnation. Greenspan couldn't see the wolves of depression and stagnation hiding in the woods.

Investors began to believe the world was safe. Unwittingly, however, policy-makers had created a huge moral hazard problem. If nothing could really go wrong – if recessions were now milder, inflation permanently lower and depression now only an artefact of economic history – it was worth taking more risk.

The West's economic illusion was most obviously reflected in persistent increases in asset prices relative to the size of economies. Asset prices reflect a set of beliefs about the future. Asset price gains suggest the future may be brightening whereas asset price falls suggest the opposite. Of course, reality is a bit more complicated than that: the level of interest rates, for example, has an influence on the current value of expected future profits and, thus, can change today's asset values even in the absence of a shift in perceptions about corporate earnings. Profits, meanwhile, may be generated either domestically or, thanks to globalization, from elsewhere in the world. Nevertheless, the general principle still holds: asset prices supposedly allow us to peer into a nation's economic future.

Or so we like to think. There is, however, an obvious problem. Our views of the future are amazingly unstable. Keynes's animal spirits – the ups and downs of economic and financial confidence – completely dominate. Collective waves of optimism and pessimism, reflected in asset market volatility, surely say more about how we make judgements of each others' beliefs today than about whether those beliefs are, in aggregate, an accurate forecast of tomorrow's reality. Yet, up until the financial crisis, we were quite happy to accept today's beliefs as an accurate portrayal of tomorrow's reality. It was like coming up with a weather forecast based not on atmospheric pressure, wind direction and so on but, instead, on a survey of people's opinions. Asking people whether it will be sunny or cloudy tomorrow will, however, make no difference to tomorrow's weather.[6]

Those beliefs were reflected not only in ever rising asset prices. They also were associated with substantial increases in debt: borrowers were happy to borrow more because their assets (housing, for example) had risen in value, while lenders were happy to lend – often at ridiculously low interest rates – confident that the loans were backed by suitable collateral (housing, again) and secure in the belief that the world economy was not about to fall off a cliff. After all, this is what politicians and central bankers had promised.

The gains in asset price and debt were extraordinary, at least relative to underlying economic performance. In the US, the Case-Shiller house price index more than doubled between 2000 and 2006. American households took on vast amounts of additional debt. As a share of (rising) household income, mortgage debt rose more than 50 per cent over the same period. The UK's experience was more or less identical.

Yet, in policy-making circles, these extraordinary changes were casually brushed to one side. In 2004, Charlie Bean, at the time the Bank of England's chief economist, argued that there was nothing amiss: he regarded house price gains and the associated increase in household indebtedness as merely 'a transfer of lifetime wealth from younger generations to their parents'.[7] In his view, first-time buyers and those trading up were both willing and able to take out larger mortgages, thanks to lower interest rates and an increase in available mortgage finance. Those lucky parents who were selling their houses at inflated prices were not, however, using their windfall gains to do anything rash, preferring to hold their gains in the form of financial assets than to go on a spending spree. As a result, inflation was mostly well-behaved and the economy was supposedly froth-free. There was, apparently, no reason to question why the supply of mortgages had increased so readily because, in the absence of significant inflationary pressures, the economy was supposedly not in any great danger.

A year later, the President of the Federal Reserve Bank of San Francisco, Janet Yellen, provided her own, rather more robust, reasons for not becoming excessively worried about the booming US housing market, offering pithy responses to three key rhetorical questions:

> First, if the [housing] bubble were to deflate on its own, would the effect on the economy be exceedingly large? Second, is it unlikely that the Fed could mitigate the consequences? Third, is monetary policy the best tool to use to deflate a house-price bubble?
>
> My answers to these questions in the shortest possible form are, 'no', 'no', and 'no'.[8]

In the event of a deflating house price bubble, Yellen was prepared to concede the possibility of a 'good-sized bump in the road' but 'the impact of a gradual spending slowdown could well be cushioned by an easier [monetary] policy'. As it turned out, the US economy came off the road altogether and no amount of monetary stimulus has, to date, led to a return to business as usual.

Their casual dismissal of these gains in illusory wealth might, in hindsight, seem extraordinary but it did these two senior central bankers no real harm: Charlie Bean was appointed Deputy Governor of the Bank of England in 2008, while Janet Yellen became Vice-Chair of the Board of Governors of the Federal Reserve System in

2010, answering only to Ben Bernanke, the Fed's Chairman since 2006. Bean and Yellen chose not to contemplate the future of an economic illusion because, for them, there was no illusion. For all I know, they might also believe a magician genuinely saws a woman in half before putting her back together again.

Bean and Yellen were, of course, in good company. The majority of central bankers believed much the same sort of thing. And, because central bankers had become the high priests of public policy – they were happy to claim the credit, after all, for achieving many years of decent growth with low inflation – their views were, for the most part, accepted by others. Politicians dispensed their fiscal largesse, assuming that the good times would continue to roll. Barney Frank, a Democrat Representative on the House Finance Committee, drew attention in 2005 to:

> an excessive degree of concern right now about home ownership and its role in the [US] economy ... those who argue that house prices are a bubble are missing an important point ... We are talking here about ... homes where there is not the degree of leverage that we have seen elsewhere. This is not the dot.com situation ... You're not going to see the collapse that you see when people talk about a bubble ... Those of us on the [Finance] Committee will continue to push for home ownership.[9]

Households took on bigger and bigger mortgages. Savers, meanwhile, happily purchased all manner of mysterious IOUs, confident in the idea that defaults were either a thing of the very distant past or, alternatively, limited only to untrustworthy nations in the emerging world. They piled into US mortgage-backed securities and all manner of Greek, Spanish, Portuguese and Irish government debt, sowing the seeds for the problems facing the global economy today.

Part of this confidence was linked to the widely held view that the West knew how to avoid Japanese-style economic stagnation. The 2000 stock-market crash certainly looked ominous but, through the copious use of monetary and fiscal policy, its impact on the broader economy was swatted away with apparent ease.

Unfortunately, there was a significant fiscal cost. At first, this was seen mostly in the US and the UK. At the end of the 1990s, both countries appeared to be in rude fiscal health. Excluding interest payments on existing debt and adjusting for the stage of the economic cycle, both were running budget surpluses of around 3 per cent of national income, a truly impressive result relative to performance in earlier decades.

Within a handful of years, however, this admirable restraint had unravelled. Long before the onset of the financial crisis, the 3 per cent surpluses had turned into 3 per cent deficits. In the US, the culprit was a mixture of tax cuts and big increases in public spending: government revenues fell from well over 35 per cent of national income in 2000 to less than 32 per cent two years later, while public spending increased by 2 per cent of national income over the same period. In the UK, the fiscal deterioration was almost entirely the result of huge increases in public spending, as I argued in the previous chapter.

A good fiscal principle is for governments to save during the good times to make sure they have room to borrow during the bad times. That principle was completely abandoned in both the US and the UK and, as it turned out, in almost all countries within the eurozone. In hindsight, the early years of the new millennium were the good times. They were hardly vintage years – the earlier stock-market crash had put paid to that – but, under the circumstances, they were perhaps the best we could hope for. Yet, despite a return to reasonable growth, governments chose to run bigger and bigger deficits, confident in the idea that ever rising prosperity was guaranteed. Not content with low interest rates alone, the reckless pursuit of fiscal stimulus even as households ran up huge debts was, to say the least, misguided. Governments became addicted to fiscal pump-priming long before the financial crisis gained traction.

Indeed, the fiscal stimulus offered prior to the financial crisis was bigger than the stimulus offered afterwards, at least in the US and the UK. This was not so much the result of post-crisis caution – government debt rose uncontrollably across the Western world in the years following the 2008 Lehman Brothers collapse – but, rather, because Western economies were on fiscal life support long before the crisis happened. The assumption was always that growth would bail us out. That proved to be hopelessly wide of the mark.

Long into the crisis, the policy debate has descended into an undignified argument between those who favour austerity and those who believe stimulus is the way forward. It's certainly true that, in some cases, austerity policies have made matters worse: in southern Europe, budget cutbacks have led to economic collapse, which, in turn, has reduced tax revenues, increased expenditure on unemployment benefit and, hence, had a counterproductive effect on the budget deficit and the trajectory of government debt, a process that investors have been swift to punish. Yet problems in southern Europe also reflected an absence of financial flexibility: put another way, there was no central bank to act as 'lender of last resort' to governments in dire financial straits. Elsewhere, the same constraints didn't hold. Yes, the UK delivered fiscal austerity in 2011 and 2012 and it turns out that the economy performed poorly. However, back in 2010, most forecasters – including the Office for Budget Responsibility, the independent fiscal watchdog – concluded that loose monetary policy alone would lead to a decent recovery in economic activity that, in turn, would allow room for some kind of fiscal contraction without too much collateral damage. It wasn't so much reckless fiscal austerity that threw the UK economy off course but, rather, the impotence of monetary policy.

Von Mises would have regarded this attempt to kick-start Western economies through ever more desperate monetary measures as the failed pursuit of illusory, not real, prosperity – claims on future economic activity that might never materialize. Yet our societies have not been prepared to make the 'real' versus 'illusory' distinction. We think we've discovered the secrets of ever rising prosperity partly because we're terrified of the consequences should prosperity crumble in our hands. We'd rather stick to the illusion of prosperity than the reality of having to live within our means.

The economic and financial crisis, however, is slowly putting paid to that illusion. Today, nation-states are still shell-shocked, seemingly unable to come to terms with persistent economic and financial disappointment. Policy-makers continue to promise a return to prosperity sooner rather than later. All the while, however, levels of economic activity remain surprisingly muted. Interest rate cuts, fiscal stimulus, quantitative easing and exhortation have all been used to kick-start economic activity, all seemingly to no avail. There is no quick fix. And policies designed to generate recovery may only be prolonging painful stagnation.

We are becoming addicted to policy-making drugs. They may now be doing more harm than good.

CHAPTER FOUR

STIMULUS JUNKIES

We hope our monetary and fiscal drugs will cure us but they may only be making our problems easier to live with, at least in the short term. Their persistent use, however, may be associated with unwanted side-effects.

For the most part, monetary and fiscal policies have, rightly, been regarded as the equivalent of drugs designed to fix the underlying problem. Interest rate cuts are normally temporary – what comes down eventually goes back up again. Big budget deficits designed to kick-start an economy automatically recede as the subsequent economic recovery tops up tax revenues and reduces social expenditures. Just like a course of antibiotics, economic stimulus is only needed for so long. The economic patient eventually makes a full recovery.

Even when recovery isn't complete, it doesn't mean to say the policy drugs haven't worked. The recession that followed the failure of Lehman Brothers in 2008 was bad enough but it could have been a lot worse. The policy stimulus on offer was far greater than anything provided during the Great Depression and, thankfully, the economic outcome was – partly as a consequence – a lot better. The overall peak-to-trough decline in US national income, for example, was 5.1 per cent compared with a whopping 30 per cent or so during the Depression.[1]

Yet we're not satisfied with this 'success'. That things could have been a lot worse is not the kind of argument that wins votes. We have hopes, aspirations and entitlements that need to be met. Stagnation, understandably, isn't good enough. We'd rather hear that economic recovery is just around the corner. And we'll happily believe anyone who can, apparently, lead us to the Promised Land. In the process, we have become addicted to policy-making drugs. We're no longer sure, however, whether they're really doing us any good. Yes, they may be hiding the pain but, in a world of excessive debts and aggressive deleveraging, is there any evidence that policy drugs are fostering lasting economic recovery?

Painkillers come in all shapes and sizes, from the humble aspirin through to powerful morphine. Across nations, however, there is significant disagreement over which painkillers can be used, either over the counter or through prescription. Vicodin, a trade name for a combination of hydrocodone bitartrate and acetaminophen, is available via prescription in the US but, alongside heroin, cocaine and LSD, is categorized as a Class A drug in the UK and is, thus, illegal. Hydrocodone is an opioid agonist and, as such, can be 'abused and [is] subject to criminal diversion'.[2] In the US, the benefits are seen to outweigh the costs: in the UK, the reverse argument applies.

Put another way, painkillers can be used, but they can come with unwelcome side-effects either for the individual (acetaminophen can lead to liver failure or death) or for society as a whole (Vicodin is too often used as a recreational drug and, thus, associated with criminal activity). The same is true of economic stimulus. Used sparingly, it can be effective, but used for a sustained period of time, it may only cause lasting damage. Western nations have become hooked on the economic equivalent of painkillers. Do these drugs offer salvation or are we merely suffering from a damaging policy addiction?

In March 2009, UK bank rate – the interest rate set by the Bank of England – fell to a mere 0.5 per cent, the lowest since records for this particular series began in the 1970s. Three years later, bank rate remained at this – by historic standards – absurdly low level. By that stage, the UK government's long-term borrowing costs had dropped to well below 2 per cent, the lowest since records began in the early 1700s.

The UK's experience was hardly unique. At the end of 2008, shortly after the collapse of Lehman Brothers, US Fed funds – the equivalent of UK bank rate – dropped more or less to zero. And, as with the UK, US government borrowing costs plummeted. The same was happening in parts of continental Europe, notably Germany.

Initially, central bankers hoped remarkably low borrowing costs would kick-start economic growth. It didn't work. Success would have allowed interest rates to have gone straight back up again. Their failure to do so tells us a great deal about the implications of the financial crisis. An interest rate is, after all, a payment for consumption foregone. Those who wish to invest for all our futures are prepared to pay a higher interest rate on any borrowings – to encourage us to defer consumption – if the future is seen to be particularly bright. If, on the other hand, the future is regarded as decidedly murky, interest rates are likely to remain persistently low, reflecting an absence of capital investment.

At first sight, this might seem a little odd. Interest rate cuts are, after all, designed to boost growth. They do so, however, primarily by making it cheaper to borrow, all other things equal. For a given – *ex ante* – view of the future, lower interest rates may encourage additional risk-taking and, hence, make the – *ex post* – future a little brighter. If, however, our collective view of the future becomes ever more miserable for other reasons, interest rates will simply end up at rock bottom and stay there. In those circumstances, interest cuts from central banks merely corroborate our collective gloom. Just think of Japan's experience during its lost decades.

Persistently low interest rates are, therefore, a sign of ongoing economic failure rather than a harbinger of future economic recovery. The post-financial crisis world is a deeply worrying place not so much because interest rates came down to such low levels initially but, instead, because the circumstances in which they might eventually go up again seem increasingly difficult to imagine. Central bankers know all this, which is why they have resorted to the use of increasingly unconventional monetary policies. They certainly don't want to admit to be caught in the so-called liquidity trap. Originally defined by Keynes as a situation where increases in the money supply would make no difference to the prevailing level of interest rates, the liquidity trap has been reinterpreted since Japan's experience of zero interest rates and deflation in the 1990s to imply that monetary policy becomes impotent once interest rates drop to zero. Central bankers have no desire to admit to their impotence in these circumstances so they've had to think of something else.

For the most part, it's been quantitative easing in one form or another. The idea is simple enough. Western banking systems are broken. They can no longer easily channel funds from savers to borrowers. Hence there is a serious shortage of money. Knowing this, the natural response by households and companies is to hang on to the money they've got, stuffing it under the proverbial mattress. Quantitative easing is designed to overcome the perceived shortage by directly injecting money into the economy at large, without having to go through the banking system. If we all believe money is then easily available, we'll no longer carry on hoarding it, and spending will inevitably rise.

How does it work in practice? The central bank creates new money not so much via a printing press but, instead, via an entry on a computer screen. The money is then used to purchase bonds (IOUs) already owned by investors. In the US experience post-Lehman, these bonds initially included a large amount of consumer and automobile debt – stuff that had become increasingly toxic during the subprime crisis – while, in the UK, the focus of attention was largely on government bonds (gilts) – primarily because the UK asset-backed securities market was still in its infancy.

Increased central bank asset purchases boost demand for those assets and, hence, raise their price. As the price is, in effect, the inverse of the yield, a higher price necessarily implies a lower yield. And if yields on asset-backed securities and government bonds are heading lower, the current holders may decide to look elsewhere for higher returns. Demand for riskier assets – equities, real estate – may then increase. Listed companies can then raise funds more cheaply – via the stock market – and households can, in theory, borrow more easily against the – now-rising – value of their properties. As such, the economy should be able to pick itself up from off the floor and return to a reasonable rate of economic growth.

As Mervyn King, the Governor of the Bank of England between 2003 and 2013, explained in late 2009:

> [Asset] purchases are aimed at injecting additional money directly into the economy. Investors will look to use some of this money to diversify into assets that have a higher return. And that in turn will boost the prices of those assets, reducing yields and the cost to companies of raising funds in financial markets. Ultimately, that will help stimulate spending, smooth the necessary rebalancing of the economy, and keep inflation close to target.[3]

It sounds simply marvellous, but does it actually work? Of course, we cannot be sure about what might have happened in the absence of quantitative easing. What we can be sure of, however, is that economic outcomes have been worse than the proponents of quantitative easing themselves foresaw.

In mid-2010, for example, the Federal Reserve's top policy-makers thought US economic growth would be in a range of between 2.9 per cent and 3.8 per cent in 2010 and between 2.9 per cent and 4.5 per cent in 2011. The actual outcomes were 3.0 per cent and 1.7 per cent respectively.[4] In other words, the US economy's performance in 2011 was significantly worse than even the most cautious of the forecasts offered by the Federal Reserve in the middle of the previous year. The Bank of England was similarly optimistic, believing that the most likely outcome for economic growth in the UK in 2011 was around 3 per cent, a view conditioned on £200 billion of asset purchases (in other words, quantitative easing). The actual outcome was a rather more modest 0.7 per cent. Admittedly, the Bank had accepted that there was a small risk of stagnation but it regarded growth of around 5 per cent as equally likely.[5]

The evidence strongly suggests that quantitative easing, in its various forms, is not the magic wand it was often made out to be. Why didn't it deliver the promised recovery?

Monetary policy works for the most part through its impact on people's expectations. None of us employs a perfectly calibrated economic model but we intuitively know what the likely reaction to an interest rate cut is going to be. Mortgage rates come down, homeowners with a mortgage are, as a result, better off, companies' borrowing costs drop and, thus, spending begins to revive: if we all believe this, a rate cut can become a self-fulfilling event. Quantitative easing, unfortunately, doesn't offer the same intuitive message: for many, it sounds distinctly suspect, has no personal relevance and, thus, makes little difference to economic behaviour. And with economic performance far worse than the protagonists of quantitative easing expected, the credibility of such esoteric measures has steadily withered on the vine.

One reason for increased scepticism relates to the impact of lower long-term interest rates – thanks to quantitative easing – on pension fund deficits. As Charlie Bean, the Deputy Governor of the Bank of England, explained in a May 2012 speech:

> Quantitative easing does not inherently raise pension deficits. It all depends on the initial position of the fund, with the movement in liabilities and assets likely to be broadly comparable when a scheme is fully funded. But the more a scheme is underfunded to begin with, the more it will find its deficit increased . . . By reducing [gilt] yields, QE increases the cost of purchasing a given future stream of income.
>
> So if a fund starts off relatively 'asset poor', the sponsors will now find it more costly to acquire the assets to match its future obligations . . . A corollary of this is that the cost of provisioning against additional pension entitlements being accumulated by currently serving staff unambiguously rises.[6]

This would, perhaps, be a small price to pay if, as a result of quantitative easing, the economy quickly recovered, allowing quantitative easing to be reversed. In that case, bonds held by the central bank as a result of quantitative easing would be sold back to the market, yields would rise and the pressure on pension deficits would be alleviated. Yet this hasn't happened. Compared with a typical period of recession, during which interest rates fall rapidly only to rise swiftly thereafter, the absence of meaningful recovery leaves pension funds facing the prospect of permanently lower interest rates and, thus, growing difficulties in meeting their obligations.

While low interest rates are not the fault of QE alone, there can be no doubt that the persistence of low interest rates has left many pension funds seriously in deficit. That, in turn, threatens changes in behaviour elsewhere within the economy that are ultimately inconsistent with economic recovery: individuals save more (or borrow less), aware that they are at risk of suffering a pension shortfall; companies choose to divert profits into their pension funds instead of investing in the capital that might kick-start economic growth; and governments have to raise taxes or cut public spending as they bid to satisfy the expectations of the boomers.

Meanwhile, the benefits of QE have a nasty habit of being channelled to precisely those parts of the economy that are unlikely to respond in a positive way. If, for example, lowering bond yields leads to a rally in stock prices, it will be easier for big blue chip companies to raise funds. Most of these companies, however, are already very profitable and don't need the extra money. Indeed, given the uncertain economic environment, many of them are choosing to return funds to their shareholders in the form of higher dividends or bigger share buybacks. Small and medium-sized companies that have little or no access to capital markets and, instead, remain dependent on bank lending have, however, derived little or no benefit.[7] The same arguments apply to households. By lowering long-term interest rates, quantitative easing should, in theory, boost the value of government bond portfolios (the price of bonds goes up) as well as the value of other, riskier, assets (with government yields now lower, other assets are relatively more attractive.) Yet, in the UK, the vast bulk of these assets are owned by the mature and the rich: those over 45 own around 80 per cent of financial assets (excluding pensions), while the richest 5 per cent of households own 40 per cent of those assets. Put another way, the rich become even richer even as the economy as a whole remains weak. And, on the whole, the rich tend to have a low marginal propensity to consume.

And there's no guarantee that the benefits of quantitative easing stay at home. We live in a world where finance can flow across borders at the click of a button. Printing money is all very well but the institutional funds that receive it in exchange for central bank asset purchases may choose to invest in other parts of the world where growth prospects appear, rightly or wrongly, to be superior. Indeed, as we saw in the aftermath of the Lehman collapse, the process can become self-fulfilling: while growth rates remained at rock bottom in the West, the rest of the world bounced back with considerable aplomb. That, in turn, led to pressures from an unexpected source. Strong demand from China and other fast-growing emerging nations boosted commodity prices. For the West, this was an unfortunate outcome: higher commodity prices, combined with rising unemployment and very low wage increases, led to a significant squeeze on real incomes, making the repayment of existing – excessive – debts even more difficult.

Wilful manipulation of government bond yields also means that the anchor for all asset values is slowly corroding. That surely means that capital will increasingly be at risk of being misallocated as a result of mispricing within financial markets, undermining long-term growth prospects. Most obviously, quantitative easing has allowed governments to avoid being penalized by the so-called bond market vigilantes. We have ended up with both incredibly low interest rates and incredibly large amounts of government debt. In the modern era, only Japan has previously managed to pull off that trick. Yet its economy has gone from one disappointment to the next.

LIVING WITH POLICY PAINKILLERS LONG TERM

As with Vicodin, excessive use of policy painkillers may eventually prove dangerously addictive. Economic incentives may change in ways inimical to long-term prosperity. Here's why.

Before the financial crisis, monetary and fiscal policies were, in most countries, conducted separately. This was a reaction to the excess inflation of the 1970s, a period during which central banks were too often required to do the bidding of their political masters. For a while, inflation was endemic, leading to losses for those on fixed monetary incomes – most obviously pensioners – and huge distortions to the price mechanism – Adam Smith's 'invisible hand'. By making central banks independent, and thus no longer subject to the temptations of the electoral cycle, the hope was that inflation would eventually be brought back under control, leaving the world a much happier place.

The financial crisis has destroyed this separation of monetary church from state. By altering the yield on government debt, quantitative easing has, in effect, brought governments and central banks back together again. As a result, policy incentives have begun to change and, once again, central bankers are in danger of returning to an overly intimate relationship with their political masters.[8]

No government wants to run out of money, to be starved of funds by its creditors. Those that are in danger of doing so often resort to printing too much money and, as a result, suffer from hyperinflation. Zimbabwe provides the best twenty-first century example: in July 2008, the inflation rate stood at a modest 231,150,888.87 per cent.[9]

Western nations surely will not plan to go down that route. Populations are ageing, grey power is on the rise and no vote-seeking political party would advocate an excessive dose of inflation that might, in turn, destroy the real spending power of pensioners. There is, however, another alternative. Governments can jump to the front of the credit queue, pushing to the side other would-be borrowers. They can engage in 'financial repression', siphoning funds to themselves that might otherwise have gone to, for example, small and medium-sized companies.[10] Quantitative easing provides one mechanism to allow them to do so.

To be fair, this was not the intention. As I've already argued, the idea was to kick-start economic growth via quantitative easing, creating a virtuous circle of rising activity, higher tax revenues, falling social expenditures, reduced budget deficits and, hence, stable – or, even better, falling – levels of government debt. The underlying assumption was that our economic problem was merely a shortage of demand and credit and that, with the appropriate monetary medicine, the economy would return to some kind of normality. The medicine, however, hasn't worked. Quantitative easing has delivered little in the way of normality. It has, instead, contributed to what might best be described as four 'traps': the fiscal trap, the exchange rate trap, the 'zombie' trap and the regulatory trap.

The Fiscal Trap

The failure of quantitative easing to deliver recovery has, naturally enough, left investors feeling underwhelmed. One consequence of this has been a lack of economic risk-taking: profits may be high but capital spending is low. Put another way, companies are no longer interested so much in growing their businesses, focusing instead on trying to avoid losing money and, in the process, often returning cash to their shareholders. They, in turn, end up investing in what they regard as 'safe' assets less likely to fall in value. For the most part, that's been government bonds.

Admittedly, quantitative easing has delivered the occasional temporary shot in the arm for riskier financial assets – most obviously, equities. It hasn't, however, led to the broader economic recovery that might have sustained such initial gains. Each time equity markets have rallied – as investors anticipate the positive effects of quantitative easing on the broader economy – they have subsequently stalled in the light of persistent economic gloom.

At the same time, already large budget deficits have, inevitably, ended up larger still thanks to economic outcomes weaker than finance ministries had expected. As a result, government debt has continued to rise as a share of national income. Whereas, in normal economic circumstances, governments might be penalized for such profligacy via a higher cost of borrowing, quantitative easing prevents that from happening. The government knows the central bank will not want to see higher interest rates – that might hinder recovery – but, in the absence of higher rates, there is no real pressure on the government to make tough budgetary choices.[11]

In other words, fiscal slippage can be accommodated because bond yields simply won't be allowed to rise, even while the government's credit status is deteriorating. Standard & Poor's, the ratings agency, downgraded US government debt on 5 August 2011 from triple-A to AA+, at the same time placing it on negative watch. It was the first such downgrade in the 70-year history of US government debt ratings. The day before the downgrade, 10-year Treasuries yielded 2.56 per cent. A year later, despite the downgrade and a blistering attack by S&P on the US Treasury Department's fiscal plans, yields were a full percentage point lower. Alongside the effects on risk appetite of the eurozone crisis, quantitative easing had worked its magic.

In effect, central banks are underwriting government debt, whether or not the public finances are in a healthy state. Investors know that the value of government bonds is guaranteed by central banks, at least in nominal terms. That guarantee makes government bonds even more attractive to risk-averse investors. They end up following the central bank's lead. But, by implication, if government bonds are now more attractive, other assets are less so. The government ends up awash with credit, but, at the same time, the rest of the economy is starved of it. This is a form of financial repression, a way of ensuring that the government is able to rig credit markets to suit its own aims even if the economy as a whole may perform less well as a consequence.

Quantitative easing may originally have been designed to improve economic performance but it has also allowed governments to raise debt on the cheap. With economic stagnation, quantitative easing has merely allowed governments to postpone the fiscal 'day of reckoning'. And the longer stagnation persists, the worse the reckoning will eventually be. Quantitative easing is a useful way of masking persistent increases in government debt, as if those increases come at no economic cost. It is also, by implication, a useful way of allowing governments to muscle their way to the front of the credit queue: with the value of government bonds in effect 'ring-fenced' by the actions of central banks, quantitative easing in a risk-averse world will only encourage more and more investors to invest in government bonds. Sovereign IOUs may not make much money but, in a world of persistent economic disappointment, they offer for domestic investors a neat way of avoiding losing money, one reason why, during the depths of the eurozone crisis in the summer of 2012, investors took their money out of southern Europe, investing it instead in Treasuries and gilts.

The Exchange Rate Trap

While central bankers may have no intention of creating excessive inflation, arguing that, with plenty of spare capacity, quantitative easing will have a bigger impact on output than on prices, they may be more relaxed regarding the exchange rate. Continuous printing of money, other things equal, should depress the value of the currency on the foreign exchanges. While this may encourage some degree of 'rebalancing' away from domestic consumption towards exports, it is really no more than a hidden tax on domestic income. A falling exchange rate leads to higher import prices and hence reduces a county's purchasing power over internationally produced goods and services. Quantitative easing that fails to bring stagnation to an end simply leaves a nation worse off. The more it's used, the more incomes will be squeezed in real terms. It is the equivalent of the Peronist tariffs in Argentina, a mechanism of slow, but inevitable, suffocation. The UK's experience since sterling's dramatic decline at the end of 2008 is a case in point: the devaluation lifted import prices, raised inflation, squeezed real spending power yet did little to reinvigorate export performance. It was, thus, a stealthy way of lowering living standards and, hence, made the repayment of debt more problematic.

The process also, however, threatens the outbreak of so-called 'currency wars'. Any policy-maker engaged in printing money in a bid to lower the exchange rate is, in effect, trying to rebalance not only their own economy but also the economies of a nation's major competitors. A fall in sterling, for example, should encourage in the UK a shift of resources into exports and away from domestic demand. But that will only work if other countries adjust in exactly the opposite direction. Should they refuse to do so – by, for example, preventing their own currencies from appreciating too far – the benefits accruing to the devaluing nation will be muted even as international tensions are inflamed. Indeed, since sterling's 2008–9 decline, the UK's export performance has been profoundly disappointing. In 2012, Germany, France, Italy, Spain and Greece all managed to do better than the UK. China, meanwhile, is more reliant on Angola than the UK as a trading partner.

The 'Zombie' Trap

Companies and individuals that might have gone bankrupt during earlier recessions, victims of their own profligacy and the unexpected impact of a sudden fall in demand, have been kept on life support thanks to the remarkable amount of policy stimulus – low interest rates, quantitative easing – on offer since the onset of the financial crisis. Their survival, in turn, may have reduced the profitability and income of more efficient companies and harder-working individuals. Worse, they may have reduced the number of new market entrants. If banks are still lending to 'zombie' companies and individuals, they will have fewer funds left over to lend to potentially more dynamic parts of the economy. The growth rate of the economy inevitably atrophies: surviving is not the same thing as thriving.[12]

The Regulatory Trap

Quantitative easing provides one way for governments to jump to the front of the credit queue. It is not, however, the only way. Regulations designed to reduce the risk of financial implosion are another useful device to divert funds into the hands of government. Again, the intention may never have been there initially, but that, however, is not really the point. Like quantitative easing, regulation can trigger the law of unintended consequences. The Basel III regulations provide a good example. Even with the revisions announced on 6 January 2013,[13] which relaxed the constraints on banks, the rules still make it easier for governments than other would-be borrowers to raise funds from the banking system. To understand why, it's worth taking a look at the Liquidity Coverage Ratio (LCR), defined as the ratio of high quality liquid assets (HQLA) to total net cash outflows over the next 30 days and designed to protect an institution in the light of a 2008-style liquidity stress scenario. What exactly are these high quality liquid assets?

In the words of the Basel Committee on Banking Supervision:

> HQLA are comprised of Level 1 and Level 2 assets. Level 1 assets generally include cash, central bank reserves, and certain marketable securities backed by sovereigns and central banks, among others. These assets are typically of the highest quality and the most liquid, and there is no limit on the extent to which a bank can hold these assets to meet the LCR. Level 2 assets . . . include certain marketable government securities as well as corporate debt securities, residential mortgage backed securities and equities that meet

certain conditions. Level 2 assets are typically of slightly lesser quality and may not in aggregate account for more than 40% of a bank's stock of HQLA.

In other words, sovereign paper is regarded as both safer and more liquid than other kinds of bonds. Regulation thus forces banks to lend proportionately more to governments than to other potential borrowers, *whether or not the governments are, themselves, a good credit risk*. Regulations designed to prevent banks from experiencing severe liquidity shortages have, unintentionally, morphed into arrangements that enable governments to receive preferential treatment from creditors whether or not their fiscal plans are sustainable. Governments have jumped to the front of the credit queue.

THE CONSEQUENCES OF QUEUE JUMPING

Quantitative easing and enhanced liquidity buffers for banks in effect work in opposite directions. Together, they offer a 'push-me-pull-you' approach to the financial crisis: quantitative easing is designed to get more cash into the private sector while enhanced liquidity buffers put pressure on financial institutions to reduce lending to the private sector. While both policies may make sense in isolation – economic stimulus is no bad thing, while higher liquidity buffers may provide some protection against bank failure during a future systemic financial crisis – it is difficult to reconcile one with the other. Indeed, one consequence of this 'push-me-pull-you' approach has been a severing of the relationship between so-called narrow money – the stuff the central bank can control, made up of notes and coin in circulation and banks' balances at the central bank – and broad money – the money created within the banking system, including lending to the private sector. In the UK, narrow money growth picked up rapidly post-crisis thanks to quantitative easing, but broad money – which really matters for the health of the broader economy – barely budged. As the Japanese discovered with their own quantitative easing experiments during their two lost decades, you can only lead a horse to water.

Yet this 'push-me-pull-you' problem pales into insignificance compared with the long-term implications of addiction to quantitative easing combined with persistently high government borrowing and ever higher levels of government debt. The 'subsidy' received by government – reflecting the underwriting of the value of government bonds by the central bank – only diverts funds to government from other parts of the economy. One obvious implication of this is a widening spread between the low interest rates paid by governments benefiting from quantitative easing and the higher interest rates paid by other would-be borrowers. Households in both the US and the UK ended up paying much higher interest rates than their respective governments in 2011 and 2012 even though, unlike their governments, households had at least repaid some debt. Internationally, Spain's fiscal position was, in 2012, better than the UK's yet, thanks to the constraints imposed by the eurozone, its borrowing costs were shockingly high. International investors were happier to flock to the 'underwritten' bonds of the US and the UK, notwithstanding possible long-term currency risk.

If quantitative easing fails to deliver a lasting recovery in economic activity, it shifts from being part of the solution to becoming part of the problem. It provides an incentive to governments to borrow excessively, it perversely induces risk-averse behaviour among financial investors and it may even lead to a higher cost of borrowing within the private sector. It is also, unfortunately, highly addictive. If the economy should fail to strengthen, the central bank will be under pressure to deliver more quantitative easing but, by doing to, the vicious cycle may simply repeat itself.

Yet bringing quantitative easing to an end is hardly straightforward. Imagine, for example, that a central bank decides quantitative easing has become dangerously addictive and indicates to investors not only that the programme will be put on hold – which both the Federal Reserve and Bank of England have signalled from time to time – but that it will come to a decisive end. The likely result is a rise in government bond yields as the central bank's underwriting comes to a conclusion. If, however, the economy is still weak, the rise in bond yields will surely be regarded as a threat to economic recovery. The government will then blame the central bank for undermining the nation's economic health and the central bank's independence will then be under threat. Far better, then, simply to continue with quantitative easing or even, perhaps, to expand the central bank's remit.

There are two ways of doing so. The first is for the central bank to buy a much wider range of assets – not just government paper but also asset backed-securities, corporate bonds, foreign currency or maybe even equities. Central banks have dabbled in all of these areas in the past and many continue to do so today.[14] There is, however, an obvious drawback. A central bank simply doesn't have the resources to manage credit risk. Allocating capital is supposed to be the job of the invisible hand, not the long arm of the central banker. Widening the range of assets to be purchased turns a central bank slowly but surely into the financial equivalent of a state planner. It is not an edifying vision.

The second option is to dig holes or to send for the helicopters. Quantitative easing is designed to bypass the banking system in a bid to put cash directly in people's pockets. One reason why it hasn't been particularly successful is simply that people already feel heavily indebted and have no desire to borrow any more. There thus needs to be a 'borrower of last resort'. That involves Keynes's idea of digging holes in the road or, alternatively, Milton Friedman's idea of dropping money from helicopters onto the population at large.

In practice, the most obvious way of doing all this is for the government to sell newly issued debt to the central bank and to use the money so created to fund increases in public spending (the equivalent of digging holes in the road) or reductions in taxation (the equivalent of a helicopter dropping dollar bills into a bank account). In other words, the government would have to increase its borrowing even further and fund the incremental increase not by borrowing from creditors but, instead, by asking the central bank to print money.

This not only allows the government to borrow cheaply. It also, in theory, has a positive impact on spending in the private sector. The level of demand depends not only on current but also expected future interest rates. Those taking out a mortgage, for example, need to think about the interest payments on their loan not just this year and the next, but also in many years' time. For monetary policy to work, the central bank needs to change the public's perceptions of where those future interest rates will be. If interest rates are already at zero, they clearly cannot decline any further in nominal terms. In real terms, however, interest rates may decline if, in the future, inflation rises and the central bank deliberately chooses not to respond. In other words, to convince the public today to borrow more, the central bank has to promise not to raise interest rates in the event of a future rise in inflation. As and when prices and wages eventually rise, the real cost of borrowing will then decline, rewarding those who took out big loans during the difficult times.

While the economic logic is sound enough, the commitment not to raise interest rates – in other words, the commitment to allow inflation to rise – needs to be completely credible. Instead, it sounds counterintuitive. All over the world, central banks have committed themselves to meeting inflation targets.[15] If inflation rises, the public have been told – time and time again – that central banks will respond by raising interest rates. To escape from a liquidity trap, however, this is precisely what central banks must not do: and, moreover, the public have to be completely convinced that central banks will not do it.[16] Many people, however, will presumably think that, with the first whiff of inflation, central banks would immediately shift interest rates back up again. Central bankers are, after all, conditioned to be the monetary equivalents of Pavlov's dogs: when the inflationary bell rings, they immediately start to salivate.

That reflex needs to be switched off. But how? The public needs to be convinced that central bankers will not behave in their old-fashioned ways, in the same way that a lion tamer needs to convince himself that the lions won't bite. Few people, however, volunteer to be lion tamers and those who do sometimes end up missing a limb or two.

There is, however, one way in which a commitment to higher inflation could be made credible. The government could impose a higher inflation target on the central bank – or at least commit to a big increase in the price level – and, at the same time, begin to issue a lot more government debt. Should inflation then fail to rise, the government would be left with a much higher real value of debt with all sorts of nasty consequences for taxation. In that sense, the commitment to higher inflation would be credible because the costs of not delivering higher inflation would be politically costly.[17]

Yet today, it's difficult to see what the political rationale in favour of higher inflation might be. Those who would object most vociferously to higher inflation – pensioners and would-be pensioners on fixed incomes – are the boomers who typically cast the largest number of votes in elections. In the 2010 UK General Election, for example, only 44 per cent of 18–24 year olds voted, while well over 70 per cent of those aged above 55 popped down to the polling stations.[18] It would be a brave politician indeed who sought power promising higher inflation as a means to solve our economic problems.

In any case, the relationship between unconventional monetary policy and the broader economy is, at best, unpredictable, as the UK found to its cost when, in attempting to lift demand after the financial crisis, it only managed to raise inflation instead. And when the central bank is printing money to fund excessive government borrowing, it can lead not so much to economic recovery but, instead, to rapidly rising prices: just think of the aforementioned Zimbabwe or, perhaps, 1980s Brazil, post-war Hungary or the Weimar Republic. A central banker who jumps into bed with a finance minister too often ends up with a nasty dose of hyperinflation.

In the *General Theory*, Keynes famously wrote: 'Practical men, who believe themselves to be quite exempt from any intellectual influence, are usually the slaves of some defunct economist.'[19] Today, it seems, we have become slaves of central bankers whose defunct ideas reflect their waning mystical powers.

The policy drugs being dispensed by central bankers are more addictive painkillers than cures, more Vicodin than antibiotics. Persistently low interest rates are a sign of lasting economic failure, not a harbinger of future economic success. Central bankers – alongside politicians – continue to claim they have unlocked the secrets of future economic wealth but, collectively, they appear to be suffering from a delusional 'optimism bias'. Year after year, economic outcomes are worse than expected, leading to more and more near-term stimulus.

This has left central bankers in an unfortunate political position. Once regarded as merely monetary technicians, their decisions today have less influence on the level of economic activity and more on its distribution. Central bankers are, slowly but surely, being dragged into the world of politics. Quantitative easing and other associated macroeconomic 'quick fixes' are, it turns out, proving to be not much more than mechanisms to redistribute income and wealth, even though central bankers are, like modern-day royalty, supposed to stand above the political fray.

An ongoing commitment to deliver low interest rates penalizes savers even as it benefits borrowers. Regulations designed to improve bank liquidity reduce lending to the private sector even as lending to the public sector is increased. Continuous weakness of the exchange rate robs households of spending power even as export prospects improve. This is redistribution by stealth, the equivalent of imposing taxes on people in the absence of any kind of democratic mandate or proper political legitimacy. It is a process not so much of kick-starting an economic recovery but, instead, of redistributing the spoils of past economic success and failure.

Mervyn King, the Governor of the Bank of England from 2003 to 2013, more or less admitted as much at the beginning of 2011 in explaining why the UK was better off accepting – temporarily – an above-target rate of inflation:

> If the Monetary Policy Committee [of the Bank of England] had raised Bank Rate significantly, inflation may well have started to fall back this year, but only because the recovery would have been slower, unemployment higher and average earnings rising even more slowly than now. The erosion of living standards would have been greater. The idea that the MPC could have preserved living standards, by preventing the rise in inflation without also pushing down earnings growth, is wishful thinking.
>
> Of course, it is possible to argue that the current recession should have been even deeper in order to keep inflation closer to the target. But that proposition ... [is not] consistent with the remit given to the MPC which states that 'the actual inflation rate will on occasions depart from its target as a result of shocks and disturbances. Attempts to keep inflation at the inflation target in these circumstances may cause undesirable volatility in output'. The MPC has stuck to its remit ...

...At some point Bank Rate will have to return to a more normal level. When that time comes, it will I know be a relief to many people dependent on income from savings.[20]

King's argument was mostly couched in aggregate terms: inflation could have been brought down to a lower level but only at the expense of a bigger fall in activity that, in the Bank's judgement, would have been not only unwelcome but also inconsistent with its inflation targeting remit. Yet there is something disconcerting about King's remarks. If inflation was allowed to overshoot target post-crisis thanks to the effects of higher import prices, why wasn't it encouraged to undershoot pre-crisis when import prices were unusually soft? There appears to have been an inconsistency of approach that, arithmetically, has delivered a higher-than-target inflation rate over the long term. If so, the Bank's actions are tantamount to ensuring savers lose out: it is a breach of trust.

Savers, meanwhile, must be wondering whether the day will ever arrive when interest rates return to more normal levels. If quantitative easing fails to stimulate economic recovery and, instead, ends up simply as an addictive economic painkiller, its side-effects will eventually dominate the headlines. The creation of winners and losers was never supposed to be part of a central bank's remit yet the process is increasingly moving to centre stage.

Central bankers are not elected politicians. They are mostly selected for their economic and financial skills, not because they know how to please an electorate. Yet they are increasingly making decisions that are inherently political. By allowing inflation to be temporarily higher than target, or by choosing to buy government bonds or other pieces of financial paper, they are making some of us better off and others worse off. In a stagnant economy, quantitative easing and other such exotic policies have only ended up robbing Peter to pay Paul. It is as if a morally indifferent Robin Hood had suddenly arrived on the scene, chaotically redistributing income and wealth using neither rhyme nor reason.

Not surprisingly, these kinds of tricky political decisions, combined with ongoing economic stagnation, have undermined public confidence in central banks. A GfK/NOP Inflation Attitudes Survey conducted on behalf of the Bank of England revealed in August 2012 that the balance of those more satisfied than dissatisfied with the Bank's performance had dropped to +6, the lowest reading since the survey was first conducted in November 2009 and well down from peaks of +54 in November 2001 and +52 in November 2005.

THE POWER BEHIND THE THRONE

Whether they like it or not, central bankers have become 'the power behind the throne'. They are the modern-day equivalents of Sir Thomas More or Rasputin. Power without legitimacy is an awkward commodity yet it is precisely the gift that's been bestowed upon the Federal Reserve, the Bank of England and the European Central Bank. No longer are our central bankers mere technicians. They are now making inherently political decisions over winners and losers within society.[21]

Their lack of democratic legitimacy is, however, a major problem. Following the financial crisis, politicians have been increasingly willing to criticize the central banking fraternity. In his autobiography, *Back from the Brink*,[22] Alistair Darling, the UK's Chancellor of the Exchequer between 2007 and 2010, observed that Mervyn King's 2009 Mansion House speech

> would be seen as evidence of a deep division between him and me. It was a blatant bid for the Bank to take over the regulation of banks – and what seemed to me to be a rewriting of recent history ... but whether Mervyn liked it or not, the design of the regulatory

system and the primacy of the Bank . . . are matters for the government, not the Bank.

Darling's view was simple: King, he thought, was happily ignoring
the government of the day because, according to Darling, the
Governor of the Bank of England regarded Labour's days in office as
numbered.

Darling is not the only politician to criticize the behaviour of
central bankers. From a completely different political perspective,
Ron Paul, the US Congressman and a candidate for the Republican
nomination for the 2012 presidential election, had this to say:

> The financial crisis has exposed the intellectual bankruptcy of the
> world's central bankers . . . like their predecessors in the 1930s,
> today's Fed governors behave as if the height of the credit bubble
> is the status quo to which we need to return. This confuses money
> with wealth, and reflects the idea that prosperity stems from high
> asset prices and large amounts of money and credit . . . The Fed's
> response to the crisis suggests that it believes the current crisis is a
> problem of liquidity. In fact it is a problem of poorly allocated
> investments caused by improper pricing of money and credit . . .[23]

Von Mises would have been proud of him.

Admittedly, Darling made his comments after leaving office and
Paul, having thrown his hat into the presidential ring, didn't get it
back. Their comments, however, are not merely the actions of
rabble-rousers. They reflect a growing unease about the power and
influence of central bankers at a time when politicians are receiving
a big chunk of the blame for persistent economic failure.

Nowhere is this strain between political legitimacy and central
bank power more obvious than within the eurozone. In a press
conference following a regular European Central Bank meeting on

3 May 2012, Mario Draghi, the ECB President, offered the following observations:

> Collectively, we have to specify a path for the euro. How do we see ourselves ten years from now; what has to be in place in ten years' time? If we want to have a fiscal union, we have to accept the delegation of fiscal sovereignty from the national governments to some form of central body, but how do we get there? Talking about a transfer union cannot be the starting point of this path. That is why the fiscal compact is so important, that is the starting point. But we also have to highlight what this path is and what conditions have to be in place in order to see what will happen to the euro in ten years' time. In other words, clarity about our future, about our common European future, is one important ingredient of growth.[24]

The implication is clear. To make the single currency a success, to prevent the occurrence of one financial crisis after another and to create the institutional conditions for lasting economic growth, Europe (or, at least, members of the eurozone) will have to accept 'delegation of fiscal sovereignty from the national governments to some form of central body'.

There's nothing particularly wrong with this conclusion from the perspective of either economic logic or, indeed, the history of successful and failed monetary unions. After all, the United Kingdom has a successful monetary union bolstered by an enduring fiscal and political union,[25] while, after the 1991 break-up of the Soviet Union and the ensuing fragmentation of political and fiscal systems, the legacy 'rouble area' lasted not much more than a year.[26] The peculiarity lies more in the idea that an unelected central banker should be urging politicians to take the right steps. How should people in individual nation-states react to the impression that European political architecture is being shaped not by politicians but by unelected central bankers operating behind the scenes? How should those people in southern Europe suffering from year after year of grinding austerity come to terms with the perceived unwillingness of the European Central Bank to provide any kind of financial support until and unless various austerity measures have been agreed upon? And how should the mass unemployed in Spain come to terms with not only economic but also political disenfranchisement?

To understand these issues, we need a bit of history.

CHAPTER FIVE

THE LIMITS TO STIMULUS
Lessons from History

Whether through interest rate cuts or quantitative easing, monetary decisions create both winners and losers. In the normal course of events, these decisions even out over time. Savers win during periods of high interest rates, while borrowers gain during periods of low interest rates. Even if quantitative easing makes it easier for governments to borrow in the near term, success should ultimately allow private sector activity to recover, thereby raising tax revenues, reducing public spending on unemployment benefit and, hence, paving the way for a cyclical fiscal improvement. In this sense, monetary policy might be regarded as 'neutral' through the course of an economic cycle.

In reality, however, the choice of monetary regime makes a huge difference to society, creating both winners and losers, particularly during times of economic upheaval. It has an effect on both the level and distribution of income and wealth. The monetary regime becomes politically charged, particularly as the pursuit of increasingly unconventional monetary options blurs the distinction between monetary and fiscal policy.

To see why, it's worth examining two previous episodes of monetary mayhem: the UK's re-attachment to gold in the 1920s, and the Great Depression of the 1930s. Both periods saw politics and monetary policy become intimately entwined and both offer lessons for today's monetary debates, notably those concerning the eurozone and the relative merits of stimulus versus austerity.

It's important, however, to draw the right conclusions. It turns out that the differences between Western economies today and in the 1930s are vast, both because the outcomes this time around have, for the most part, been much better than in the 1930s and because fiscal positions today are so much worse than was the case back then. The proponents of 'New Deal' economics may be keen to seduce us with their demands for ever more stimulus but their siren voices should be treated with caution. Stimulus has its limits.

STERLING IN THE 1920S

In the 1920s, the UK found itself at a monetary crossroads. Heavily in debt, newly unionized, full of fat cat businessmen, suffering persistent economic stagnation yet determined to keep its creditors happy, Britain decided in 1925 to rejoin the Gold Standard at the pre-war parity, which left sterling seriously overvalued in international markets. The balance of trade was, as a result, constantly under pressure, forcing UK governments to deliver dose upon dose of austerity.

With the onset of Depression at the beginning of the 1930s, the situation only got worse. It was, so it seemed, time for some serious belt-tightening. The May Report, written by members of the Committee on National Expenditure and published on 31 July 1931, concluded that, with taxes already too high, the only way to balance the budget was to enact serious reductions in public spending, including cuts in unemployment benefit. Yet not all Committee members agreed. In the weeks that followed, as sterling came under pressure on the foreign exchanges, a split within the Cabinet on whether to introduce either tariffs or unemployment benefit cuts triggered the resignation of Ramsay MacDonald's Labour government on 24 August. A National Government, led by MacDonald but supported by both Conservatives and Liberals, was then formed.

On 10 September 1931, Philip Snowden, the then Chancellor of the Exchequer, delivered his – now infamous – Budget. His proposals were remarkably draconian. As John Maynard Keynes argued a few days later:

> The incomes of well-to-do people have been cut by 2½ to 3½ per cent. The school-teachers are cut 15 per cent, in addition to the extra taxes which they have to pay. It is a monstrous thing to single out this class and discriminate against them, merely because they happen to be employees of the Government.[1]

The Royal Navy – or at least some of its junior ratings – reached a similar conclusion, only much sooner. Returning to port at Invergordon from their adventures on the high seas on 11 September, they quickly discovered that, thanks to Snowden, they were facing severe pay cuts. For junior ratings who had enlisted before 1925, the reduction threatened to be a staggering 25 per cent. On 15 and 16 September 1931, some of the sailors mutinied. The stock market duly crashed, foreign investors headed for the exit and, on 20 September, sterling left the Gold Standard, the fixed exchange rate system that had become the 'anchor' for monetary policy across the industrialized world. This was a humiliation for the government of the day and has served as a warning to British governments ever since. Eighty years later, in the midst of a new period of economic stagnation, Snowden's Budget continues to haunt policy-makers fearful of facing similar disgrace.

Why did the policy have to be so draconian? Why did it fly in the face of advice from Keynes – who thought 'the Government's programme is as foolish as it is wrong' – and other luminaries?

The standard answer is to blame everything on the so-called 'Treasury View', which called for balanced budgets, the conventional wisdom of the day and an idea that is still embraced in some of the more Germanic nations and, indeed, by those who favour aggressive budget deficit reduction in other parts of the world. Keynes may have been completely opposed to this view but, in the early 1930s, he was regarded more as a cantankerous outsider than someone to be taken seriously by the establishment: back then, his views didn't always pass muster. As Keynes later admitted – in the introduction to his *Essays in Persuasion* – 'the volume might have been entitled "Essays in Prophecy and Persuasion", for the Prophecy, unfortunately, has been more successful than the Persuasion.'

The Times, at least, liked Snowden's September 1931 Budget, failing to foresee any kind of difficulty in its implementation. The day after the Budget, its leader was gushing in its praise – and hopelessly wrong about the implications for the exchange rate:

> Mr Snowden has neither flinched nor wavered in his unpleasant task. With draconian severity, he has set himself to balance the Budget . . . This is certainly an heroic achievement which should leave no doubt in the minds of our foreign creditors that at any rate we are thoroughly prepared to pay our way by living within our means . . . there need no longer be any fear that the pound sterling will be overwhelmed by budgetary instability.[2]

This extraordinary enthusiasm stood in marked contrast to the attitude towards Snowden's effort in April of that year, which the *Times* caustically labelled 'A Makeshift Budget':

The taxpayer is at best in the position of the patient who has escaped for the moment the more painful attentions of the dentist, only to leave the real business of the operation until the next visit ... The outstanding features of Mr Snowden's Budget ... are a quite unwarranted optimism and a misplaced fertility of makeshift expedients ...

His deficit is due in the main to an increase in current expenditure which shows no signs of abating: nor is there any solid reason whatever for supposing that any such marked recovery as he anticipates is likely to take place during the next twelve months. However deplorable any increase in taxation may be, there is at least one thing more deplorable still, and that is increased expenditure uncovered by current revenue.

Today, Snowden's Budget and the 'Treasury View' that underpinned it are roundly condemned. As Ed Balls, the Shadow Chancellor of the Exchequer, argued in 2010: 'And the result [of Snowden's Budget]? The promised private sector recovery failed to materialise as companies themselves sought to retrench. Unemployment soared. The Great Depression soured world politics and divided societies.'[3] This is, if you like, the new conventional wisdom. It is also mostly wrong. Snowden's budget certainly didn't cause the Great Depression: by late 1931, the Depression was already well under way. In any case, the Depression was a far bigger problem in the US and elsewhere than it was in Britain. And, remarkably enough, even as other economies continued to contract, the UK economy was, by 1932, showing the first signs of recovery. That year, per capita incomes in the UK rose 0.2 per cent in contrast to declines of 13.8 per cent in the US, 7.9 per cent in Germany and 6.5 per cent in France. The recovery gained considerably more momentum in the following two years: in 1933, per capita incomes rose 2.5 per cent even as the US economy continued to collapse and, in 1934, incomes rose a further 6.3 per cent.

What accounted for the UK's recovery? Snowden's Budget was important not so much because its austerity was ever likely to work but, instead, because it inadvertently revealed the political impossibility of maintaining a monetary arrangement that persistently imposed costs on British citizens even as the government attempted to maintain the UK's credibility in the eyes of international financiers. No longer did the UK have to set interest rates to please foreign creditors: the cheap money policies that followed sterling's departure from the Gold Standard enabled the UK government to reduce the cost of servicing its debt, encouraged the (healthy) banks to lend more and triggered a boom in housing construction. Nor did the government have to limit domestic consumption or capital spending to keep the balance of trade in check. Instead, the exchange rate could take the strain, thanks in part to the resounding political and financial rejection of Snowden's Budget triggered by the Invergordon mutiny. Put another way, Snowden's budget revealed that, after years in which Britain attempted to play by the rules of the Gold Standard, the game was finally up.

Snowden's Budget was, in fact, only the final nail in the coffin. Foreign investors were pulling their money out of Britain long before Snowden unleashed his austerity plans. Oddly, during this earlier period, the Bank of England was remarkably reluctant to raise interest rates. Its reluctance, however, is more easily understandable in the light of persistently high unemployment. The last thing the Bank wanted to do was to face the opprobrium of Parliament, the press and the people. Arguably, then, sterling was fatally undermined even before Snowden forced Britain onto a diet of cod liver oil and leeches.[4]

Snowden's Budget signalled the end of an era. Political reality got in the way of conventional economic thought. In the mêlée that followed, politics won and economics – at least of the conventional variety – lost. Arguably, Snowden's budget was the inevitable 'final step' in a story that had seen the British economy lurching from one crisis to the next. The First World War alone had severely weakened the UK's competitive position: wealth was reduced by between 10 and 15 per cent.[5] But the UK also faced other challenges that preceded the outbreak of hostilities in 1914.

The longer-term problem partly related to industrial unrest and a general lack of competitiveness. Long before the First World War, industrial relations were rapidly deteriorating. The number of days lost as a consequence of strikes and lockouts increased from around 3.5 million in the early 1900s to 12 million in 1910 and a remarkable 38 million in 1912. There was a mixture of frustrations: wage increases lagged behind price increases, there was a reluctance to invest in new technologies and there was unease regarding the apparent success of the US and German economies. Part of the problem – hardly unique in twentieth-century British economic history – was an absence of productivity gains. Miners were a case in point. From the onset of the First World War though to 1926, the year of the General Strike, coal exports fell by around 25 per cent in total, even though the number of miners employed rose by around 10 per cent.

Britain's coal miners were partly victims of international circumstance. Thanks to the Treaty of Versailles, Germany was obliged to pay reparations to the Allies. With its economy in tatters, the only way Germany could do so was to pay via the export of 'free' coal, which it duly did thanks to the 1924 Dawes Plan. Unfortunately – at least for the British mining industry – this inevitably led to a much lower international price for coal, thereby undermining British mining competitiveness.

The miners' situation was compounded by Winston Churchill's decision, as Chancellor of the Exchequer, to rejoin the Gold Standard. Churchill was certainly in good company. By the end of 1925, 28 out of a possible 48 currencies had been pegged to gold.[6] Yet having seen a bucket-load of inflation during and immediately after the war, the level of UK prices and wages was, by the mid-1920s, simply too high to enable the UK to be competitive in international markets at the pre-war exchange rate, particularly given that the French had engineered an undervalued exchange rate, leaving the UK at a relative disadvantage.[7] As Keynes put it:

> Failing a fall in the value of gold itself, nothing can retrieve [the exporters'] position except a general fall of all internal prices and wages. Thus Mr Churchill's policy of improving the exchange rate by 10 per cent [to return it to the pre-war parity] was, sooner or later, a policy of reducing everyone's wages by 2 shillings in the £.[8]

Now anarchy threatened: miners naturally resisted the threat of draconian wage cuts while the mine owners – regarded by many as no more than exploitative fat cats – insisted on the need for big profits to keep their shareholders happy (at the miners' expense). In a bid to keep the peace, the Conservative government provided a short-term subsidy to support miners' wages while the Samuel Commission deliberated on likely next steps. Sir Herbert Samuel and his colleagues concluded that, alongside a massive restructuring of what had become a hopelessly inefficient mining industry, the workers themselves would have to accept pay cuts of around 13.5 per cent. In many cases, the mine owners demanded even greater sacrifice, threatening lockouts unless workers accepted new terms and conditions. The scene was set for the General Strike, called by the Trades Union Congress in support of the miners. In early May 1926, the British economy temporarily shut down.

Although the General Strike lasted only a handful of days – the government was well prepared whereas the TUC was not – it was hardly the end of the affair. Woefully poor competitiveness left Britain with a painfully high double-digit unemployment rate, a terrible balance of trade, a growing dependency on the willingness of the Federal Reserve to keep US interest rates low, thereby limiting capital flight from Britain, and a persistently disappointing growth rate. Between 1920 and 1929 – in other words, before the onset of the Great Depression – the UK saw per capita incomes rise a mere 21 per cent compared with gains of 45 per cent for Germany, 46 per cent for France and 24 per cent for the US, a nation that at least had the excuse of already being in – mild – recession in 1927 and 1928.

Long before the Wall Street Crash and the subsequent Great Depression, the UK was, thus, already in big trouble. It had been living beyond its means, it had terrible industrial relations and it had a stupidly uncompetitive exchange rate. The Snowden Budget, rather than being purely an act of folly – as is now commonly argued – was the inevitable next step in a process that had already been under way for more than a decade, a process that resulted from faulty economic thinking, a persistently poor productivity performance and an attachment to a monetary system well past its sell-by date. Fortunately, at least from a British point of view, the Budget proved a bridge too far.

The Invergordon mutiny, more than anything else, proved that it was near enough impossible to force workers to take swingeing pay cuts. If, however, competitiveness could not be improved via a fall in domestic wages and prices, the only other realistic option was a fall in the exchange rate. Britain's membership of the Gold Standard was, thus, doomed. The Snowden Budget offered pain aplenty but, thanks to the rebellious actions of naval ratings in a remote part of Scotland, a safety valve was found, namely a decline in sterling and, by implication, the delivery of an independent domestic monetary policy. People power had undermined the interests of government and the captains of finance.[9]

In the light of the terrible events of the 1930s, the traumas of the 1920s, at least from a British perspective, are too often ignored. Yet they relate much more closely to the difficulties facing many Western economies today. Most obviously, the problems facing the UK back then – high unemployment, an absence of decent growth, a dependency on foreign creditors and an inability to improve competitiveness via domestic wage and price cuts – are almost identical to the difficulties facing the peripheral nations of the eurozone today.

NEW DEAL, NEW PROBLEMS

Thanks to Milton Friedman and Anna Schwartz, we now have a better idea of what led the US from a Great Recession in 1930 and early 1931 into the Great Depression that followed. In their view, the problem was a serious shortage of money. As bank after bank went to the wall and money, inevitably, became scarce, those lucky enough to have dollars in their pockets chose to keep them there. Spending collapsed. Yet, at the time, there was little understanding of what to do next.

Andrew Mellon, the US Treasury Secretary under the Hoover administration, offered the following infamous advice:

> liquidate labor, liquidate stocks, liquidate farmers, liquidate real estate . . . it will purge the rottenness out of the system. High costs of living and high living will come down. People will work harder, live a moral life. Values will be adjusted, and enterprising people will pick up from less competent people.

As one of the richest people on the planet, it was easier for Mellon to give this advice than for others to receive it. Friedman and Schwartz, however, took a very different view. Rather than suggesting people merely should opt for the moral life – the equivalent of medieval priests suggesting their peasant congregations should suffer in the name of God – they rightly recognized there had been a monumental failure of monetary policy. The Federal Reserve had the option of 'printing money' to make sure there was no hint of any cash shortfall – in effect, the option of departure from the Gold Standard. By refusing to do so, however, the Fed merely encouraged a belief in monetary shortage that, inevitably, led to more bank failures and, hence, the beginnings of a self-fulfilling prophecy.

Intriguingly, the Federal Reserve's monetary failures were not so obviously part of the political discourse of the time. Instead, politicians opted for partisan point scoring. Franklin Delano Roosevelt, elected US President in 1932, offered the following thoughts in New York's Madison Square Garden on 31 October 1936 – throwing down a 'trick or treat' gauntlet to his Republican rivals ahead of the forthcoming presidential election:

> We have not come this far without a struggle and I assure you we cannot go further without a struggle. For twelve years this Nation was afflicted with hear-nothing, see-nothing, do-nothing Government ... For nearly four years you have had an Administration which instead of twirling its thumbs has rolled up its sleeves. We will keep our sleeves rolled up. We had to struggle with the old enemies of peace – business and financial monopoly, speculation, reckless banking, class antagonism, sectionalism, war profiteering. They had begun to consider the Government of the United States as a mere appendage to their own affairs. We know now that Government by organized money is just as dangerous as Government by organized mob.[10]

In other words, the Depression was a consequence not so much of monetary failure but, instead, of an excessively cosy relationship between previous (Republican) administrations and the money men on Wall Street, a relationship that stank of 'organized money'. For Roosevelt – at least in his public pronouncements – the Depression reflected not systemic economic and financial failure but, instead, a toxic conspiracy. He was, in effect, invoking biblical judgement: 'And Jesus went into the temple of God, and cast out all them that sold and bought in the temple, and overthrew the tables of the moneychangers, and the seats of them that sold doves.'[11] For voters, this narrative was understandably tempting: Roosevelt won the second of four victories in 1936 thanks not only to the New Deal but also to his rejection of the money men. It's a narrative that is also tempting today.

Yet Roosevelt's story is hardly a satisfactory explanation. It fails to establish why the Depression was such a pulverizing event: the late 1920s were hardly the first instance of speculation and reckless banking yet the subsequent economic collapse was uniquely terrible, at least by the standards of American late nineteenth and early twentieth-century history. And if the behaviour of money men was so obviously reprehensible in the 1920s, why was no one able to spot the oncoming disaster? Irving Fisher, the great American economist, declared in 1929, just ahead of the Wall Street Crash, that 'stock prices have reached what looks like a permanently high plateau'. Keynes wasn't much better, opining in 1927 that 'we will not have any more crashes in our time'.

The wholesale failure to spot the impending crisis and the sense that nothing in the Roaring Twenties, with its new technologies and F. Scott Fitzgerald-style wealth, could possibly go wrong suggest that, for humanity, hubris too often comes before nemesis. When things do go wrong, however, a culture of blame often follows. Someone, somewhere, must be at fault and be made to atone for society's sins. In the mid-1930s, not content merely with the New Deal and blaming the money men, Roosevelt and his acolytes relentlessly pursued Andrew Mellon through the courts, accusing him of tax evasion. Mellon was eventually exonerated only after his death in 1937.

Still, Roosevelt was able to establish his monumental reputation with the New Deal, an inspiration to Keynesians ever since. In one of his early fireside chats, President Roosevelt offered the following commitment as he attempted to grapple with the Great Depression:

> The Administration has the definite objective of raising commodity prices to such an extent that those who have borrowed money will, on the average, be able to repay that money in the same kind of dollar which they borrowed. We do not seek to let them get such a cheap dollar that they will be able to pay back a great deal less than they borrowed. In other words, we seek to correct a wrong and not to create another wrong in the opposite direction. That is why powers are being given to the Administration to provide, if necessary, for an enlargement of credit, in order to correct the existing wrong. These powers will be used when, as, and if it may be necessary to accomplish the purpose.[12]

Roosevelt's point was simple. During Hoover's last term in office, commodity prices had dropped 26 per cent. With interest rates at zero, the real cost of borrowing (the interest rate minus the inflation rate) was painfully high. Roosevelt wasn't merely committing to stop prices from falling. He was promising that prices would rise back to where they were before deflation took hold, thus giving debtors enough dollars to be able to pay their loans. He was thus willing to encourage a – temporary – period of unusually high inflation. And he backed his commitment up with an extraordinary (by the standards of the time) increase in government borrowing that, thanks to America's recent departure from the Gold Standard, could be financed by printing dollars.

The policy appeared to work. The 30 per cent decline in national income during the Depression was reversed. In Roosevelt's first term in office, output rose 39 per cent. Prices also rose, up 13 per cent over the same period. Between 1932 and 1934, total government spending rose from 5.6 per cent of national income to 12.2 per cent. The budget deficit, meanwhile, jumped from 2.2 per cent of national income to a remarkable 9 per cent.[13] This was Keynesian pump-priming even before the *General Theory* had been published.

LESSONS FOR TODAY

For the UK in the 1920s, the issue was not so much recession but, instead, the persistence of continuously weak growth that required swingeing cuts in public spending or increases in taxation to make the fiscal numbers add up and to keep foreign creditors happy: we see echoes of the 1920s all around us today. Yet, in Britain's case, ongoing austerity did little to help: the more the budgetary screws were tightened, the weaker the economy became. Ultimately, with the onset of the 1930s Depression, the economic framework of the day – with sterling tied to the Gold Standard – proved to be politically unsustainable. With departure from gold, the unthinkable happened: sterling fell dramatically and the UK economy recovered. If there is a modern-day corollary, it would be an individual nation's departure from the eurozone, reflecting a rejection of ongoing austerity, a series of defaults or, perhaps, the eurozone's complete collapse.

This conclusion, however, has to be treated with care. In the second half of 2008, sterling itself collapsed. In July of that year a pound would buy more than $2. By the beginning of 2009, a pound could only buy $1.37, a drop of over 30 per cent, almost identical in percentage terms to the decline in the months following Snowden's September 1931 Budget. Yet whereas 1932 saw the beginnings of a sustained British economic recovery – even as the rest of the world remained trapped in depression – the situation since sterling's 2008 decline has remained remarkably poor. In 1933, UK national income was only 2.3 per cent below the peak four years earlier, thanks in part to Britain's departure from the Gold Standard. In 2012, four years after the equivalent peak, UK national income was still 4.3 per cent lower. The mistakes of the 1920s and 1930s in large part may have been avoided but seemingly to no avail. It's easy enough – and politically convenient – to blame Britain's current difficulties on developments in the eurozone or excessive fiscal austerity domestically. Yet, despite its ongoing problems, the eurozone is nothing like as weak as the industrialized world was in the early 1930s and the fiscal austerity offered by the UK's coalition government from 2010 onwards has been nothing like as draconian as that offered by Snowden in 1931. Back then, devaluation worked. This time around, it hasn't. Back then, monetary policy had teeth. Today, it doesn't.

For those who advocate exchange rate flexibility and who regard the modern-day euro as being little different from the Gold Standard, this is surely a puzzling result. Take, for example, the views of Bernanke and James:

> The basic proposition of the gold standard-based explanation of the Depression is that, because of its deflationary impact, adherence to the gold standard had very adverse consequences for real activity . . . Between 1932 and 1935, growth of industrial production in countries not on gold averaged about seven percentage points a year better than countries remaining on gold, a very substantial effect . . . there was a strong link between adherence to the gold standard and the severity of both deflation and depression . . . increased freedom to engage in monetary expansion was a reason for the better performance of countries leaving the gold standard in the 1930s . . .[14]

No mention there of the limited impact of either monetary policy or exchange rate changes as a consequence of weakness elsewhere in the world. No mention, either, of the role of fiscal policy. Monetary policy, apparently, did the trick. Yet, in the modern era, it hasn't quite delivered the goods. Central bankers and governments have found, much to their irritation, that monetary policy no longer seems to have the potency of old.

Reduced sensitivity to the exchange rate in the modern era doubt-less reflects a number of key structural changes in the second half of the twentieth century. In the UK, for example, manufacturing is now a much smaller share of national income than it was in the 1930s, down from 28 per cent to a mere 10 per cent. So, too, is the share of exports. The price sensitivity of exports has slowly declined over the years: other influences – design, after-sales service, distribution, brand value, advertising – have steadily become more important. And goods are nowadays produced by multinationals on a strategic basis. Location decisions are unlikely immediately to change as a consequence of a sudden shift in the exchange rate, particularly now that corporate treasury departments use hedging strategies to insure against unanticipated movements in the currency markets.

And there is another big difference. The US may have had a huge banking crisis in the 1930s but the UK did not. Monetary policy therefore could feed through to the broader economy relatively easily. That no longer applies: in the UK, thanks to an enormous banking crisis, the monetary drugs no longer appear to have the power of old.

Despite these objections, there are plenty of people who argue that what the world needs now is a bigger dose of 1930s medicine, another New Deal, another period of economic stimulus to match the policies of the Depression era that reversed the earlier attach-ment to austerity and liquidation. For them, the dosage of policy drugs should be increased, not so much through extra monetary stimulus alone but, instead, through additional government borrowing funded through more quantitative easing, thus invoking the spirit of both Roosevelt and Keynes.

Paul Krugman, the Nobel Prize-winning economist, argues precisely this in his *End This Depression Now!* – a polemic that rightly attacks the idiotic statements made by those who disagree with him but, oddly enough, glosses over the occasional idiotic statements made by those who just happen to be on his side.[15] For example, he approvingly quotes the aforementioned Janet Yellen, the Vice Chair of the Federal Reserve, when she talked in 2009 of 'a Minsky meltdown', ignoring the fact that she, among others, had trivialized the threat stemming from the housing bubble that preceded it.[16]

Krugman argues that the position we're now in is 'essentially the same kind of situation that John Maynard Keynes described in the 1930s' and backs this up with estimates from the Congressional Budget Office that claim that 'the US economy is operating about 7 percent below its potential'. These 'output gap' estimates are, however, notoriously unreliable, suffering dramatic revisions from one year to the next. In the past, they have often led to bad policy decisions. One reason why the Japanese were slow to offer stimulus in the early 1990s was that official estimates at the time – both from the Japanese themselves and from esteemed international institutions – suggested that the Japanese economy was operating well above its potential, wrongly indicating an incipient threat of inflation.

None of this worries Krugman: he thinks we're facing merely 'a technical problem, a problem of organization and coordination', that 'the sources of our suffering are relatively trivial in the scheme of things, and could be fixed quickly and fairly if enough people in positions of power understood the realities'. In other words, our economic problems result only from the stupidity of those in charge. He backs up his argument by pointing to occasions during which big increases in government spending led to a booming economy and plunging unemployment, almost all of which occurred during wartime. He happily concludes that, in peacetime, the effects would be larger still, because the rationing of wartime would not be necessary.

Alongside Lord (Richard) Layard, Krugman went on to claim in a 2012 'Manifesto for Economic Sense' that 'today's government deficits are a consequence of the crisis, not a cause', thereby justifying further extravagant increases in government borrowing.

His arguments, however, are remarkably misleading. As I noted in chapter 3, structural budget positions, at least in the US and the UK, had deteriorated hugely even before the onset of the financial crisis, which is a problem given that not even the most optimistic forecaster today believes that we are likely to see a return to a pre-crisis economic trajectory. The idea that we can simply grow our way out of the hole we're in therefore seems to be misguided: problems with debt surfaced long before the crisis took hold. For Krugman, however, the starting point seemingly doesn't matter: whether government debt is 10 per cent or 200 per cent of national income, more stimulus is required.

Krugman's wartime claims are notable specifically for what they omit to mention. In *How to Pay for the War*, Keynes certainly didn't see the outbreak of hostilities in 1939 as an opportunity for a 'Keynesian' stimulus.[17] He was much more worried about the possibility of inflation, a problem that had plagued the UK during the First World War and, indeed, during plenty of earlier campaigns. Despite the fact that the UK economy had barely grown over the previous ten years, leaving the unemployment rate still in double digits in 1939,[18] Keynes regarded the increase in military spending as a sure-fire way of creating inflation, not as a way of closing some kind of spurious output gap. To prevent inflation, he recommended higher taxes on the wealthy and a form of 'compulsory saving' for everybody else: in effect, a process of deferred consumption. As it turned out, the UK government – and many others – resorted instead to rationing. Either way, for many countries, wartime was a period of miserable austerity. Worse, the process continued long after the war came to an end: rationing didn't end in the UK until

1954, long after the U-Boats had stopped wreaking havoc. Britain was basically bust, thanks to huge debt-fuelled increases in public spending.

Krugman is quick to emphasize the similarities with the 1930s but silent on the many differences. Back then, the collapse in US nominal demand – the *value* of national income – was far greater than the collapse in real demand – the *volume* of national income. In other words, the US in the 1930s was suffering from what Irving Fisher described as *debt deflation*. Today, the situation is entirely different. Relative to the expectations of economists whose job it is to forecast such things, there has most definitely been a shortfall in the volume of US national income. However, even allowing for the impact of the financial crisis, there has been no significant shortfall in the *value* of national income.

In other words, while output has been consistently lower than expected, inflation has been consistently *higher* than expected. This was true long before the financial crisis took hold and has continued to be the case ever since.[19] Rather than there being only an absence of demand, it appears that there has also been a gradual deterioration in the US economy's supply potential. While the economy may appear to have plenty of spare capacity, that capacity is in all the wrong places.

Through the early years of the twenty-first century, ahead of the financial crisis, the US experienced a seismic restructuring of its labour market. While overall jobs growth was good – with around 10 million net new jobs created between 2000 and 2007 – the aggregate numbers hid two offsetting trends: over 2 million jobs were lost in manufacturing and transportation while a similar number were created in construction. Put another way, the outsourcing and offshoring pressures stemming from globalization that contributed to the loss of a huge number of manufacturing jobs were counterbalanced through a domestically generated housing boom. Productive work went elsewhere in the world while the US economy lived in a financial bubble of its own making. The UK's experience was much the same: jobs were created only in three areas – financial services, construction and the public sector. When the bubble burst, the jobs market simply wasn't diverse enough to offer new opportunities. Western nations had foolishly put their economic eggs in very few baskets, reflecting the co-dependency between housing and finance.

This raises an obvious problem. If jobs were created in only a narrow range of sectors that are now in decline, how can new jobs be easily created elsewhere simply as a result of broad macroeconomic stimulus? The answer, it turns out, is that they can't. Instead, the financial crisis has been associated in the US with an extraordinary rise in so-called 'long-term' unemployment, those who have been out of work for at least six months and, in an increasing number of cases, for more than a year. This is sadly familiar territory for nations in Europe but it is a new, and very unwelcome, experience for the US. And it isn't a problem restricted merely to those who have lost their jobs. Approaching a quarter of 16–19 year old American school leavers available to work have found themselves unemployed since the onset of the financial crisis, by far the highest number in post-war history. It is a staggering reflection of sustained economic failure. And, as unemployment persists, many are simply giving up: the so-called US participation rate – a measure of those of working age either in work or actively seeking work – has hit rock bottom. High unemployment is, in itself, bad enough but high long-term unemployment is a much more challenging condition: it cannot so easily be fixed through simple macroeconomic stimulus.

Inflation, meanwhile, has been higher than expected largely thanks to the impact of unusually buoyant commodity prices. Again, it's a reflection of developments elsewhere in the world – notably the emergence of millions of new consumers and thousands of new industries throughout the emerging nations – but it's also an unintended consequence of attempts to stimulate demand in the Western world: printing money has helped raise commodity prices as investors try to offload their cash and buy something more likely to hang onto its value. However, the process has made the task of reinvigorating Western economies that much harder: higher commodity prices have had an impact on real incomes equivalent to an increase in indirect taxes. Those parts of the world producing commodities have, of course, won but it is scant consolation to know that Saudi Arabia, Australia, Venezuela and Russia have ended up richer thanks to misguided attempts to boost activity in the West.

None of this matters to Krugman. Having argued in a debate hosted by Richard Layard in the Houses of Parliament in October 2012[20] that the US should expand its budget deficit in the order of 4 per cent of GDP in order to sustain recovery, he appears to think that there is no limit to the benefits of expansionary government spending: 'changes in government spending move output and employment in the same direction: spend more, and both real GDP and employment will rise: spend less, and both real GDP and employment will fall.'[21]

The argument starts with the idea that conventional monetary policy has run out of steam – because interest rates are at zero. These were precisely the conditions facing Roosevelt in the early 1930s. Roosevelt, however, was able to grab hold of monetary policy – by leaving the Gold Standard and by persuading the Federal Reserve to do his bidding – in part because the earlier period of deflation – both in the US and elsewhere – had been so devastating. The modern-day equivalent would be for the administration to take away the Fed's independence and to insist on a radical redrawing of the rules governing monetary and fiscal policy. Yet, in the absence of earlier deflation, the justification for doing so is not immediately obvious. Whereas, in the 1930s, the value of national income dropped 50 per cent from peak to trough, the value of national income at the end of

2012, four years after the collapse of Lehman Brothers, was already almost 10 per cent higher than it had been at the previous peak. There is simply no comparison. Outside the eurozone periphery, there is no deflation, no depression and no persistent economic collapse. Those who claim otherwise are confusing the disaster of depression with the melancholy of stagnation, two completely different concepts.

In any case, the ammunition available to Roosevelt no longer exists. The Hoover administration may have been economically foolish but it left Roosevelt with one key advantage: he inherited a fiscal position that was relatively healthy. Today's politicians are not so fortunate. Whereas the Roosevelt-era budget deficit peaked at around 9 per cent of national income, budget deficits in 2012 were already at around that level. Admittedly, deficits could be increased further, financed via printing money, but we would be moving into territory totally without precedent. Roosevelt could do what he did only because those who went before him had been proponents of fiscal conservatism: the same simply doesn't apply today. In 1934, US public sector debt amounted to around 38 per cent of national income; in 2012, across all branches of government, it had risen to over 100 per cent of national income.[22]

Krugman and his acolytes appear to suffer from a Depression fetish. They continuously insist we've gone back to conditions not dissimilar to those seen in the 1930s. They continuously insist that only with massive stimulus will there be a recovery. In Krugman's words:

> The basic point is that the recession ... wasn't a typical postwar slump, brought on when an inflation-fighting Fed raises interest rates and easily ended by a snapback in housing and consumer spending when the Fed brings rates back down again. This was a prewar-style recession, a morning after brought on by irrational

exuberance. To fight this recession the Fed needs more than a snapback; it needs soaring household spending to offset moribund business investment ... I just don't understand the grounds for optimism. Who, exactly, is about to start spending a lot more? At this point it's a lot easier to tell a story about how the recovery will stall than about how it will speed up.

There's only one problem with this argument. Krugman wrote these words in August 2002, at the beginning of what became known as the subprime boom.[23] Too much stimulus, it turns out, can create its own problems.

TWO FUNDAMENTAL CONCLUSIONS

The opportunities open to Roosevelt in the 1930s are no longer available and, even if they were, it would be foolish to use them. A commitment to sustained higher inflation cannot be easily made in the absence of earlier deflation. Deficit expansion has already happened: it isn't plausible to argue that deficits could be increased by a further 7 percentage points of national income, as Roosevelt managed during his first term in office: with quantitative easing, there probably wouldn't be a bond market crisis but there could easily be a dollar crisis instead. Public spending in the US is already up to 40 per cent of national income and, in other nations, is higher still. And, on any sensible medium-term assessment of Western fiscal outlooks, deficits under current plans are already in danger of running out of control.

Meanwhile, money cannot easily be separated from politics. Monetary regimes create both winners and losers and, at the limit, can lead to social fragmentation. Admittedly, the task facing today's Federal Reserve and Bank of England is easier than that confronting the European Central Bank – which has the unenviable task of running monetary policy for a group of unruly nation-states – but the experiences of the interwar period emphasize that monetary decisions are either political in themselves or lead to – sometimes unintended – political consequences. The idea that monetary policy is politically neutral is a convenient fiction rather than a reflection of reality. Yet it is often only during periods of economic and social upheaval that the fiction is exposed. Today, monetary policy works not so much by reinvigorating the economy but, instead, by redistributing wealth and income: it is no more than a stealthy form of redistributive taxation. We're back to the idea of winners and losers.

CHAPTER SIX

LOSS OF TRUST, LOSS OF GROWTH

If macroeconomic policies – of either the conventional or unconventional kind – cannot deliver a return to 'business as usual', what's gone wrong? Is it simply that we expect too much? Or is it that the problems facing Western economies are not easily resolved simply through an interest rate tweak, a money-printing measure, a tax cut or a big increase in public spending?

Something more fundamental is amiss. Macroeconomic policies are more likely to succeed if we believe the underlying economic foundations are still intact. Yet those foundations are in danger of collapsing. Central banks are now busily engaged in income and wealth redistribution as opposed to conventional pump-priming. Governments don't know whether to deliver stimulus or austerity. And markets of all kinds – from the humble vegetable stall through to the complex world of credit default swaps – are in serious trouble. Central banks, governments and markets thrive on trust. With the onset of the financial crisis, however, trust has fallen by the wayside. Without trust, it's difficult to see how Western economies can easily bounce back.

Indeed, in the absence of trust, human interaction becomes increasingly corroded.

On a recent trip to Jerusalem, I went on a guided tour to take in all the major sights: the Western Wall – and the Western Wall Tunnels – the Dome of the Rock, the Church of the Holy Sepulchre and the Via Dolorosa. Whereas the entrance to the Tunnels is adjacent to the Western Wall in the Jewish quarter, the exit is in the Via Dolorosa in the Arab quarter. From an archaeological perspective, the Tunnels are a goldmine, revealing more or less the entirety of the Western Wall, the longest of the four walls that surrounded King Herod's Temple, eventually destroyed by the Romans in CE 70.

Yet, whatever the archaeological importance, the religious sensitivity is obvious. The Tunnels connect two parts of Jerusalem symbolizing the entire Israeli–Palestinian conflict (while Jerusalem as whole symbolizes the near-continuous conflict between the world's three major monotheistic religions). First explored by British archaeologists back in the 1860s, the Tunnels begin in the Jewish quarter but they pass directly under the Arab quarter (constructed directly on top of ruins left by the Romans). The Via Dolorosa exit was created only in 1996, on the instructions of Binyamin Netanyahu during his first stint as Israel's Prime Minister. The response was instantaneous: a Palestinian uprising that led to around 80 deaths.

The events of 1996 revealed, not for the first time, the total lack of trust between Israelis and Palestinians. Was the exit created merely to encourage more tourists to visit this extraordinary sight? Given its inconspicuous nature, should the exit's creation really have mattered to anyone? Wouldn't the exit increase tourist trade for those living in the Arab quarter? Was it a deliberate provocation by Binyamin Netanyahu, the Israeli Prime Minister, to Muslims living in Jerusalem? Was it an attempt by the Israelis to use ancient history to make territorial claims today? Were the Palestinians too willing to suppress historical evidence, fearful that their own territorial claims might be undermined? Was the newly formed Palestinian Authority – its soldiers armed (ironically) by the Israelis – looking for an excuse to go on the rampage? Both sides had their well-articulated points of view but their different perspectives ultimately reflected a total lack of trust in the other side's stance. In situations like this, a lack of trust prevents any kind of engagement. And second-guessing the other side's underlying intentions may only make the situation worse.

Not all breakdowns of trust have terrible consequences. Yet they can just as easily lead to lost opportunities.

On leaving the Tunnels, I headed along the Via Dolorosa towards the Church of the Holy Sepulchre, supposedly built over the tomb of Christ, and then on through the hundreds of market stalls that vie for tourist business. As any sensible visitor to the Old City knows, there's little point buying souvenirs without haggling. I, however, was faced with an additional problem. My guide was recommending specific stalls to me, suggesting their proprietors could be trusted to give me a good price. What, however, if my guide received a kickback from these proprietors? If so, his recommendations would be next to useless. Yet, if I went to other stalls, not recommended by my guide, he might then take offence.

I eventually decided the simplest thing to do was to refrain from buying anything. Thus the proprietors lost out, my guide lost out and I lost out, returning home empty-handed. A lack of trust prevented a transaction from taking place. This was a classic example of market failure: all parties wanted a transaction to take place but a lack of trust meant that it was impossible to strike a deal.

My experience is not so different from George Akerlof's market for lemons. In his seminal paper published in 1970,[1] Akerlof investigated an obvious peculiarity associated with the value of second-hand cars. Why did the value of a brand new car immediately drop as soon as it was driven off the forecourt? The answer was simple: the seller, having owned the car, would know something about its idio-syncratic strengths and weaknesses that the would-be buyer would, inevitably, be clueless about.

Imagine the would-be purchaser is faced with a choice of ten second-hand cars sold through a variety of dealers. One or two of these cars might well be 'lemons', cars poorly made in Detroit first thing on a Monday morning or last thing on a Friday evening when workers were either too exhausted from having enjoyed their weekend or too focused on preparing for their weekend. Each of the sellers knows whether his car is a lemon – he's driven it, after all – but none of the sellers will admit it to the buyer: if any of the sellers did so, they'd be stuck with the lemon. Each seller will thus proclaim that the car on sale is perfectly reliable, a 'good little runner'. Yet the would-be buyer – who wisely doesn't trust the dealers – knows there's a chance he might be buying a lemon: therefore he will only pay a price that offers compensation for taking that risk. The asymmetry of information – sellers knowing more than buyers – leads to an outcome that fails to reflect the true value of totally reliable cars – which will be inappropriately underpriced – and 'lemons' – which will, of course, be grossly overpriced. At the limit – where risk-averse buyers simply refuse to transact – the second-hand car market might collapse altogether.

In the absence of economic growth, it is easy to see how trust can evaporate. In Adam Smith's melancholy state, for example, where one person's gain is necessarily another's loss, it is hardly surprising that people eye each other warily. They become increasingly suspicious of 'bad behaviour', whether illegal, immoral or otherwise undesirable. During prosperous times, bad behaviour may go unpunished, shrugged off because it appears to have little effect on anybody else. During melancholy times, however, bad behaviour, no matter how trivial, becomes a dominant theme. It provides a narrative for those who seek to blame others for their own misfortune and an escape route for those who want to get rich quick. Bad behaviour, in turn, allows an atmosphere of mistrust to fester. Without trust, however, markets begin to fragment and malfunction. Economic stagnation is then locked in.

Nowhere is this more obvious than within the financial system. The word 'credit' is derived from the Latin *credere*, which means 'to trust' or 'to believe'. Because the financial system necessarily involves time, the transactions that take place within it have to involve trust: if either borrowers or lenders prove to be fickle, changing their minds from one day to the next, or are downright dishonest, it's difficult to see how a financial system could easily function.

There are plenty of surveys of trust. For the financial industry, they mostly make for grim reading. Gallup, for example, has asked Americans on a regular basis since the end of the 1970s about their confidence in banks.[2] The percentage of respondents answering positively – ranging between 'quite a lot' and 'a great deal' – stood at 60 per cent in 1979 and fell to a low of 30 per cent in the early 1990s during the first (and, it now seems, minor) credit crunch before rebounding to 53 per cent in 2004. At its nadir in late 2010, however, only 18 per cent responded positively. Meanwhile, although generally sceptical about the legislative programme in Congress, American citizens have been unusually supportive of one particular area of legislation, namely 'increased government regulation of banks and major financial institutions'. If politicians and regulators want to absolve themselves of blame for their own part in the financial crisis, they know where to turn.

Not surprisingly, levels of trust vary with the economic cycle: during the good times, bankers are held in – relatively – high esteem whereas during the bad times they're often treated more like toxic waste. A Federal Reserve Bank of San Francisco study published in March 2011 calculated that 'two-thirds of the recent decline in trust [in banks] is explained by the cyclical downturn'.[3] Put another way, trust in banks and the financial system adjusts along with the ebb and flow of the economy more generally. In theory, then, trust in banks and bankers should automatically rise as and when the US economy next recovers. That, however, may be too cavalier a conclusion. Should a lack of trust *prevent* recovery from materializing, the cyclical argument would no longer hold.

In 2012, that certainly appeared to be a valid interpretation. Five years after subprime entered the public consciousness, Bob Diamond, the high-profile chief executive of Barclays Bank plc, was forced to resign, thanks to an interest rate-rigging scandal affecting the London interbank offered rate (Libor) – the interest rate paid daily by banks for funds from other banks – which, during the financial crisis, became a key barometer of the health or otherwise of individual banks. Fiddling with Libor denied relevant information to investors about the solvency or otherwise of financial institutions, thus increasing the likelihood of inappropriate financial decisions. Barclays was hit with a fine of £290 million for its role in this unfortunate episode. Later, UBS AG reached a settlement of $1.5 billion for its part in the scandal. That the Bank of England also got caught up in the story – having chosen to ignore advice provided to them by the New York Federal Reserve – only served to compound the problem.

Meanwhile, HSBC – my own employer – was involved in a particularly distasteful money laundering scandal concerning Mexican drug money, ending up with a deservedly heavy fine of $1.9 billion from the US authorities. Even without fines, many financial institutions ended up in trouble thanks to a lack of trust. Spanish caixas – savings banks with, it seems, an unhealthy interest in property investment – were unable to persuade anyone that their underlying financial positions were in any way secure despite protestations to the contrary both from themselves and from a Spanish government keen to maintain its own credit rating in international financial markets.

On its website, Barclays offers a short history of a once-venerable financial institution:

> Private banking businesses were commonplace in the eighteenth century. Clients' gold deposits were kept secure and credit-worthy merchants received loans. In 1896, 20 such businesses collaborated and formed a joint-stock bank.
>
> The leading partners of the new bank, which was named Barclay and Company, were already connected by a web of family, business and religious relationships. The company became known as the Quaker Bank reflecting the tradition of the founding fathers . . .
>
> . . . Today, Barclays has grown from a group of English partnerships to a global bank represented in Europe, the USA, Latin America, Africa, the Caribbean, Asia, the Middle East and Australia.[4]

There is nothing in this history about trust. Another part of the Barclays website, however, offers the following thoughts: 'We expect the highest ethical standards to be maintained and seek compliance with the law and regulations. We acknowledge mistakes and encourage constructive disagreement. In everything we do, we focus on the processes and controls to protect the Barclays brand and our shareholders.'[5] This kind of statement is, of course, utterly meaningless. A large institution would never choose to say anything else. Imagine if Barclays had said 'we do not expect the highest ethical standards to be maintained' or 'we do not seek compliance with the law and regulations'. Missing from the statement is any significant reference to Barclays' longer-term values. What were its Quaker traditions? And do they still have relevance today?

The founder in 1690 of the bank that was, eventually, to become Barclays was John Freame. He hoped 'to implant in [young] minds a sense of piety and virtue, and to train them up in the best things.

This would prove more advantageous to children than getting a great deal of riches for them.'[6] Bank deposits were taken from customers not so much to speculate in subprime real estate or the Libor market but, instead, to help fellow citizens' businesses. There was a good reason for this cooperative arrangement. Quakers – alongside Ranters, Muggletonians and Seekers – had suffered at the hands of King Charles II in the second half of the sixteenth century, a time of rampant religious experimentation sufficient to put the fear of God in the ruling elite. There had already been one Civil War and, unlike his father, Charles presumably had no intention of losing his head.

This sense of common purpose, of mutual support, meant that the vast majority of Quaker companies survived the rigours of the eighteenth century even as other companies – led by morally weaker men who too often succumbed to avarice – fell by the wayside. Quaker bankers would, today, be regarded as supporters of a 'stakeholder society', one in which the interest of borrowers, depositors, staff and owners would all be taken into account. You certainly wouldn't catch an eighteenth-century Quaker banker spending his fat bonus on a Ferrari and a crate of Bollinger. Even though early Quaker businessmen included a very successful brewer, Thomas Fowell Buxton (1786–1845), temperance became de rigueur for Quakers as the nineteenth century progressed.[7] Meanwhile, Quakers kept business local, making sure that the banker knew his client. It may not have been efficient but it was, it seems, a far better way of building trust than observing the world via a computer screen.

Back then, bankers were trusted pillars of the community. They have since fallen a long way. The general public's loss of faith in the industry is hardly surprising.[8]

Yet despite the general public's dismay over the operation of the financial system, the problem for economic growth lies not just with

the general public's perceptions – the sort of thing regularly measured by Gallup and captured in newspaper headlines – but, also,
from lack of trust from within the financial system itself. Without
'internal' trust, the financial system is next to useless. Yet, today,
bankers no longer trust each other.

While Northern Rock grabbed all the headlines in 2007 thanks to
the vast queues of worried depositors who gathered outside, understandably fearing the loss of their savings, its public failure was only
the final chapter in a whole volume of – sometimes self-imposed –
mishaps. The loss of trust in Northern Rock reflected four factors:
(1) a loss of faith in the pieces of paper – the IOUs – which banks
released into the capital markets – so-called wholesale funding – to
support lending to high risk households; (2) a sense that Northern
Rock's own business model – unusually dependent on wholesale
funding – was no longer sustainable; (3) a sudden panic on behalf of
equity investors who recognized that, in the absence of wholesale
funding, Northern Rock was no longer a viable concern; and (4) in
the absence of sufficient deposit guarantees – and after a leak to the
BBC[9] – a recognition on behalf of Northern Rock's depositors that
their money was no longer safe.

For the banking industry more generally, a further complication
came with the formation of so-called conduits and related structured investment vehicles (SIVs), which typically created a contingent – albeit hidden – liability for banks. Conduits would typically
make their money by purchasing a wide range of assets (including
the aforementioned credit transfer instruments) funded through the
issuance of asset-backed commercial paper, typically on a 30-day
rolling basis. Typically, they could only do so if they were 'underwritten' with credit lines from commercial banks. Often, the
banks themselves would create their own conduits and SIVs to
overcome regulatory constraints: these offered a way of boosting
returns without having to hold more capital because the vehicles

were 'off balance sheet' and therefore invisible from a regulatory point of view.

Underneath all this, however, was a key assumption, namely that the ultimate 'real' assets underpinning all of this paper wealth – in the main, US housing – were actually worth something. Specifically, the belief was that US housing would never fall in value: after all, it had never done so since the Second World War, so there was, apparently, little reason to think that a sudden decline was imminent. Yet, as a consequence of financial innovation, combined with political momentum in favour of a wider property-owning democracy, the nature of the US housing market was changing: borrowers were becoming increasingly 'subprime' and, thus, were slowly but surely becoming a bigger credit risk. Yet, with the system slicing and dicing credit risk into so many tiny parts, it was difficult for any one observer to spot the risk to the system as a whole. The belief in an ever rising housing market, however, increasingly became an act of faith because, in the event of a reversal, the whole system was in danger of collapsing – and that, surely, wouldn't be allowed to happen.

The system duly did collapse. And with the collapse came an extraordinary loss of trust. Bank-sponsored conduits and SIVs could no longer issue asset-backed commercial paper because underlying investors no longer trusted the backing assets. Banks were obliged either to provide funds to the conduits and SIVs or – as time went on – to bring the assets of those vehicles onto their own balance sheets. The inevitable deterioration in asset quality left banks short of capital. Equity investors no longer trusted banks: as a result, share prices collapsed. Meanwhile, banks stopped trusting each other. As property portfolios went belly up, some institutions found access to the interbank market – the market that, on a daily basis, allows banks to deal with liquidity shortfalls and excesses – increasingly difficult. And, as interbank rates rose, so equity investors sold even more shares, believing that those operating in the interbank market might have had 'inside knowledge' of the state of an individual bank's solvency. Meanwhile, the underlying investors who now owned huge amounts of collateralized debt obligations and the like began to realize they were sitting on a pile of toxic waste: and without the appetite to buy more of the stuff, banks lost a key source of funding for lending. Credit creation came to a grinding halt and so, too, did Western economies.

This was yet another example of an age-old banking problem. No bank ever has sufficient funds immediately available to be able to return cash to all of its depositors at once. In moments of panic, when those who fund banks fear the game may be up, bank failure is in danger of becoming a self-fulfilling prophecy. History offers plenty of examples, from Overend, Gurney and Co. in 1866 through to the 1907 failures of the National Bank of North America and the Knickerbocker Trust Company, and from the 11,000 US banks that failed during the Great Depression through to the 1,000 US Savings and Loans companies that collapsed in the 1980s. There were failures of regulation, fraudulent activity, financial malfeasance and all manner of other unspeakable sins. In each case, there was also a complete failure of trust. It even happened in *Mary Poppins*, with a run on the Dawes, Tomes, Mousley, Grubbs, Fidelity Fiduciary Bank.

Mary Poppins is set in 1910, a handful of years before the outbreak of the First World War, at a time when cross-border capital flows had reached a level not to be seen again until the beginning of the 1980s. The degree to which international capital markets were integrated – thanks, in part, to the political arrangements associated with empire – is captured remarkably well in 'Fidelity Fiduciary Bank', a *Poppins* song. The lyrics for that song, in turn, were inspired by an essay titled 'Money London' by a Mr Turner in a book titled *Living London* edited by a Mr Sims and published in 1903. In the essay, Turner offered the following thoughts:

It is not possible to realise without much thought the industrial power that is wrapped up in money London. Railways through Africa, dams across the Nile, fleets of ocean greyhounds, great canals, leagues of ripening corn – London holds the key to all of these, and who can reckon up what beside.

Economically and financially, the world returned to the conditions seen in *Mary Poppins* in the 1980s. Politically, however, it did not: we no longer live in a world of empires. In the absence of cross-border legal and regulatory control, trust becomes a particularly valuable commodity – and it can too easily be abused. As Kenneth J Arrow, the Nobel Prize-winning economist, noted in 1970:

> trust has a very important pragmatic value, if nothing else. Trust is an important lubricant of a social system. It is extremely efficient: it saves a lot of trouble to have a fair degree of reliance on other people's word … Trust and similar values, loyalty or truth-telling, are examples of what the economist would call 'externalities'. They are goods, they are commodities, they have real, practical, economic value; they increase the efficiency of the system, enable you to produce more goods or more of whatever values you hold in high esteem. But they are not commodities for which trade on the open market is technically possible or even meaningful.[10]

Arrow's key point is that, with trust, economic efficiency increases: in other words, resources are allocated more effectively, offering the potential for everyone to be better off. Without trust, economic efficiency decreases. As Arrow observed:

> among the properties of many societies whose economic development is backward is a lack of mutual trust. Collective undertakings of any kind, not merely governmental, become difficult or impossible

not only because A may betray B but because even if A wants to trust
B he knows that B is unlikely to trust him.[11]

The loss of trust witnessed in recent years – from within the financial
system – has been nothing short of extraordinary. Pre-crisis, faith in
the power of the market – and its invisible hand – was sky high. That
faith, however, depended on the idea that the market could somehow
be trusted to deliver not just outcomes better than under any alternative system of resource allocation but also outcomes that were
genuinely good for all. Yet, slowly but surely, trust has been chipped
away, so much so that financial markets are no longer capable of
delivering the outcomes of old. Creditors and debtors – and all those
who lie in-between – eye each other with suspicion. All the while, the
supply of credit ebbs away.

Pre-crisis, confidence in financial alchemy manifested itself in all
sorts of ways: strange innovations within capital markets; the huge
expansion of carry trades as investors could borrow cheaply in, for
example, Japanese yen and invest in sterling, the New Zealand dollar
or the Turkish lira, all of which offered much higher interest rates;
rapacious bankers who were happy to bet the house (or, more likely,
their bank) on ever more outlandish deals; and, for the man and
woman on the street, a massive increase in mortgage debt as dream
homes became part of a new, credit-frenzied, reality.

At the height of the subprime boom, when investors were falling
over themselves to purchase allegedly safe assets with returns higher
than those available on low-yielding government bonds, the connection between ultimate borrower and ultimate lender became increasingly tenuous: the homebuyer in Arizona had little idea that her
mortgage had, ultimately, been provided by Norwegian savers putting
money aside for their future pensions. And the Norwegian savers
had no reason to think their savings had been invested in the
Arizonan real estate market, where some subprime borrowers never

intended to repay their loans. This disconnect, however, supposedly didn't matter. Financial innovation had led to the growth of credit risk transfer instruments – including credit default swaps and structured credit products such as collateralized debt obligations – which allowed hitherto unmanageable risks to be spread ever more thinly.

This, though, meant that the financial institutions that originated credits no longer had to hold them on their books. Instead, credits could be repackaged and sold off into the capital markets, allowing a distant but ultimately fragile link to be created between the subprime mortgage customer in Arizona and the contributor to a Norwegian pension fund.

This was an extraordinary process. Money saved in one part of the world was increasingly being channelled to investment opportunities in other parts of the world, whether or not those investment opportunities were attractive, risky or appropriately diversified. The dangers associated with such large cross-border financial flows were getting bigger day by day. Both creditors and debtors chose to ignore them. The tell-tale signs were certainly there. Some countries were borrowing like crazy. Greece was, no doubt, the most extraordinary example. In 2007, before the onset of the financial crisis, Greece was running a balance of payments current account deficit of over 14 per cent of national income, bigger than any of the Asian deficits before the 1997 Thai baht crisis. But it wasn't the only nation borrowing heavily from the rest of the world. Spain ran a deficit of 10 per cent of national income, Ireland and the US ran deficits of around 5 per cent, while the UK clocked up a deficit of 2.5 per cent of national income.

A current account deficit simply implies that a nation is investing more than it is saving. It therefore has to borrow from abroad. For every current account deficit, there has to be a surplus somewhere else. Put another way, for every country that is investing more than it is saving, others must be saving more than they are investing. The world doesn't do business with Mars or Jupiter. And, for every crazy borrower, there has to be an equally crazy lender.

In 2007, the main surplus nations included China, Saudi Arabia, Russia, Japan and Germany. What was their justification for investing their money in a US housing boom or a super-inflated Spanish property market rather than investing back at home? Were their savers even aware of where their money was eventually ending up?

China, Russia and Saudi Arabia had – and still have – poorly developed financial systems relative to those in the West. In particular, consumer credit facilities are rudimentary. The inevitable result is that consumer demand is constrained. Those with good income prospects cannot easily borrow to consume now and pay later. Inevitably, their money is invested in liquid assets – the sorts of things that can be sold on a whim with no significant loss. US Treasuries fit the bill nicely. But, in the early years of the twenty-first century, demand for Treasuries simply left US interest rates lower than they needed to be, removing the discipline that might otherwise have constrained borrowing by both US households and government.

Japan's story, at least since the onset of its stagnation in 1990, is rather different. Awash with excessive amounts of debt and with profits shot to pieces, companies chose not to invest but, instead, to repay debt. As repaying debt is a form of saving, Japan has inevitably run repeated current account surpluses over the years, a consequence of persistently weak domestic demand. As a result, Japanese interest rates have remained remarkably low, allowing international investors – at least those prepared to put currency risk to one side – to borrow remarkably cheaply in yen and reinvest the proceeds elsewhere. That money helped fund excessive borrowing in other parts of the world.

Germany offers another variant on the surplus story. Its financial system can hardly be described as rudimentary, its companies are not facing huge debts and its households, if they wanted to, could presumably spend freely. Like Japan, however, Germany's population is rapidly ageing – and shrinking. In 2010, it had a population of 82 million. The United Nations projects that, by 2075, Germany's population will have dwindled to 70 million. Meanwhile, its old age dependency ratio – the ratio of those above standard retirement age to those of working age – is rising rapidly: according to the UN, it's set to jump from 31 per cent in 2010 to a remarkable 55 per cent by 2035. That's an awful lot of elderly people who will need looking after: and, before they retire, they're all busily saving to make sure they don't end up in impoverishment.

Money put aside, however, is also money that, ultimately, will eventually be invested. The alternative of putting it under the mattress is hardly attractive: mattresses, in general, don't pay interest or earn a profit.

Germans didn't invest all of their savings at home. Ignoring the opportunities to put their money into Germany's fabled industrial machine, they ended up investing abroad, sometimes unwittingly.

It wasn't just individuals who parked their savings in the local Sparkassen, which, in turn, became a conduit for investment abroad. Industrial companies placed their well-earned profits into the banking system, preferring to earn interest than to invest in additional capacity, either in Germany or, indeed, elsewhere. The banks, in turn, searched for the highest yields associated with minimal risk: they, after all, wanted to keep their savers happy. And, like many other financial institutions, they looked abroad for safe assets. Emerging markets were mostly spurned: there had been too many burnt fingers in the past. Instead, the assets of choice included US mortgage-backed securities and southern European government debt. These were supposedly safe: after all, the US housing market had continued to rise in value decade after decade, while no Western industrial nation had defaulted since before the Second World War.

Yet Germany's saving behaviour – and that of the Chinese, the Saudis and the other surplus nations – ultimately subsidized excessive borrowing in other nations, which, in turn, allowed the entitlement culture to grow year by year. All those purchases of government bonds and mortgage-backed securities were driving interest rates down to lower and lower levels. The actions of the savings nations were providing the incentive for the deficit nations to borrow more and more. And they did so with considerable aplomb. The savers turned a blind eye to the dangers for three reasons. They didn't know – and nor did they ask – where financial intermediaries were investing their savings. Their ageing populations were prepared to ignore the risks. And they trusted particular financial assets, notably government bonds and, in the US, mortgage-backed securities.

It was the Freudian illusion at work again. The investment philosophy adopted by millions of savers was one involving a heavy dose of wish-fulfilment. Many of those savers had no idea of what, ultimately, they were investing in. Even the more sophisticated didn't stop to think. All they cared about was maximizing their returns. By doing so, however, they removed market discipline from the system. Those who borrowed too much, who allowed their housing markets to spin out of control, who sanctioned continuous increases in entitlement spending, could do so partly because of the generosity of the world's savers. And the borrowers themselves were hardly sensible: even when interest rates were incredibly high, most obviously on credit cards, many were happy to take on even more debt. Years into the crisis, borrowers' behaviour was still questionable: Wonga, a credit company, was offering short-term loans in the UK in 2013 with an interest rate of 1 per cent per day: expensive money indeed.

Of course, on the assumption of continued economic expansion – the Freudian illusion – the debtors could always repay their creditors. The creditors thus could afford to ignore risk and hence were prepared to lend to the debtors at remarkably low interest rates.

The economic and financial crisis, however, has put paid to that illusion.

Before the Second World War, a country's creditors and debtors were mostly home grown: those who put money aside for a rainy day would, in effect, be lending to those in their own country who wanted to spend now and pay later (given restrictions on consumer credit, the borrowers were typically governments and companies, not individuals). An economic crisis could be handled democratically if only because both creditors and debtors both had a voice in a nation's economic and financial affairs.

That's not to say that everyone was treated equally. In the nineteenth century, debtors had a nasty habit of ending up in prison, as described by Charles Dickens – in a paean to his own debt-encumbered and incarcerated father – in *Little Dorrit*:

> Thirty years ago there stood, a few doors short of the church of Saint George, in the borough of Southwark, on the left-hand side of the way going southward, the Marshalsea Prison. It had stood there many years before, and it remained there some years afterwards; but it is gone now, and the world is none the worse without it. It was an oblong pile of barrack building, partitioned into squalid houses standing back to back, so that there were no back rooms; environed by a narrow paved yard, hemmed in by high walls duly spiked at top. Itself a close and confined prison for debtors, it contained within it a much closer and more confined jail for smugglers. Offenders against the revenue laws, and defaulters to excise or customs who had incurred fines which they were unable to pay, were supposed to be incarcerated behind an iron-plated door closing up a second prison, consisting of a strong cell or two, and a blind alley some yard and a half wide, which

formed the mysterious termination of the very limited skittle-ground in which the Marshalsea debtors bowled down their troubles.

Among the big losers in the UK in the first half of the twentieth century were the landed gentry, many of whom were undone by the impact of death duties, one reason why the National Trust now looks after 'over 350 historic houses, gardens and ancient monuments'.[12] The Trust purchased its first property – the Alfriston Clergy House in Sussex – for a mere £10 in 1896 but other properties soon followed as the rich were inevitably squeezed to fund the costs of two world wars and an intervening depression. Above a certain threshold, property rights were mostly ignored. Rich creditors lost out, even as national income for the most part continued to expand.

In the second half of the twentieth century, both debtors and creditors could more happily live side-by-side thanks to persistently rising living standards. Rising incomes gave at least some creditors a reasonable return – banks and bondholders both did incredibly well as the inflationary 1970s gave way to the price stability of the 1980s and beyond – while debtors could sleep easily, knowing that higher living standards would easily allow them to pay off their debts, with both interest and little financial pain.

Without growth, however, the relationship between creditors and debtors becomes a lot more problematic. The creditors want their money back, but the debtors may no longer have the ability to repay. Economic stagnation understandably leads to mistrust, to poorly functioning credit markets, to credit shortages and debt default.

At the beginning of the twenty-first century, however, there is an added complication. The creditors of China have lent to the debtors of the US. The creditors of northern Europe have lent to the debtors of southern Europe. Without growth, how can the creditors demand repayment from the debtors? In today's international capital markets, there is no Marshalsea to punish debtors in difficulty and, thus, to encourage the wayward to live within their means.

The financial crisis has left Western income levels at very depressed levels: the ability and willingness of debtors to repay their foreign creditors – and creditors to extend more loans to foreign debtors – are no longer what they used to be. Yet none of this sits well with our addiction to the bailout, the quick fix and the Keynesian stimulus. We live in fear of the cold turkey that awaits should it turn out we are living off illusory, not real, prosperity. But what happens if, as a consequence of ongoing economic disappointment, creditors and debtors cannot agree on the next steps? What happens if creditors are no longer prepared to fund the financial drugs debtors crave, or debtors are no longer willing to keep their creditors happy?

MISTRUST SPREADS

The mistrust seen first of all within the financial system has now spread to parts of the public sector. The argument in favour of fiscal stimulus was always that, unlike companies, governments could not really go bust: blessed with the coercive power of taxation, governments could always repay their creditors, at least in nominal terms. It's one reason why, pre-financial crisis, foreign creditors were happy to lend to the likes of Spain and Greece at remarkably low interest rates – and, of course, one reason why Spain began to suffer a real estate bubble.

Between 2010 and the beginning of 2012, the Greek economy contracted 16 per cent, a result that turned Greece into a latter-day depression-era nation. Its decline reflected, in part, a breakdown of trust. The Greeks had borrowed heavily from the rest of the world, partly in a bid to sustain various rather generous entitlement programmes. To do so, the Greek government had cooked the books. Its true fiscal position was far worse than it had claimed. It had deceived its creditors, both domestic and foreign (with a little help from Goldman Sachs[13]). Once the scam was revealed, Greece's creditors headed for the exit. No longer were they prepared to extend credit to Greece on such generous terms. Interest rates started to rise, the economy slowed down, tax revenues haemorrhaged and the Greek people were suddenly faced with either the prospect of years of biting austerity or the ignominy of (partial) default. As it turned out, they eventually ended up with both.

Greece's problems rapidly spread to other parts of the eurozone. It wasn't obvious that other countries had been quite so economical with the truth. Nevertheless, a pattern had been set. Creditors were losing faith in debtors. More disturbing politically, creditor nations were losing faith in debtor nations. Persistently soft economic growth had left governments with weakening fiscal positions, a reflection of tax shortfalls and the maintenance of public spending commitments. Sluggish economic activity had also left banks with rapidly deteriorating balance sheets: good loans were turning bad. In response, regulators insisted banks should improve their capital ratios, a process that simply reduced bank lending, making activity even more sluggish.

This wasn't the first time that governments had ended up with huge amounts of debt. Expressed as a share of national income, government debt levels had risen on three occasions during the twentieth century: immediately after the First World War and during the 1930s, when the ratio of government debt to national income in the advanced economies peaked at around 70 per cent, and immediately after the Second World War, when the ratio peaked at around 90 per cent. On each of these occasions, debt levels came down very quickly, a result either of inflation (Germany in the 1920s), default (some European nations and near enough the entirety of Latin American nations in the 1930s), or a combination of rapid economic growth, artificially low interest rates and accelerating inflation (the Western world's so-called golden age in the 1950s and 1960s). In each case, those who lent to governments ultimately lost out.

On all three occasions, there was a ready explanation for why debt levels were so high relative to national income. Either it was the cost of war (forcing debt levels up) or the despair of depression (forcing debt levels up and incomes sharply lower). Wartime debts would inevitably come down so long as countries were subsequently able to maintain the peace: cutting military expenditure is an easy way to bring public spending under control. Depression-era debts were not so easy to tackle – partly because countries were locked into the Gold Standard, a monetary straitjacket not so different from the disciplines associated with the euro. Depression-era debts, however, ultimately ended up folded into the much bigger debts associated with the Second World War. We'll never know what would have happened to those debts if the author of *Mein Kampf* hadn't ended up in the Reichstag and the Japanese hadn't decided to bomb Pearl Harbor.

While, then, there are precedents for the high levels of government debt built up in the first decade of the new millennium, there are three important differences that, all too often, are ignored.

First, high levels of public spending today reflect not temporary increases in military expenditures associated with the foolishness of war but, instead, persistent increases in entitlement expenditures associated with the comfort of peace.

Second, governments today borrow heavily internationally whereas, in the interwar period, throughout the Second World War and in the 1950s and 1960s, they had to make do mostly with domestically generated funds: protectionism and isolationism were hardly conducive to sizeable cross-border capital flows.

Third, at least in wartime, governments were able to issue edicts – restrictions on freedom – to ensure their borrowing could be funded: rationing, for example, may not have been much fun but it was a useful way to coerce British citizens during the Second World War to lend their hard-earned income to the government rather than to spend it on consumer fripperies. Powdered egg, a severe limit on tobacco and a complete absence of silk stockings were the least of it: paying for all those Hurricanes, Spitfires and Lancasters required austerity on a massive scale. Even after the war, rationing continued, not ending completely until 1954.

Today's model creates a mismatch between the interests of domestic debtors – those who have an inflated sense of entitlement – and foreign creditors – who want to be paid interest and ultimately expect to get their money back. Indeed, the mismatch could more accurately be termed a democratic deficit. Democratically elected politicians need votes. Promising entitlements is one way of winning those votes. Borrowing money cheaply – whether directly or via private finance initiatives that create a contingent liability for the state – allows those entitlements to be provided. Promising foreign creditors they'll get their money back – with interest – is relatively easy to do. Meeting that promise is a lot more difficult if, subsequently, economic performance disappoints. Politicians will then surely listen more to their domestic voters than to their foreign creditors. After all, unlike their Victorian forbears, today's creditors do not have the ability to throw debtors into the Marshalsea prison. Creditors and debtors reside in different parts of the world.

Of course, for much of the second half of the twentieth century, economic performance didn't disappoint. Western economies were wealth machines, perfectly capable of delivering rising incomes year by year. Creditors didn't have to worry about default because rising incomes meant debtors could always repay. For many years, the democratic deficit could easily be sustained.

No longer is this the case. A country that has borrowed heavily but that is then unable to grow will end up imposing a huge burden on either taxpayers, recipients of public services or its creditors. Worse, a country that has borrowed heavily, is unable to grow and then discovers its banks are up to their eyeballs in bad debts may then need to borrow even more to bail out its financial institutions just at the point when its creditors are beginning to think 'enough is enough'. If neither banks nor government are then able to raise sufficient funds, something will have to give.

At the onset of the financial crisis, the problem seemed to be one of overwhelming complexity. It simply wasn't possible to value pieces of paper that had sliced and diced risk in so many different ways: the alphabet soup of modern international finance was beyond comprehension. Yet, as the crisis developed, a problem of complexity was replaced by a problem of simplicity. There aren't many financial assets simpler than government bonds – mere IOUs backed by future tax revenues – yet even in this simplest of areas, trust – or the lack of it – was becoming a major problem.

Government borrowing costs began to vary. In part, this reflected differing levels of national savings. The German and Japanese governments had room to borrow from their own residents. Other countries – most obviously the US and the UK – had the option to print money to fund government borrowing. The Spanish and Greeks, however, had no choice but to borrow from abroad. The combination of burgeoning budget deficits, weak banking systems and a lack of economic growth meant that it wasn't long before creditors began to worry about default. With neither sufficient savings nor access to a printing press, southern European nations found themselves at the mercy of international capital markets.

As private investors became increasingly reluctant to lend to debtor nations, public investors – in the form of the International Monetary Fund, the European Central Bank and others – plugged the gap. In the event of a subsequent partial default, however, it seemed that these big public sector institutions – funded, in effect, by taxpayers – would enjoy seniority. In other words, they would get their money back – at last in part – even if other investors lost the shirts off their backs. Not surprisingly, private investors became even more agitated. Yields on government debt rose still further, requiring even more in the way of official help. Southern European nations were in danger of turning into the financial equivalent of client states, dependent on the – reluctant – generosity of taxpayers in northern Europe and elsewhere, as opposed to the judgement of financial markets, to keep themselves technically solvent.

What had been a funding arrangement involving millions of private sector decisions – ranging from subprime customers through to cautious savers putting money aside for their retirement – had turned into a series of multilateral government-to-government deals. In the absence of properly functioning and democratically accountable political arrangements within the eurozone – most notably, in the absence of some form or another of fiscal union – trust in the entire eurozone project began to falter. How could southern European nations remain client states of those in the north? How could northern European taxpayers dip into their pockets continuously to fund southern nations whose people had, over the years, worked too little and paid themselves too much?

The answer, it seemed, was for investors no longer to trust the euro. Although the single currency area remained intact, and euros were in use all over the eurozone – and, at least in the hands of the world's reserve managers, in many other nations too – this was no more than a thin veneer. Fear of either euro break-up or the creation of a disorderly queue of departing nations led to banks, companies and even individual savers removing their funds from southern European banks and taking their money north. Mostly done via a flick of a switch rather than with suitcases stuffed with used €100 notes, the consequence was a flight of cash that left southern European banks short of cash, global investors seriously worried about the solvency of southern European banks and borrowing costs for anyone in southern Europe – government, company or individual – far higher than those set by the European Central Bank in Frankfurt. There may have been one currency but the eurozone monetary system was split asunder. Eventually the European Central Bank had to step in with the promise in 2012 of 'outright monetary transactions' – in effect, a commitment to purchase southern European government debt to reduce excessively high borrowing costs – to restore a semblance of order. Even then, it was no more than the application of yet another monetary sticking plaster: the troubling relationship between debtors and creditors remained unresolved.

AND THE WINNERS ARE . . .

The collapse in confidence in southern Europe led to exaggerated flows of capital into so-called 'safe-havens'. The cost of borrowing in the US, Germany and the UK tumbled, prompting some commentators to argue that even more fiscal stimulus was justified. Yet there was, surely, a major problem with this view. The cost of borrowing had declined dramatically in Italy, Spain, Portugal and Greece during the euro's early years, a reflection of their ability to attract capital flows from abroad. These countries duly borrowed more, either via bigger budget deficits or through big increases in property loans. In hindsight, this was a major mistake. The economies didn't perform as well as expected. The returns from excessive borrowing were, as it turned out, often negative. And, as creditors realized the error of their ways, the debtors were no longer able to service their debts at reasonable rates. It wasn't just borrowers making mistakes. Lenders made mistakes too.

Lower yields may provide a justification for additional government borrowing but, as in Japan's case, there is no guarantee that the additional borrowing will deliver the right results. Worse, instead of being a vote of confidence in a nation's anti-inflation capabilities, persistently low interest rates may simply imply that investors have lost all appetite for risk or for adding to capacity. Riskier assets then lose value, investment is increasingly constrained, the economy slumps and inflation ends up too low. Rather than paving the way towards sustained economic recovery, low interest rates become a symptom of a deep economic and financial malaise. It is tempting to believe that, with remarkably low borrowing costs, the US, UK and German governments are trusted by creditors to spend wisely. Yet does it make sense to succumb to the siren voices of fickle creditors interested only in protecting the value of what they have and not in taking excessive risk? Governments, after all, no longer retain the trust of old.

Earlier, I referred to Gallup polls that showed a dramatic loss of trust in the financial system, only some of which could be explained by the economic downturn. But the loss of trust is not restricted to the financial system alone. It has become endemic across almost all aspects of life. In a report released in September 2011, Gallup declared that 'Americans express historic negativity toward US Government'.[14] Overall, 81 per cent of those polled declared that they were dissatisfied with the way in which the nation was being governed, the worst result (by far) since data were first collected in 1971. Confidence in Congress was at an all-time low with only 31 per cent of those polled saying they had either a great deal or a fair amount of trust in Capitol Hill, down from 72 per cent back in 1972. Consistent with this bleak message was a complete loss of faith in the performance of public officials, 'the men and women in political life . . . who either hold or are running for public office'.

The lack of trust extends to public spending. In another poll,[15] Americans were asked: 'Of every tax dollar that goes to the federal government in Washington DC, how many cents of each dollar would you say are wasted?' In 2011, those polled reckoned that more than half of their money was being poured down the drain. Admittedly, there were biases across those polled: the elderly were less trusting of government spending than those just entering adulthood, and those benefiting from a higher level of education were more likely to give the federal government the benefit of the doubt. The overall picture, however, is clear: Americans of all political persuasions – Democrats, Republicans, Liberals, Moderates and Conservatives – have serious doubts about the direction Washington is heading in.

A lack of political trust is neither confined to Washington nor uniquely American. The 2012 Edelman Trust Barometer[16] shows that, across many developed and emerging nations, governments were trusted less than businesses, while political leaders were trusted less than their business equivalents, a result most likely of governments failing to deliver on their promises. 'Yes we can' perhaps can be rephrased as 'perhaps we can't'.

It doesn't end there. Financial institutions, government and central bankers may be bad enough, but mistrust has now spread through society more broadly. Jimmy Carr, a multimillionaire British comedian, was discovered by *The Times* in 2012 to be paying a marginal tax rate of only 1 per cent thanks to an offshore accounting device, a scam in all but name. His shame was compounded by the unearthing of a Channel 4 comedy sketch in which he had lampooned Barclays Bank for doing much the same thing.[17] Tax dodging is hardly new – Leona Helmsley, the New York hotel owner and self-styled 'Queen of Mean', was convicted of tax avoidance, thanks in part to her observation that 'only the little people pay taxes' – but with successful comedians as opposed to bruiser businesswomen involved, it is difficult to know where it will all end. At around the same time, the Leveson inquiry was uncovering the underhand tactics of those in the media who had decided that hacking into people's mobile phones to listen to their messages might be a good idea. And British MPs had been dragged through the mud as a consequence of an expenses scandal that, in other professions, would have led to mass sackings.

If people trust each other, and the institutions they represent, they are more likely to trade. That means more in the way of profitable exchanges and, hence, greater opportunities to specialize. And with heightened levels of trust, there is less need for bureaucracy: rules, regulations and legal enforcement can be reduced without wider costs. Meanwhile, higher levels of trust are also associated with more effective financial markets: savers are prepared to put their money into projects with uncertain returns believing, rightly or otherwise, that they will be fairly treated. And higher levels of trust in financial markets will surely facilitate the cross-border movement of funds between creditors and debtors, allowing savers to hunt for the best global returns and, thus, allowing capital to be allocated in the most efficient way to maximize income.

Without trust, economic growth will be in short supply. And with neither trust nor growth, society is in danger of disintegrating.

CHAPTER SEVEN

THREE SCHISMS

To understand the challenges stemming from a breakdown of trust – in particular, when the breakdown is linked to economic disappointment – it's worth going back to the thoughts of Alexis de Tocqueville (1805–1859), author of *Democracy in America* and *The Old Regime and the Revolution*. In the latter, he argued that, well before the 1789 French Revolution:

> public prosperity began to develop with unexampled strides. This is shown by all sorts of evidence. Population increased rapidly; wealth more rapidly still. The American war [of independence] did not check the movement: it completed the embarrassment of the state, but did not impede private enterprise: individuals grew more industrious, more inventive, richer than ever.
>
> . . . measurably, with the increase in prosperity in France, men's minds grow more restless and uneasy; public discontent is embittered; the hatred of the old institutions increases. The nation visibly tends toward revolution.

...The regime which is destroyed by a revolution is almost always an improvement on its immediate predecessor, and experience teaches that the most critical moment for bad governments is the one which witnesses their first steps toward reform ... Evils which are patiently endured when they seem inevitable, become intolerable when once the idea of escape from them is suggested.

...No one in 1780 had any idea that France was on the decline: on the contrary, there seemed to be no bounds to its progress. It was then that the theory of the continual and indefinite perfectibility of man took its rise. Twenty years before, nothing was hoped from the future: in 1780, nothing was feared. Imagination anticipated a coming era of unheard-of felicity, diverted attention from present blessings, and concentrated it upon novelties.

In other words, de Tocqueville's view of revolutionary upheaval was based not so much on the Marxist idea that the proletariat were being exploited but, instead, on the idea that rising prosperity naturally breeds hope and optimism for the future, which, if not then satisfied, provides a serious challenge to the ancien régime. In the event of subsequent setback, the ancien régime gets the blame. De Tocqueville's view thus allows for the role of expectations and the impact on the political system if those expectations are not met.

De Tocqueville's view of expectations and their impact on political stability captures many of the upheavals seen in the non-democratic world since the end of the 1980s, including the fall of the Berlin Wall, the subsequent collapse of the Soviet empire and the Arab Spring. But de Tocqueville also has something useful to say about the problems now facing Western economies. Economic stagnation need not make anyone worse off but it certainly has left expectations unmet. Reductions in public spending plans, rises in education costs, increased retirement age, bigger pension contributions and lower stock-market returns are all part of the same story: stagnation prevents us from delivering on the promises we have made to ourselves. When the money runs out, there is only disappointment. And from disappointment comes hardship, tragedy and anger.

All three came together in terrible circumstances in November 2012 when Amaia Egana, a 53-year-old woman, took her own life as she was being evicted from her home in the Basque town of Barakaldo. This wasn't the first eviction-related suicide in Spain but, thanks to a wave of public protests in the days that followed – including a banner unveiled at a soccer match stating 'They're not suicides. They're murders. The banks and politicians are accomplices. Stop the evictions!' – the story dominated the newswires.[1] Between 2008 and Egana's 2012 suicide, almost 400,000 Spanish homes had been repossessed even though Spain's banks had received significant support from the Spanish government and, hence, from the Spanish taxpayer. A poisonous cocktail was made worse by Spain's obligations to its foreign creditors and by the growing divide between the national government in Madrid and the semi-autonomous regions. Indeed, following the results of a regional election on 25 November 2012, Catalonian separatist parties demanded a referendum on independence, even though Catalonia was heavily in debt, was unable to tap into international capital markets and had – reluctantly – become dependent on credit lines from Madrid.

While, today, anger is mostly directed at politicians and 'fat cat' bankers, de Tocqueville was more concerned with fat cat monarchs, in particular Louis XVI, beheaded in 1793. According to Jean-Baptiste Cléry, the king's manservant, Louis cried out as the blade of the guillotine dropped because 'his head did not fall at the first stroke, his neck being so fat'. The King of France was, then, the prototypical fat cat, an enormously rich man disconnected from the difficulties and challenges his nation faced. Unfortunately – for him, at least – his nation eventually reconnected with him in a most brutal manner – by disconnecting his head.

More than anything else, France's ancien régime lost the trust of its people. Economic progress in the late eighteenth century had created expectations that cried out for political reform. Yet, as de Tocqueville argued, the ancien régime was no longer fit for purpose. It was unable to cater for the mass of middle-class expectations riding the crest of an industrial wave. Even if, as de Tocqueville argued, the regime under Louis XVI was an improvement compared with, say, the despotic Louis XIV, the improvement only fermented demand for further change.

There were, of course, other things happening at the same time that only added to revolutionary fervour. The American War of Independence – which some might argue was triggered over the price of a cup of tea – surely offered a warning to complacent monarchs and nobility across the whole of Europe. After all, Thomas Jefferson had stated as early as 1775 that 'all men are created equal and independent, that from their equal creation they derive rights inherent and inalienable, among which are the preservation of life and liberty and the pursuit of happiness'. For Europe's increasingly nervous nobility, this was a sacrilegious statement. Meanwhile, in philosophical circles, Enlightenment thinkers held sway, happy to reject the idea of monarchy deriving its power directly from God.

At the same time, French policy-makers exhibited staggering incompetence, largely thanks to a struggle between the monarchy and the nobility. The French economy in the late eighteenth century was horrendously short of money. The French national debt tripled between 1774 and 1789, in part a reflection of the costs of supporting the American War of Independence against the British. Those who lent to the French state had no guarantee of when, if ever, interest would be paid. To prevent complete bankruptcy, something had to be done.

Charles-Alexandre de Calonne, the French Director-General of Finance, proposed the imposition of a permanent land tax that, unlike most existing taxes, would not be replete with the usual exemptions for the ruling upper classes. Inevitably, therefore, the tax would fall most heavily on the fat cat nobility and clergy who, between them, owned most of the land. Via the Assembly of Notables and the Paris *parlement*, the nobility and clergy not surprisingly rejected Calonne's proposal – both when he proposed it and, later, when it was submitted by Calonne's successor, the Archbishop of Toulouse. From the nobles' perspective, the argument was simple, if self-serving: it would be wrong, in their view, to allow the power of taxation to be concentrated in the hands of the king, living a life of luxury in Versailles, and his advisers. Inevitably, the battle for power between monarchy and aristocracy both left the French fiscal position in tatters and ignored the interests of peasants, the urban poor and, in some cases, the newly emerging industrialists.

Despite rising prosperity in Paris and other French cities, the majority of citizens – mostly the underprivileged – were still vulnerable to sudden spikes in food prices. The first such occasion, in 1775, resulted from reforms enacted by Anne-Robert-Jacques Turgot, the controller-general and an early free-market fan, who lifted price controls on flour. The price of flour inevitably jumped, in turn triggering the uprising of the *guerre des farines*. The second food price spike, in 1788, came courtesy of a spring drought followed by July hailstorms that, together, destroyed the annual wheat harvest. As the price of bread soared, the urban poor of Paris were in big trouble. Things only got worse with the onset of a brutally cold winter.

Jean-Baptiste Réveillon, a manufacturer of luxury wallpaper,[2] wrote in an essay the following year: 'Since bread was the foundation of our national economy, its distribution should be deregulated, permitting lower prices. That in turn would allow lower wage costs, lower manufacturing prices and brisk consumption.'[3] Despite his good intentions – he only hoped for a lower price for bread – his remarks were sadly misinterpreted. The comments on wages were taken completely out of context, and led eventually to the destruction of his factory, his home and his wine cellar by an angry mob. It was the first real act of violence in what eventually became the French Revolution. Had the mob been aware that Marie Antoinette was one of his more important clients, Réveillon's situation might have been even worse.

Even with the onset of Revolution – signalled by the meeting of the Estates General – the financial situation failed to improve. Having seized land from the aristocracy and the clergy – often through the use of supreme and barbaric violence – the revolutionary authorities attempted to create an eighteenth-century version of asset-backed securities, raising money through the issuance of pieces of paper – *assignats* – backed by the newly acquired spoils of revolutionary upheaval. Inevitably, as more and more *assignats* were issued, their value collapsed. There was only one thing for it: following the Terror and the death of Robespierre, France ended up solving its problems by going to war. Via multiple military conquests, Napoleon Bonaparte attempted both to overthrow ruling ancien régimes elsewhere in Europe and loot their treasures all in the name of *liberté, égalité, fraternité*. Much of the loot is now on display in the Paris Louvre.

Despite all its late eighteenth-century progress, France was a country living beyond its means. It had no ability to balance the fiscal books and became reliant on naive creditors whom it simply could not repay. *Assignats* were a typical example of financial innovation designed to hide the underlying fiscal problem but ultimately proved worthless. France was also a nation split asunder: the so-called Third Estate – the common people – had no political voice yet were required continuously to support the excesses of both clergy and aristocracy: for France, there had been no equivalent of England's 1688 Glorious Revolution, which triggered a Bill of Rights leading to the ascendancy of Parliament over monarchy.[4]

France, then, was a nation where the wealthy had run off with many of the spoils yet were so busy squabbling with each other that they were unable to observe the growing disquiet among the common people. There was a total failure to deal with the implications for the masses of poor harvests and rising food prices. Enormously indebted, the ancien régime simply didn't have the political ability to cope with the strains that ultimately led to revolution. The assumption was too casually one of 'business as usual'.

Guillotines may be long gone but echoes of pre-revolutionary France can still be heard today. The combination of rising food and fuel prices – thanks, in part, to strong demand from the emerging Asian superpowers – and Western economic stagnation has led to a serious squeeze on real incomes. Trust in government has fallen dramatically, yet there is little agreement within government as to the next course of action. Ideological divisions have led to huge ruptures in American politics, with those advocating large tax increases to improve the nation's finances at loggerheads with those determined to push for the much smaller involvement of government in society. In the eurozone, the 'Third Estate' taxpayers and unemployed of the southern European nations are in the firing line of economic adjustment even if, in many cases, they are hardly to blame for the behaviour of their governments, their banks, their foreign creditors and, as the eurozone crisis has gathered momentum, the single currency's rule-makers in Brussels, Berlin, Frankfurt and Paris. As austerity bites, so political extremism reappears. The family silver – in the form of major companies rather than swathes of land – is slowly being sold off to foreign buyers. Meanwhile, governments are awash with debt and have no obvious strategy to deal with it, other than hoping that growth will miraculously return.

Revolution and beheading may not be uppermost on the list of challenges facing Western nations today but, like the rulers of the ancien régime, today's policy-makers seem at a loss to be able to fix our problems. As trust in our institutions – both public and private – fades, policy-makers have yet to confront the de Tocquevillean gap that's opened up between our supposed entitlements – built on the assumption of ever rising income – and our new, and stagnant, economic reality.

That gap is set to get worse, thanks to the widening of three schisms that have become central features of economic and political life at the beginning of the twenty-first century: haves and have-nots, intergenerational conflict and the aforementioned creditor/debtor rivalries.

During earlier periods of rapid economic expansion, these schisms didn't matter too much. Even as some were becoming a lot better off, few were ending up worse off. With economic stagnation, however, the game has changed. Someone, somewhere, will lose out. We have made promises to ourselves that are far beyond the capacity of our economies to deliver. As reality sets in, there will be a fight over the spoils. That fight, in turn, will undermine trust still further, leading to a climate of blame rather than of cooperation. As such, stagnation is in danger of becoming a trait hard-wired into our collective consciousness.

THE FIRST SCHISM: INCOME INEQUALITY

Countries with high levels of trust among their citizens tend also to be countries that enjoy high living standards. Intriguingly, countries with high levels of trust tend also to be countries with low levels of income inequality. Within the OECD, Norway, Sweden, Denmark, Finland and Switzerland all have high levels of trust, high living standards and low levels of income inequality. At the opposite end of the spectrum, Turkey, Mexico and Portugal have low levels of trust, low living standards and high levels of income inequality. It would seem to follow, then, that reducing income inequality should raise levels of trust and, at the very least, make societies a bit happier.

Plenty of people have been happy to make the argument. In *The Spirit Level*, Richard Wilkinson and Kate Pickett argue powerfully in favour of greater equality, concluding:

> We know that greater equality will help us rein in consumerism and ease the introduction of policies to tackle global warming. We can see how the introduction of modern technology makes profit-making institutions appear increasingly anti-social as they find themselves threatened by the rapidly expanding potential for public good which new technology offers . . . We have seen that the rich countries have got to the end of the really important contributions which economic growth can make to the quality of life . . .[5]

If only things were that simple. Even if the conclusions were right, it is not at all obvious how governments can successfully engineer a smooth shift from high to low levels of income inequality, particularly when so many of the sources of inequality – most obviously, the forces of globalization – are beyond the control of any individual government. Moreover, while rich economies with low levels of inequality may deliver high levels of trust, they often struggle to grow: countries in the OECD with high per capita incomes and low levels of income inequality – most obviously those in Scandinavia – have typically experienced only very slow rates of economic expansion since the 1980s.[6] Put another way, self-satisfied societies whose citizens are too trusting may lack the necessary impetus to take risks that, in turn, might foster economic expansion. That might not be a problem for the likes of Sweden but it is a problem for those nations with geopolitical interests, notably the US. In any case, without expansion, the risk of Smith-style melancholy becomes that much greater. At the same time, economies with low per capita incomes and rising income inequality may be able to expand relatively easily if, for example, there is support for political reform to allow a faster rate of economic growth. Think, for example, of China's economic success – thanks to reforms launched by Deng Xiaoping – since the 1980s. Even with high levels of income inequality, rapid growth can keep Smith's melancholy at bay.

Indeed, China's success has been accompanied by a persistent rise in income inequality. Fast-developing economies typically go through a period of rapidly rising inequality as the new urban 'rich' see their incomes fast outstripping those of the rural poor, thanks to higher levels of productivity in manufacturing than in rural endeavours. Eventually, however, this process should go into reverse: a rapid reduction in the number of people working on the land leads to an increase in productivity for the remainder, allowing their incomes to catch up with those available in the distant metropolis.

Admittedly, political institutions have to develop to facilitate this process: those who aren't able to jump onto the first rung of the development ladder have to be patient. The Arab Spring suggests that, in the absence of those political institutions, anger eventually spills over into revolutions and uprisings. Tunisia, for example, wasn't a particularly poor country but much of its wealth was in the hands of one man, President Zine al-Abidine Ben Ali, deposed in January 2011 thanks, in part, to a lavish lifestyle funded by billions of (allegedly) stolen dollars hidden away in Switzerland and elsewhere.

In per capita terms, however, neither China nor Tunisia has made it into the economic premier league and their levels of income inequality are not atypical for developing nations. The rich West, however, is facing a rather different challenge. Whereas economic growth in the first few decades after the Second World War was distributed among its citizens fairly equally, the same hasn't held since the 1980s. For the US and the UK, in particular, the spoils of economic success have accrued mostly to the very few rather than the many. In the event of stagnation, this threatens to create a significant political problem. Those who have gained will want to hang on to their wealth while those who have yet to gain will suddenly realize they have missed the boat.

Most of us mix in social circles linked to income levels: we know few people either a lot richer or a lot poorer than we are. In a world of stagnation, where there are both winners and losers, that lack of connection inevitably leads to low levels of trust. And, in the absence of trust, it is all too easy to establish a culture of blame. Rather than focusing on the systemic causes of economic and financial failure, it is politically more convenient, instead, to blame the behaviour of specific individuals and groups. At that point, trust in society is in danger of disintegrating, locking in stagnation for the long term.

While both Argentina and Japan made the transition from growth to stagnation, Argentina's experience, to date, has been far worse than Japan's. I argued in chapter 1 that this underperformance reflected, among other things, an isolationist economic dogma and a relatively high level of income inequality. Indeed, since the beginnings of Argentina's relative economic decline in the post-war period, income inequality has gone from bad to worse. Already high by international standards in the 1950s and 1960s, it went into the stratosphere in the 1990s and beyond.

Consistent with the idea that stagnation and inequality in combination make reform a lot more difficult, Argentina ranks poorly as a place to do business. Out of 183 countries ranked by the World Bank, Argentina came a lowly 113th in 2012 for 'ease of doing business', with a particularly poor reputation for dealing with construction permits, business start-ups and tax collection. In contrast, Japan ranked twentieth, despite its economy having endured two lost decades.[7] Trust, it seems, is much higher in Japan than it is in Argentina.

If trust is sorely lacking in Argentina, might the West be heading in the same direction? Certainly, the income inequality figures are, in many cases, disturbing. Between 1979 and 2007, average real after-tax household income for the 1 per cent of the US population with the highest incomes went up almost threefold. For the remainder of the top 20 per cent, income rose by around two-thirds. Those in the middle of the income scale – from the 21st through to the 80th percentiles – saw their income rise by around two-fifths. For those in the bottom 20 per cent, income rose by only one-fifth.

Remarkably enough, between 2005 and 2007, the total after-tax income received by those in the top 20 per cent of the population exceeded that received by the bottom 80 per cent. The top 1 per cent alone saw their share of after-tax income rise from 10 per cent of the total in 1979 to a staggering 20 per cent by 2007. In effect, the already rich became the super-rich. Admittedly, others ended up better off, but the gap between rich and not-so-rich widened enormously. The spoils of US economic success went mostly to those who already were very well off.[8] It's no wonder that, following the financial crisis, the Occupy movement has become so popular.

For the UK, the top 1 per cent of income earners saw their share reach a trough of around 6 per cent in the mid-1970s. Thereafter, the share rose dramatically, reaching a peak of over 15 per cent in 2007, close to ratios last seen before the Second World War. On this particular metric, the UK is not so different from Argentina. The land of the pampas saw the share of the richest 1 per cent hit a trough in the mid-1970s before rising rapidly thereafter. Japan, in contrast, has seen little change over the years. In the post-war period, the share of the richest 1 per cent always remained below 10 per cent of the total.[9]

High levels of income inequality need not, in themselves, be a source of concern. In the late nineteenth century, it was commonly believed that income inequality was, in fact, good for growth: the rich typically saved more than the poor and, by doing so, provided the resources for more investment. More investment, in turn, meant that new technologies would come on stream more quickly, thereby boosting economic growth. On this argument, higher levels of income inequality were ultimately synonymous with improved living standards for the many, not the few. Not surprisingly, this line of thought was particularly popular with the ruling upper class.

By the late twentieth century, the argument was mostly abandoned, largely thanks to cross-country comparisons. As we've seen, many of the world's richest nations – measured through per capita income – had low levels of income inequality. Some of the world's poorest nations, meanwhile, had very high levels of income inequality. In some cases, their ruling elites had established *de facto* kleptocracies. Sierra Leone and the Central African Republic are two obvious examples.

Yet for each example, there is a counterexample. Hong Kong – a wealthy, dynamic and fast-growing economy – has one of the highest levels of income inequality in the world. Brazil and China – paragons of economic success at the beginning of the twenty-first century – are not far behind.[10] In itself, a high level of income inequality appears to be a constraint neither on economic growth nor, indeed, on average living standards.

Another way to demonstrate this is to split the US up into its constituent states. Across the US, there are huge variations in income inequality yet there is no obvious correlation with living standards. The richest state – if it can be called a state – is the District of Columbia, with post-tax per capita incomes in 2011 of almost $64,000. It is also the most unequal state (or district) with regard to income distribution. Second richest is Connecticut, which also happens to be the second most unequal state. Mississippi has the fifth highest level of income inequality across all US states yet is the poorest state. Utah has the lowest level of income inequality yet is the fifth poorest state. Across the US as a whole, there is no obvious link between average living standards and levels of income inequality.[11]

A moment's thought shows why. What matters is not so much whether a society is unequal but, rather, *why* it is unequal. Did the wealthy enrich themselves unfairly? Were the poor exploited? Or, instead, did inequality arise through voluntary exchange, in which case there might be little need to worry?

One such example of voluntary exchange involves the UK's National Lottery. Each Saturday night, the draw for the lottery takes pace. Every so often, a person – or syndicate – wins millions of pounds when their lucky number comes up. The money for the draw comes from the contestants themselves who buy Lotto tickets during the week. Only around 50 per cent of the money raised is redistributed back to the winners. Of the rest, 28 per cent goes to 'good causes': health, education, various charities, the arts and, among other sporting successes, the Great Britain Olympic cycling team. Lottery Duty takes 12 per cent, and 5 per cent goes to retailers. The remainder covers costs.[12]

There are two odd things about this arrangement. First, it's a bit like a voluntary tax: in aggregate, the contestants will definitely lose money because only half of what they pay in is recycled back to the lucky winners. Second, the lottery leads – admittedly on a very small scale – to an entirely voluntary redistribution of income. A tiny handful of those who take part become multimillionaires while the rest end up worse off: having paid for their lottery tickets, they are left empty-handed. Yet there are few complaints.[13]

Arguably, that's because the system is entirely fair and transparent: everyone enters the competition with their eyes open and, while most don't expect to win, many doubtless hope to emulate those who have won. After all, the National Lottery's strapline at one point was 'It could be you'. The lottery can only work, however, if, for the vast majority of contestants, 'it absolutely cannot be you'. That doesn't stop people playing the game every week hoping that, one day, their numbers will come up: a lottery ticket offers a chance to dream – for a small weekly price.

The lottery offers a very transparent and rules-based version of inequality. Everyone knows in advance how the rules work, no one is forced to take part and those who 'lose' do so without feeling that, somehow, their pockets have been picked.

Other sources of inequality can be equally transparent but, in the absence of clear rules, the outcome may not be quite so savoury. The aforementioned kleptocracies are a good example: in their case, inequality results from larceny on the grandest of scales. Transparency alone provides no guarantee that inequality is acceptable. Fairness is also important.

Fairness and market forces, however, do not always make happy bedfellows. Take, for example, soccer. The average weekly salary of soccer players in English football's top division was around £34,000 in 2010. Back in 1966, the year in which England won the World Cup for the first – and, so far, only – time, the average weekly salary was a mere £44, which, adjusted for inflation, would be around £672 in today's money. In real terms, then, football players in the modern Premier League are paid 50 times more than their 1966 counterparts, even though, in international competitions, English players have since utterly failed to emulate the success of Moore, the Charltons, Hurst and Ball.

Is this fair? Hardly. It is, however, a perfectly reasonable reflection of market forces, specifically those unleashed as a result of new technologies. The number of players in England's top soccer division is – and always has been – necessarily constrained but the demand for the players' footballing 'services' has gone through the stratosphere. Satellite and cable broadcasting have dramatically increased the global audience for Premier League soccer matches and, in the process, turned today's footballing stars into multimillionaires, if not World Cup-winning legends, thanks to the brand 'power' of the top teams. Manchester United, for example, is recognized by BrandFinance as having 'huge and long-standing international appeal and is perhaps the most recognized football club brand worldwide with vast accumulated brand equity'.[14] Footballers themselves may not be responsible for the sudden increase in audience numbers but their brand value has nevertheless soared: while Bobby Charlton's most obvious physical attribute was his 'comb-over', David Beckham and Cristiano Ronaldo have become global underpants icons.

The rewards received by international footballing icons are consistent with 'superstar' theories of inequality: there are plenty of good actresses in the world but only one Angelina Jolie and plenty of aspiring models but only one Kate Moss. Superstars have won the global equivalent of the lottery. They are able to earn vast amounts more than others who, for one reason or another, have been unable to establish an equivalent brand. Some people, of course, earn vast amounts of money by simply being themselves: the majority of people would struggle financially to keep up with the Kardashians.

All of these global 'brands' have become wealthy thanks to new technologies. If those technologies, in turn, lead to rising living standards for more or less everyone, there appears to be little reason to worry: Smith's melancholia is held at bay. Soccer players may be 50 times richer today than in the 1960s but society as a whole is also richer, if not by quite the same amount.

The newly rich – soccer players, models, and so on – have seren-dipity to thank for their enhanced earnings. Their talents may be no greater than their predecessors' but they were lucky enough to be born in the right place at the right time. Few would argue that Damien Hirst is a superior artist to Van Gogh. Van Gogh, however, died in poverty while Hirst was, in 2011, worth a cool £215 million.[15]

Market forces work in many other ways to benefit some more than others. In some cases, however, there are both winners and outright losers. Globalization – an international version of market forces – has led to a significant redistribution of income, thanks to a far greater cross-border mobility of capital. US manufacturing workers can no longer be sure that US companies will invest at home when there are plenty of opportunities to invest in lower-wage countries elsewhere: as a result, US manufacturing wages come under downward pressure and American unemployment rises even as Chinese wages go up. Rising Chinese incomes, in turn, lead to higher demand for food: as people become wealthier, they typically shift from vegetarian to meat and dairy based diets, but feeding humans via animals ultimately requires a lot more crops than would be required if humans nourished themselves directly from those crops. Higher food prices, in turn, benefit the US farmer but leave the US manufacturing worker worse off. Faster Chinese growth leads to higher demand for energy, benefiting oil-producing nations at the expense of oil-consuming nations thanks to a higher oil price.

And, as globalization lifted off in the late twentieth century – thanks to open capital markets, new (and cheaper) information technologies and political reforms – so those working in the financial sector saw their incomes rise dramatically even as others saw only modest gains. Between 1950 and 1980, wages in the US financial industry stayed roughly in line with wages across the US private sector more generally. Thereafter, however, they soared, rising to levels 70 per cent above those in the rest of the private sector by 2006, just before the onset of the financial crisis. The last time such a large discrepancy had been seen was back in the 1920s in the years leading up to the Wall Street Crash.[16]

The reasons behind such a big shift are not hard to fathom. In times of rapid economic and technological change, those who claim to be able to help price complicated financial risks – including risks associated with uncertain new technologies – are likely to be in heavy demand. Put globalization and the IT revolution together and it's not hugely surprising that demand from the rest of the economy for financial wisdom – if that's the right phrase – rose so swiftly at the end of the twentieth century.

At the same time, a significant reduction in financial sector regulation in the 1980s and 1990s allowed risk-taking to increase significantly, regardless of whether those risks were in the long-term interests of society as a whole.[17] Not surprisingly, heightened risk-taking led to substantial private sector rewards, even if, later on, economies at large suffered systemic damage. Those rewards, in turn, sucked increasing numbers of educated people into finance and away from the rest of the economy, often leading to ever more ingenious risk-taking gambits. And as pay in the financial world soared, so the ability of regulators to recruit the right calibre of staff to 'police' finance inevitably declined.

Meanwhile, demand for financial services soared thanks to an increasingly aggressive hunt for yield. Investment management companies grew in size not because they had discovered the elixir of ever higher returns but, rather, because they had to find increasingly ingenious – if also increasingly risky – ways of financing pensions, health care and the other demands of ageing populations. Whether or not those investments paid off didn't matter too much: thanks to the recommendations of friendly independent financial advisers, policyholders could dream of a comfortable retirement while the advisers themselves could walk away having pocketed a tidy commission.

Underneath all this is a fundamental problem. How should output within the financial sector be measured, particularly if private affluence is eventually followed by public collapse?

One way to measure output is by totting up the cost of all the inputs: the wage bill, reflecting the cost of labour, the level of profits, reflecting the cost of capital, and the like. Yet there are two problems with this approach. First, in an insufficiently competitive market, wages and profits may overstate the output being produced: those involved may instead simply be engaged in rent-seeking behaviour. Second, whereas input costs are known today, the ultimate 'output' of the financial sector won't be known for many years, if ever. If the financial sector's role is to allocate resources efficiently over time – to meet the interests of savers and investors – we can only know tomorrow whether today's financial decisions will pay off. And, if they don't pay off, that need not be the fault of the financial system alone.

Another option – one that is now routinely used in the construction of national accounts – is to treat the income earned by banks through the gap between the 'risk-free' rate at which the more creditworthy of their ilk can raise funds and the rate at which they can then lend to customers as a reward for risk-taking. The bigger the gap, the greater is the supposed value of banking services. Yet, in the aftermath of the financial crisis, this looks distinctly odd: those banks that took more risk were apparently adding to national income yet, in hindsight, were also partly responsible for its subsequent collapse.

In reality, the financial system prices beliefs – and beliefs about beliefs – not ultimate truth. The dotcom bubble wasn't a story solely – or even mostly – about nasty financial middlemen: instead, it reflected a genuine, if false, belief that new technologies would both transform the economy and make the investors in those technologies very wealthy.

The litmus test of financial acumen – at least from society's perspective – is whether living standards ultimately rise. This, unfortunately, is inevitably a rather nebulous judgement. The Roaring Twenties gave way to the economic traumas of the Great Depression but they also provided us with mass-production techniques, the Model T Ford, the birth of General Motors, RCA Victor with its phonographs and (by 1930) vinyl, the introduction of airlines and a host of other things that came to define people's lives through the twentieth century. At the beginning of the twenty-first century, financial globalization has contributed to the strongest period of global economic growth since the 1960s, with the number of people dragged out of poverty larger than ever before. The price of financial failure, however, has fallen disproportionately on taxpayers in Western nations. Time (from the 1920s through to the second half of the twentieth century) and space (from the stagnation of the developed world through to the dynamism of the emerging world) make judgements over the success or otherwise of the financial system especially difficult. Seen this way, the problem of financial collapse is that those who benefited from the earlier period of financial expansion – the bankers themselves and the millions of people dragged out of poverty thanks to globalization – do not have to pick up the bill when things then go wrong: that cost falls directly on Western taxpayers.

Time after time, periods of rapid economic change are often associated with heightened financial risk. From the UK railway revolution of the 1840s through to the IT revolution of the 1990s, major economic transitions have been associated with extraordinary financial upheaval. Fortunes have been made and lost. Winners and losers have emerged on an entirely random basis. Yet we like to believe we control our own economic destinies and can pinpoint precisely who to blame when things go wrong. Those in the financial system who have earned vast fortunes inevitably find themselves in the firing line. Yet their riches are often no more than a reflection of society's desire to chase its financial dreams, whether or not those dreams accord with reality. When those dreams turn to nightmares, however, it's hardly surprising that mistrust spreads. Does that mistrust then destroy the innovative culture that, while contributing to financial bubbles and high levels of income inequality, ultimately allows living standards to rise for the many, not the few?

THE SECOND SCHISM: GROWING OLD DISGRACEFULLY

Income inequality may be the issue that grabs headlines, not least thanks to the efforts of the Occupy movement, whether on Wall

Street, outside the San Francisco Federal Reserve or in a campsite outside London's St Paul's Cathedral. There is, however, a second schism that, ultimately, may be more problematic because, within our democratic framework, it is so difficult to deal with. We are on the verge of an intergenerational war. Economic stagnation makes it near enough impossible to satisfy the expectations of both the baby boomers – who hope to enjoy a happy, healthy and financially stress-free retirement – and younger generations – who, increasingly, are expected to pick up the bill.

The debate on ageing is, by now, familiar territory. Old age dependency ratios – the ratio of the elderly relative to those of working age – are set to increase throughout the world, but nowhere more so than in the developed Western world. Based on dependency ratios alone, Germany, Japan and Italy appear to have bigger challenges ahead than the likes of France, Spain, the UK and the US. By 2030, roughly one-third of the adult population in Germany, Japan and Italy will be elderly, even if not in retirement, while only around one-quarter will be of similar maturity in the other four countries.

The challenges of population ageing have been hugely compounded by poor returns on financial assets – a story that began long before the onset of the financial crisis – and the much lower than expected levels of economic activity that have been generated since the crisis. Put these two factors together and suddenly it seems as though the Western world is heading towards a perfect intergenerational storm.

The UK's Financial Services Authority (FSA) requires fund managers to provide 'projections' of likely accumulated benefits for their customers over the medium to long term, based on anticipated returns on a mixture of financial assets, most obviously bonds, equities and real estate – in other words, the bread and butter of the typical UK pension fund or insurer. The FSA specifies lower, intermediate and higher nominal annual rates of return for a typical 'bundle' of financial assets. In 2012, these returns were 5, 7 and 9 per cent for products enjoying favourable tax treatment, most obviously pensions.

Pension funds tend to be invested in equities more so than other financial assets. That's fair enough. Over the very long term, equities have offered better returns than other asset classes and, as pension funds invest for the long term, that makes equities attractive. Through the twentieth century, annual real (inflation-adjusted) equity returns averaged well over 5 per cent, a handsome performance given all the upheavals over the last one hundred years. Adjusted for today's inflation rates – typically around 2 per cent per annum – that's the equivalent of a nominal return of over 7 per cent, roughly in line with the FSA projections.

Recently, however, returns have been far lower. Since early 2000, the year in which the technology boom reached its zenith, total returns on UK equities – including both dividends and capital appreciation – have averaged only around 2.5 per cent per annum in nominal terms, a pitiful result compared with the standard assumptions made by the regulators and by those operating in the pensions industry.

Adjusted for the impact of inflation – and taking into account the fees charged by funds to their customers – the 'real' return has, in many cases, been negative. That compares with a return of around 18 per cent per annum during the final 20 years of the twentieth century, a period during which pension funds were over flowing with good fortune. Unfortunately, funds didn't run surpluses during the good years, leaving many schemes hugely vulnerable in the bad years that followed. The Pension Protection Fund (PPF), which monitors the health or otherwise of UK pension schemes, announced in June 2012 that the pensions 'deficit' had risen to an extraordinary £312 billion, by far the biggest shortfall since records began.

Mind the Gap

The problem is certainly not confined to the UK. Individual American states, for example, are suffering from enormous pension shortfalls. According to a Pew Center report, also published in June 2012, the gap between the states' assets and their obligations for public sector retirement benefits in the 2010 fiscal year was an extraordinary $1.38 trillion, split between $757 billion for pension promises and $627 billion for retiree health care.[18] As with the UK, the position has deteriorated markedly in recent years: whereas, in 2000, over half of all US states were fully funded, only Wisconsin was able to make the same boast in 2010. By then, 34 states were less than 80 per cent funded. Not surprisingly, some of those performing badly found themselves in the ratings agencies' firing line: Illinois was downgraded by Standard & Poor's in August 2012, making it the worst-rated state in the US apart from California. For pessimists, Illinois is 'The Greece Next Door'.

Public sector workers on either side of the Atlantic may have rather modest pensions but their nest eggs are typically 'gold-plated'. Put another way, in the event of a financial crisis, or a period of economic stagnation, workers in the public sector may be better protected than those in the private sector. Admittedly, reform is coming through but, as the UK Audit Commission notes, it is a slow process:

> The legal basis of pension schemes influences the way they have responded to rising cost pressures. Private sector employers have more scope to adjust the benefits of pension schemes than employers in the public sector ... The types of action private employers would consider are: raising employer contributions; reducing accrual rates; reducing annual pensions increase; closing defined benefit schemes to new members; or closing defined

benefit schemes to existing members, while preserving pensions
accrual to date ... In the public sector, the benefit structures are
determined nationally ...[19]

Put another way, whereas companies can cut the pension benefits of
their current employees, if not their past employees, it's much more
difficult to do the same within the public sector. In addition to legal
restrictions, there's an obvious reason for this: it's politically deeply
unpopular. Far better, then, to let sleeping dogs lie even if, as with
Illinois's credit rating, the dogs eventually wake up and administer a
nasty bite. In the murky world of pension finance, the temptation is
too often to sweep problems under the carpet. It is the Nick Leeson
approach to dealing with bad financial news.

The implications, however, are distressing. Unless pension benefits are cut – through, for example, a significantly higher retirement
age, lower retiree income or bigger employee contributions – the
costs will fall on others, most obviously taxpayers and recipients of
public services. In other words, public pension shortfalls as a result
of poor asset returns require a tightening of fiscal policy that, other
things equal, will drain demand from the economy, lead to slower
growth and, hence, threaten a continuation of poor asset returns.
The most obvious losers are the young. Already coughing up more
for their education, in later life they will have to pay higher taxes to
fund the entitlements of those who have already staked their claim
on our scarce resources.

THE THIRD SCHISM: DECLINING TRUST BETWEEN CREDITORS AND DEBTORS

The US, the UK and many eurozone nations have one major problem
in common. Their fiscal paths are unsustainable. In each case,
debtors have had to turn to foreign creditors for sustenance. And, in

each case, those creditors have very little chance of getting their money back, at least in a form that would be economically and financially meaningful.

Unlike the southern European nations – which may eventually have to default if economic growth fails to recover – both the US and the UK have access to a printing press: their central banks can print money both to lower the yields on government paper and to devalue their exchange rates. A lower exchange rate is certainly not cost-free: as the UK discovered in 2009 and 2010, it raises the cost of imports and, hence, makes households worse off. It is also, however, a means of 'default by stealth'. If foreigners have lent to a nation in its currency – and not their own – they will lose out if that nation subsequently devalues: the assets foreigners have purchased will now be worth less in their home currency.

Imagine, for example, that the dollar falls dramatically against the Chinese renminbi thanks to persistent abuse by the Federal Reserve of the printing press. Measured in renminbi, the $1.2 trillion of Treasuries accumulated by the Chinese would now be worth a lot less than before. Meanwhile, a more competitive US dollar should, in theory, lead to stronger US export growth, higher inflation and, hence, a higher nominal value for US national income. Other things equal, the ratio of US government debt to GDP would then decline. China's loss would be America's gain. The interests of the domestic electorate would have trumped the interests of foreign creditors.

This misalignment of incentives results directly from economic weakness but also, importantly, threatens to make that weakness persist indefinitely. Again, it's a problem of trust. The electorates of heavily indebted democracies have every incentive to avoid austerity. They can pass the burden on to future generations or, instead, they can shift the pain of adjustment onto foreigners; they, after all, don't have a vote.

Until the onset of the financial crisis, there was little reason for foreigners to worry. Persistently rising living standards and recession 'bounceback-ability' ensured that both domestic voters and foreign creditors could be kept happy. Post-crisis, however, it seems increasingly likely that a *de facto* pecking order will be established. Domestic debtors – with votes – will surely trump the interests of foreign creditors. Put another way, we are about to witness the politicization of global capital flows.

This will take place under a number of different guises. Those creditors wary of getting their money back will be tempted to keep their savings at home. Money that might otherwise have gone into growth-enhancing foreign ventures may, instead, be kept under the proverbial mattress: safety will trump risk. Global imbalances will narrow, but only because foreign investors will no longer be prepared to fund the borrowing of others: the credit crunch will thus become a cross-border event. Those who want to borrow will increasingly have to go in search of funds generated domestically. In the event of a funding shortage, financial institutions will be increasingly compromised: unable to raise funds internationally on the scale seen pre-financial crisis, they will nevertheless be under pressure to lend domestically and, often, to projects that may seem to be politically expedient if not economically or financially worthwhile. The interests of shareholders, bondholders, pension and insurance policy holders and others will be increasingly compromised as a 'home bias' emerges thanks to cross-border mistrust.

Those still prepared to invest abroad will increasingly go in search of assets that cannot so easily be 'devalued' via the printing press. That means increased investment in commodities and companies that, if internationally exposed, will rise in dollar terms should the dollar fall in value. That, in turn, implies that debtor countries will increasingly have no choice other than to 'sell the family silver'. Even as quantitative easing operations encourage risk-averse domestic investors to hold more government bonds – their value ring-fenced by the actions of central banks – so foreign investors will increasingly attempt to own productive assets. The signs are already there: London and Manhattan property falling into the hands of Russians, Chinese and Saudis and, in the process, pricing domestic purchasers out of the market; European and American companies bought up by Chinese and Indian equivalents, often in search of access to superior technologies.

Meanwhile, as international trust ebbs, so nations will attempt to impose their will on others, attempting to rewrite the international rules of the game to suit their own interests. US regulators have increasingly extended their reach over dollar transactions, threatening to revoke US banking licences for institutions carrying out allegedly illicit dollar transactions between customers outside of America's borders. In time, the implied restrictions on cross-border dollar-based financial activity outside American jurisdiction may encourage the emergence of other reserve currencies to rival the dollar: China, likely to become the biggest economy in the world and with a foreign policy indifferent to the behaviour of other regimes, may find that, as it deregulates its own capital markets, the renminbi will grow to rival the dollar as a major international currency. As Western debtors and creditors continue their dispute over who, ultimately, should foot the bill for the financial crisis, the centre of gravity for the world economy and its financial markets will shift east and south, marking the end of Western dominance.

WHAT NEXT?

Without trust, it's difficult to see how economies can regain their former poise. Yet trust is in desperately short supply. Banks – deservedly in some cases – are no longer trusted. People within the financial system no longer trust each other. Politicians are increasingly treated by the public with suspicion, their venal ambition not consistent with the restoration of trust any time soon. Domestic debtors are no longer trusted by foreign creditors. Even central bankers – with their increasingly imaginative money-printing tactics – have been knocked off their pedestals. Markets no longer work well but those with the power to reform markets either are not trusted to do so or, in our increasingly globalized world, have lost the power to do so. This is no longer a debate about market versus state, of a temporary collapse in animal spirits or of a quick fix to restore a sense of economic certainty. It is, instead, a debate about how, collectively, we can find a way to live within our means having made promises to ourselves that can no longer be fulfilled. It is a debate about how best to reduce our collective entitlements in ways that will shore up trust and, thus, bring our economic stagnation to an end.

CHAPTER EIGHT

FROM ECONOMIC DISAPPOINTMENT TO POLITICAL INSTABILITY

The schisms seen in Western societies today are hardly new. Karl Marx (1818–1883) wrote about these kinds of strains 150 years ago. Indeed, those with Marxist sympathies would doubtless argue that what we've witnessed since the financial crisis is an inevitable process of worker immiseration fundamental to the capitalist model. As Marx noted in *Das Kapital*:

> Within the capitalist system all methods for raising the social productivity of labour are put into effect at the cost of the individual worker ... all means for the development of production undergo a dialectical inversion so that they become means of domination and exploitation of the producers; they distort the worker into a fragment of a man, they degrade him to the level of an appendage of a machine, they destroy the actual content of his labour by turning it into a torment, they alienate from him the intellectual potentialities of the labour process ... they transform his life-time into working-time, and drag his wife and child beneath the wheels of the juggernaut of capital.[1]

There is, however, an obvious problem with this argument, one that Marx failed to foresee as he scribbled away in the British Museum in the 1860s. Living standards have risen across the board in Western industrialized societies over the last 150 years. The situation of the worker, be his payment high or low, has, in reality, improved dramatically since Marx came up with his theory of surplus value. Perhaps rewards for capitalists (or bankers) have, on occasion, risen a lot faster than rewards for other workers, leading to substantial increases in income inequality, but workers themselves have hardly ended up worse off. Indeed, as more and more workers find themselves with occupational pension schemes, the distinction between the bourgeoisie and proletariat has inevitably become more and more blurred.

Even on an international basis, the argument no longer holds. While manufacturing facilities owned by multinationals operating in, say, China or Indonesia may not offer the working conditions available in the West, it is impossible to overlook the fact that the mobility of international capital since the 1980s has brought millions upon millions of people out of poverty. Rather than immiserating workers, the spread of capital throughout the world, associated with rapid urbanization, has provided the main escape route from rural poverty.

Persistent economic stagnation in the West has, however, made life distinctly uncomfortable again. Mervyn King, the then Governor of the Bank of England, stated at the beginning of 2011, 'real wages are likely to be no higher [this year] than they were in 2005. One has to go back to the 1920s to find a time when real wages fell over a period of six years.' Even in the absence of an 'inevitable' Marxist march towards socialism, the social strains associated with economic disappointment can become all-consuming. It might not be intentional immiseration – whereby capitalists are deliberately setting out to exploit workers – but there can be no doubt that, following the financial crisis, average living standards are, in many Western nations, making no progress whatsoever.

Admittedly, things might have been a lot worse. Had it not been for the massive stimulus provided by monetary and fiscal policy following the onset of the financial crisis, we might have ended up not with stagnation but, instead, with depression. Yet stagnation has its own costs. By attempting to live life as if nothing had really changed, by arguing that there are abundant macroeconomic 'quick fixes', by resisting the unpleasant medicine that we may all, eventually, have to take, we may be sacrificing our long-term economic health. Without economic pain, the urgency of reform is reduced but, without reform, the risk of continuing stagnation only rises.

Under these circumstances, macroeconomic policies designed merely to deliver stable growth and low inflation may lead, instead, to instability. Worse, the instability may not be of the economic variety alone. With the opening up of damaging schisms, the risk is also of heightened political instability. To understand why, it's worth travelling back through time and across geographies. Persistent economic disappointment triggers toxic political undercurrents.

Nineteenth-century monetary regimes proved to be a source not of financial calm but, instead, of continuous economic and political upheaval. The monetary rules at the time may have been simple and part of the conventional wisdom of the day but they proved unsuited to a world that was undergoing rapid change. A hundred years later – and ten years before the onset of the subprime crisis – Asian policy-makers were similarly victims of conventional economic and monetary thought. They also faced economic and political upheaval, although, luckily for them, they were eventually able to post recoveries far and away more impressive than anything seen more recently either in the US or Western Europe. In both periods, however, people wanted someone to blame. Scapegoating became an essential, if undesirable, part of rapidly evolving political narratives.

THE MONETARY UPHEAVALS OF THE 1870S

The 1870s kicked off with a bang – literally. European fault lines that had lain dormant since the Congress of Vienna in 1815 reopened. It was the usual nineteenth-century nonsense. The French objected to the possibility that a Prussian from the ruling Hohenzollern clan – even a Catholic Prussian – might end up on the vacant Spanish throne, thereby leaving France geographically isolated. A meeting in Ems between King Wilhelm I of Prussia and the French Ambassador, Count Benedetti, was reported to the press by Otto von Bismarck – in deliberately exaggerated fashion – as a discourteous demand from the French for the Prussian King to guarantee that a Hohenzollern would never grace the Spanish throne, a guarantee that Wilhelm inevitably refused to provide. The French media went potty (as Bismarck had intended), the people of Paris demanded retribution for this apparent snub and, on 1 August 1870, Napoleon III's son fired the first shot in what became known as the Franco–Prussian War.

The French doubtless hoped they could use Bismarck's Ems Dispatch as a pretext for extending their border with Germany to the Rhine. Within days, however, France was staring in the face of a humiliating defeat. A small rump of the original French fighting force continued to resist for a number of months but, eventually, the Third Republic government had no choice other than to sue for peace. It was hardly the ending Napoleon III had anticipated. He fled to London, Wilhelm I became German Emperor (in the Hall of Mirrors in Versailles, of all places), most of the German nations were united (thanks to Bismarck), Alsace-Lorraine ended up in German hands, the revolutionaries of the Paris Commune had a fleeting taste of power and the French agreed to pay huge reparations – around $1 billion – to the Germans. Germany, thinking ahead to the creation of a new monetary system, wanted its reparations in gold, taking its lead from British developments earlier in the nineteenth century.

During the Napoleonic Wars, the value of paper British money had declined rapidly: it was the early nineteenth-century equivalent of abandoning a commitment to price stability and allowing inflation to surge. After the Congress of Vienna, however, Britain moved to a gold standard. By that stage, with war no longer an excuse, holders of government bonds were unwilling to accept the inflationary losses attached to their savings and the City of London was not prepared to tolerate the instability associated with high and variable inflation rates. A precious metal standard was the obvious solution. Precious metal was – supposedly – in limited supply so any currency fixed in value against a precious metal was, itself, unlikely to lose value through a dose of inflation.[2]

But why gold? David Ricardo, the leading economist of the day, thought Britain would be better off under a silver standard. But, in 1819, in testimony to a Parliamentary Committee, he changed his mind, a reflection of his (incorrect) understanding of the impact of the Industrial Revolution: 'I have understood that machinery is particularly apposite to the silver mines and may therefore very much conduce to an increased quantity of that metal and an alteration of its value, whilst the same cause is not likely to operate upon the value of gold.'[3]

Ricardo was hopelessly wrong in his analysis of gold and silver extraction. Between 1851 and 1870, gold production almost matched the total produced over the previous 350 years. Simultaneously there was little increase in the production of silver. As a result – and thanks to a continuous leakage of silver to India and China, both of which were on a silver standard – the price of gold came down relative to silver.

While this may have undermined Ricardo's argument, the increased supply of gold made a move towards a universal gold standard more plausible. Until the 1860s, there was simply too little of it around and, as a consequence, it could not support the rapid increase in monetary transactions associated with the opening up of world trade. That all changed in the years running up to the Franco–Prussian War. An increased supply made gold more useful as an international means of exchange: while it may have fallen in value relative to silver, it was still worth a lot more per ounce. As such, a little went a long way.

Germany recognized this, one reason why the reparations it demanded from France were to be paid in gold, not silver. In 1871, after the war had ended, Germany passed a law to allow the minting of new gold coins while at the same time halting the production of large silver coins. In 1873, a further law was passed that not only established a formal Gold Standard but also ensured the demise of existing silver coins: these were then steadily withdrawn from circulation. The result was inevitable. Germany's need to hold silver for monetary purposes collapsed, a huge amount of silver was dumped into the international market and, by the end of 1873, its price had tumbled. This, in turn, created enormous problems for those countries still on a bimetallic standard: France and the other members of the Latin monetary union – Belgium, Italy and Switzerland – were obliged to buy silver at a rate far higher than that on offer on the market. Not surprisingly, they ended up swamped with silver even as they watched their gold heading rapidly for the exit. Eventually they, too, were forced to abandon the bimetallic standard.

Meanwhile, on the other side of the Atlantic, Congress passed the Coinage Act of 1873. The Act contained no reference whatsoever to the standard silver dollar, which had been part of a bimetallic monetary system (based on both gold and silver) ever since the days of

Alexander Hamilton at the end of the eighteenth century. For some, this omission was regarded as a 'crime'.[4] Others regarded the Act as a 'piece of good fortune, which saved our financial credit and protected the honor of the State'.[5] Either way, US bimetallism came to an abrupt end. By the end of the 1870s, only India and China still depended on silver. Everyone else had embraced gold.

Germany's decision to adopt a gold standard had already led to a dramatic reduction in the demand for silver. America's Coinage Act only added to the subsequent instability. The US Treasury had been stockpiling gold in anticipation of the 1873 Act and continued to do so throughout the rest of that decade. By 1879, the stock of gold held in the US – both officially and privately – had risen to 7 per cent of the world's total. Ten years later, the share was approaching 20 per cent. And, as gold production was no longer growing at anything like the pace seen in earlier decades, the increase in American gold holdings was offset by a *decrease* elsewhere.

Put another way, the combination of a wholesale shift towards a gold standard – the establishment, if you like, of a new international monetary convention – alongside continued industrialization and an absence of any significant increase in the supply of gold, led increasingly to a world gold shortage. There was only one thing for it. If the volume of output was rising but the stock of money – determined by the supply of gold – was unable to keep pace, prices of more or less everything – commodities, manufactured goods, labour – would have to fall. They duly did. Between the mid-1870s and the mid-1890s, the rate of deflation was around 1.7 per cent per year in the US and around 0.8 per cent per year in the UK.

Did this matter? At first sight, perhaps not. Although periods of deflation are often associated with economic stagnation (Japan) or worse (the Great Depression), living standards in the developed world mostly rose in the last three decades of the nineteenth century. Yet there were problems a-plenty.

185

The US enjoyed a railroad boom in the years running up to the Coinage Act, helped along by subsidies and land grants that ultimately paved the way for over-investment, excessively low returns and spectacularly high debts. Meanwhile, thanks to the reparations paid by France after the Franco–Prussian War, Germany experienced a near-term investment boom with qualities not dissimilar to those associated with the US railroad boom: the usual suspects included low returns and high debts.

Then things went rather horribly wrong. What became known as 'The Panic of 1873', triggered initially by a collapse in the Viennese stock market in May of that year, led to financial turmoil on both sides of the Atlantic. Jay Cooke and Company, an American bank with heavy exposure to the railroads, declared bankruptcy in September, triggering a series of further bank failures that, in turn, led to wave after wave of company failures. The German economy, which had been enjoying a mini-boom, hit a brick wall. Having seen living standards rise at a 1.5 per cent annual rate in the years leading up to the Panic, the newly unified nation saw living standards effectively stagnate all the way through to 1880. Meanwhile, the US economy, which had lived off the railroad boom, was suddenly looking extraordinarily vulnerable. The National Bureau of Economic Research estimates that the 'contractionary phase' of the business cycle, which began in October 1873, lasted until March 1879. At 65 months, this was longer than the contractionary phase of the Great Depression, a mere 43 months. Even the subsequent, powerful, recovery proved short-lived: a further 38-month contraction began in March 1882.[6]

The Panic, the ensuing economic stagnation and the persistence of deflation were all reflections of the now near-universal attachment of monetary systems to the Gold Standard, the nineteenth-century equivalent of inflation targeting. At first, investors in silver mines – many of which were in North America – were particularly vulnerable, reflecting the sudden loss in 'official' demand for silver. Falling prices, however, also left debtors vulnerable. Among them were many of America's farmers, who were particularly hard hit by declines in commodity prices. The Australian and New Zealand economies, major agricultural producers, suffered for the same reasons. And industrial unrest increased: in 1877, the US succumbed to the Great Railroad Strike.

Worse, at least from the perspective of long-term recovery, the events of the 1870s led to a heated debate – at least in the US – about the wisdom of remaining on the Gold Standard, an arrangement that William Jennings Bryan, the Democrat presidential candidate in 1896 – with huge support from the recently created People's Party, also known as the Populists – described in the following, less than complimentary, terms: 'You shall not press down upon the brow of labor this crown of thorns. You should not crucify mankind upon a cross of gold.'

Strong rhetoric indeed. Bryan was interested in supporting the debtor – the little man, the farmer – against the powerful Wall Street lobbies. He wasn't alone. Back in 1876, three years after the Coinage Act, the 'Greenback Party' was formed with the particular aim of encouraging the issuance of dollar notes to act against persistent deflation and, ideally, to encourage a bout of inflation: after all, rising prices would make it easier for debtors to repay their creditors (and, by the same token, reduce the amount in real, inflation-adjusted, terms that creditors would be repaid).

Put another way, the adoption of the Gold Standard created a series of schisms within US society. The economy as a whole didn't collapse, even though there were lengthy periods of mild contraction or, at best, stagnation. But, within the economy, there were clear winners and losers. As a result, the debate over whether the Gold Standard should be maintained – a weirdly technical debate in most circumstances – became a key part of US political discourse. A monetary reform that benefited some but hurt others was clearly not going to go unchallenged. Continuous sniping, however, only made matters worse.

People inevitably were unsure about the future of the new monetary regime. Had the Coinage Act gone unchallenged, the Gold Standard might have worked perfectly well in the US, as it had done in the UK. This wasn't the case. An uneasy alliance between silver miners and small farmers – particularly in the south – continuously sowed the seeds of doubt over the future of the Gold Standard. Yet as the alternative was a more inflationary silver or bimetallic standard, people naturally looked for protection against that risk. Gold, already in short supply, offered that protection. Thus, people hoarded this increasingly precious metal, contributing to even greater deflation than might otherwise have been the case and, hence, an even bigger schism between creditors and debtors. As Milton Friedman and Anna Schwartz explained in their monumental *A Monetary History of the United States, 1867–1960*:

> This entire silver episode is a fascinating example of how important what people think about money can sometimes be. The fear that silver would produce an inflation sufficient to force the United States off the gold standard made it necessary to have a severe deflation in order to stay on the gold standard.

The growing gap between creditors and debtors led to all sorts of unpleasant social strains. Those in the US left worse off as a result of the 'cross of gold' inevitably looked to blame others for their plight. Big finance was an obvious target (with, at times, more than a hint of anti-Semitism) but so, too, were immigrants, specifically those from China. The Chinese Exclusion Act, a blatantly racist piece of legislation, was signed into law in 1882. It was supposed to remain in place only for the following ten years but, in practice, was only lifted in 1943. Chinese labourers had been instrumental in supporting both the Californian Gold Rush and the later railroad boom but, with the onset of economic upheaval in the 1870s, they ended up being blamed for the low level of wages across the economy more broadly. The Act banned future Chinese immigration on pain of incarceration and eventual deportation. Meanwhile, those Chinese living in the US who chose to leave lost their right to re-entry.

In Germany, meanwhile, a new strain of intolerance towards Jews began to emerge. Those in the first half of the nineteenth century hoping for the unification of the German-speaking people faced an obvious problem, namely what to do about the various minorities living in their midst. The Burschenschaft movement pushed for the complete assimilation of minorities, under the condition that those minorities fully embraced a 'Christian-German spirit': Jews who remained Jews were not to be trusted. Later on, as theories of racial distinctiveness developed, so the idea of assimilation was slowly rejected. Even as the newly unified Germany offered Jews emancipation, a growing number of nationalists and racists were arguing exactly the opposite. With the onset of the 1873 Panic, *Gartenlaube*, a hitherto decent and upstanding journal, published a series of articles that pointed the finger of blame at Jews. At roughly the same time, Wilhelm Marr published the first edition of his virulently anti-Jewish *The Victory of Judaism over Germanism*, a pamphlet that was to be reprinted 12 times in the following six years. Within it, Marr first coined the term *anti-Semitism*. As Germany's economic and financial upheavals continued, this line of thinking became increasingly mainstream. By 1893, 16 representatives of overtly anti-Semitic political parties were sitting in the Reichstag.[7]

What eventually became known as the 'Long Depression' stemmed from an earlier period of excessive optimism. Understandably, expectations were high in Germany following its unification and its victory over France. They were equally high in the US, thanks to the railroad boom of the late 1860s. Yet, thanks partly to the monetary upheavals and associated uncertainties of the 1870s, optimism was dashed. While economic collapse was avoided, the combination of stagnation and deflation created clear winners and losers that, in turn, led to the rise of populist politicians happy to blame not only the 'cross of gold' but, increasingly, the minorities in their midst.

Looking at the world from 2000 onwards, the parallels are, sadly, obvious. The implicit mortgage subsidies on offer from Fannie Mae, Freddie Mac and other government-sponsored enterprises in the years running up to our modern-day subprime crisis were surely the equivalent of the government subsidies and land grants provided to railroad speculators in the 1860s. The inevitable over-investment in housing at the beginning of the twenty-first century was foreshadowed by railroad mania in the mid-nineteenth century, while the bank failures that followed the onset of the subprime crisis are no more than a twenty-first century version of the banking collapse triggered by the bankruptcy of Jay Cooke and Co. Subsidizing interest rates is, it seems, a recipe for financial upheaval.

The twenty-first century equivalents of a near-universal gold standard are the global dollar standard – with massive increases in foreign exchange reserves, most abundantly within the emerging world, greenbacks are no longer the preserve of the US – and, within Europe, the euro. The eurozone crisis, which kicked off in Greece towards the end of 2009 but which soon engulfed almost all eurozone member states, has its antecedents in the events of the 1870s. Yet the Gold Standard itself was born out of an earlier rejection of bimetallism: the dollar and euro might, eventually, be rejected in much the same way, signalling both a period of monetary anarchy associated with quantitative easing and 'currency wars' and, in time, challenges from the renminbi and other 'emerging' currencies.

In the late nineteenth century, the schism between debtors and creditors was mostly a problem within nations, notably within the US. Today, the same schism exists but, at least within the eurozone, it is a more of a problem between nations. Germany, a major creditor nation that wants its money back, insists on a euro that is 'as good as gold', adopting a position equivalent to that of north-eastern states in the US – and the bankers of Wall Street – in the late nineteenth century. Greece, Portugal, Spain and Italy prefer a euro that, in nineteenth-century terms, would have been part of an earlier, bimetallic, era, the equivalent of the wishes of the southern states supported by the Greenback Party, the Populists and William Jennings Bryan.

This difference in preferences, however, immediately recreates the deflationary bias highlighted by Friedman and Schwartz and threatens the euro's survival, in much the same way that the popular debate in the late nineteenth century threatened America's attachment to gold. The natural thing to do in the late nineteenth century – as a result of (in the event, unjustified) fears of inflation – was to hoard gold. The early twenty-first century equivalent is to hold euro deposits in the banking systems of those countries deemed least likely to be tempted – in the event of a euro break-up – by inflation, devaluation and excessive money printing. The result is capital flight from the southern nations to Germany and other nations that, it seems, are transfixed by a cross of euro gold. With money pouring into northern Europe, borrowing costs for Germany and other like-minded nations inevitably fall. With a monetary exodus from southern Europe, borrowing costs for the so-called 'periphery' inevitably rise. To paraphrase Friedman and Schwartz, this entire euro episode is a fascinating example of how important what people think about money can sometimes be.

Meanwhile, our modern-day version of stagnation offers the same opportunities for politicians to blame foreigners, immigrants and minorities for ongoing economic difficulties. Greece's economic and financial difficulties have led to the rise of political extremism. The success of Marine Le Pen, the French far-right politician, in the 2012 French presidential elections, points to growing unease over immigration. The Arizona Support Our Law Enforcement and Safe Neighbourhoods Act (known simply as SB 1070) requires state law enforcement offices to check on an individual's immigration status if there is 'reasonable suspicion' – whatever that means – that the individual concerned might be in the US illegally, while offering the opportunity to punish those involved in housing, employing or transporting such aliens. The opportunity for racial profiling and stereotyping, primarily aimed at immigrants from Latin America, would, for the unscrupulous law enforcement officer, be surely too good to miss.[8] It is an Act not far removed from the anti-China legislation of the late nineteenth century.

THE ASIAN CRISIS

The story of the late 1990s Asian crisis can be simply summarized: having been forced to recognize they had lived beyond their means, the nations involved took the pain up front but were then able to recover strongly. The near-term losses in Asia were, in many cases, far bigger than those seen in the West following its later financial crisis but, having been written off as hotbeds of crony capitalism and, thus, doomed to fail, Asian economies were able to bounce back in style. There was no Western-style economic stagnation but, instead, a return to economic dynamism within just a handful of years. Yet the political response varied from nation to nation.

In the early 1990s, Asian nations had increasingly adopted the so-called 'Washington Consensus', broadly speaking a commitment to low inflation, conservative fiscal policies and open cross-border capital markets. For a while, the policies seemed to work: Thailand,

Korea, Malaysia and Indonesia all enjoyed rapid income gains thanks partly to heavy inflows of foreign financial investment. Indeed, the rest of the world was perfectly happy to buy into the Asian miracle (as, indeed, it later bought into the US housing miracle and the Greek government bond miracle). Admittedly, some had offered warning that the miracle was perhaps not all it seemed[9] but few took notice. This was hardly surprising. Rates of economic growth were extraordinarily high, inflation not disastrously excessive (at least by the standards of the day) and countries mostly were running fiscal surpluses.

There was, however, a problem. Each of these countries depended on the continued willingness of foreign creditors to fund ongoing expansion. After years of rapid gains in domestic demand, Asian balance of payments deficits had soared. Thailand's was approaching 8 per cent of national income. In other words, year by year, Thailand was becoming ever more indebted to its foreign creditors. And it was Thailand that proved to be the weak link.

In 1997, life was beginning to change elsewhere in the world. US interest rates were heading higher. The US stock market was on the up, thanks in part to the emergence of exciting new technology companies. Dollar-based investors began to think twice before investing their savings in risky foreign ventures. Hopes of Japanese recovery faded; playing safe, Japanese banks stopped leading abroad. Countries that were borrowing heavily in international capital markets were suddenly vulnerable. As money headed elsewhere, Thailand found itself in an incredibly difficult position. Its currency collapsed and, in short order, so did its economy. In 1998 alone, the Thai economy shank more than 10 per cent, a remarkable fall from grace. Others followed suit: Indonesia down over 13 per cent, Malaysia down more than 7 per cent and Korea down almost 6 per cent. As this financial and economic tsunami took hold, it seemed as though the Asian miracle was now over.

Then came the fallout and finger-pointing. Western policy-makers, unable to believe there was anything wrong with the Washington Consensus, laid the blame fairly and squarely on the frailties of the Asian economic model. US Federal Reserve Governor Roger Ferguson offered the following – in hindsight, remarkable – musings on the subject at hand in a speech given in March 1998:

> One of the most important elements . . . has been the weakness of the banking sector in most of these countries. The managers of banks had not developed appropriate procedures for evaluating and extending loans. This was due, in part, to the fact that they were subject to direction by the authorities and, in part, therefore, because they expected the government to support their borrowers. But importantly this lack of procedures was because they had not developed the tools of credit risk analysis, and the system of bank supervision was not equipped to impose proper risk management practices. Thus, when economic conditions worsened abruptly, the quality of the banks' assets deteriorated. Some borrowers could not service their loans. As the banks' financial condition eroded, their creditors in turn looked at them more carefully and their access to funding began to dry up.
>
> The problems caused by poor lending practices and inadequate supervision have been compounded by two other features . . . First, standards for the transparency and disclosure of private financial information were extremely lax. Once problems arose, it was difficult for creditors to distinguish good risks from bad, and this caused them to withdraw credit from all borrowers indiscriminately. Second, creditors to banks no doubt relied to some extent on a public safety net to back up their claims. This was true not only of small depositors, but also of foreign bank creditors. As it turned out, the presumption of official support was at least to some extent misplaced, because the government did not clearly have the resources to provide that support.[10]

Many Western observers preferred to be just a little more direct. Asian countries were suffering from crony capitalism, an unhealthy relationship between government and commerce associated with endemic bribery and corruption, and they'd fooled innocent foreign creditors into lending to them.

The fact that South Korea, in particular, had delivered an extraordinary increase in living standards in previous decades was conveniently ignored. Between 1950 and the onset of the Asian crisis, Korean living standards had risen 15-fold, suggesting that crony capitalism – if that's what it was – had hardly been an impediment to rising prosperity. In any case, the problems outlined by Ferguson were, as we now know, not uniquely Asian: the Western world discovered to its cost ten years later that American – or, indeed, Western – exceptionalism was not quite so exceptional after all. In hindsight, Ferguson's comments – specifically directed at Asia's failings – look rather ridiculous.

The West's newly disparaging view of Asia was all very well but subsequent events suggest this was based on little more than a lazy imperial assumption of economic and financial superiority. In hindsight, the big surprise about the Asian crisis was not so much the economic collapse but, rather, the impressive economic recovery that subsequently followed, a recovery that for the West, following its own financial crisis, has remained out of reach.

True, some nations took longer than others to turn the corner. Whereas Korea was back to its pre-crisis level of economic activity only seven quarters following the onset of the crisis, Thailand took 19 quarters and Indonesia a staggering 22 quarters. Ten years after the implosion, however, all initial casualties were significantly better off: Indonesia, the weakest performer, was almost 30 per cent better off than it had been before the crisis, while Korea, one of the strongest performers, was 55 per cent better off. There was no Argentine failure, no Japanese lost decade and no Western-style stagnation.

Remarkably, all of this happened without any significant help from Western-style macroeconomic policies. Asia's difficulty reflected a mass panic on behalf of Asia's foreign creditors in the light of evidence – however limited – that the game was up. Someone shouted fire, the creditors ran to the exits and, in the mêlée that followed, it seemed as though Asian economies might be razed to the ground. For Asian economies, the money had genuinely run out.

A Keynesian-style fiscal stimulus wouldn't work because no one would lend to nations that, almost overnight, had become international pariahs. A Friedman-style monetary stimulus wouldn't work because exchange rates were already in free fall, leading to significantly higher import prices and, hence, higher inflation: printing money to add fuel to the fire would have been of no help whatsoever. Instead, Asians had no choice other than to knuckle down, work hard and accept their newly diminished status. They had to adjust more or less immediately to their newly straitened circumstances. They had to dispense instantly with the idea of economic entitlement – of ever rising prosperity – and accept that the world had changed.

The reaction politically, however, varied from country to country.

HOW POLITICAL RESPONSE TRUMPED ECONOMIC THEORY: THREE ASIAN STORIES

Indonesia: Goodbye Suharto

In Indonesia, the financial crisis led to political upheaval. Suharto, who had been Indonesia's increasingly totalitarian President for 31 years, was forced out of office. A former army general, he made sure that dissent was stymied where and when possible, seeking to deliver economic success alongside authoritarian rule. Opposition was squashed, patronage was handed out where necessary, and the whiff of corruption began to permeate all aspects of Indonesian society.

None of this mattered too much so long as the economy was performing well. Suharto's initial success in the late 1960s was to stamp out the hyperinflation that had proved so incredibly debilitating under his predecessor, Sukarno. Suharto's so-called 'New Order' delivered significant increases in living standards, with incomes per capita quadrupling between the mid-1960s and the mid-1990s. Nevertheless, Indonesia was still a poor country and, even before the Asian crisis, was losing ground to others. China, in particular, was catching up rapidly.

Meanwhile, on the home front, the mid-1990s saw an increase in political opposition, led by Megawati Sukarnoputri, the head of the Indonesian Democratic Party and, by happy coincidence, the daughter of Sukarno, Indonesia's former leader. Her success led in 1996 to a renewed crackdown by Suharto's henchmen, including Megawati's removal from the IDP. This alone was enough to lead to protests.

The protests became more violent, however, as Indonesia found itself caught up in the Asian crisis. The ensuing collapse in the Indonesian economy simply ratcheted up the tension, with mob violence leading to brutal attacks on Chinese communities, some of which were seen as soft targets. Ultimately, though, the Indonesian people knew whom to blame. Suharto may have been re-elected in March 1998 but everyone knew the outcome was rigged. Two months later he was gone, a victim of popular student-led uprisings, economic meltdown and, ultimately, a nation's refusal to accept ongoing political corruption. Suharto didn't cause the Asian financial crisis but he was one of its most visible casualties.

Malaysia: Mahathir Deflects Blame

Mahathir Mohamad, Malaysia's leader, adopted a rather different approach. He, too, had been in power for many years, first becoming Prime Minister in 1982. Yet he survived the Asian crisis. As with Indonesia, Malaysia had seen a fourfold increase in per capita incomes between the mid-1960s and the mid-1990s. Malaysia was, however, significantly richer, with living standards double those in Indonesia. Indeed, at over $7,000 per capita, annual incomes were high enough to suggest that Malaysia, as a nation, had escaped from poverty.

Like other Asian nations, Malaysia had become hugely dependent on foreign capital: its balance of payments current account deficit reached an extraordinary 9.6 per cent of national income in 1995. Admittedly, the deficit then began to fall but, at the onset of the crisis, Malaysia was still borrowing the equivalent of almost 6 per cent of national income. A year later, the situation completely reversed. Malaysia was in 1998 saving around 13 per cent of national income and using its newly discovered parsimony either to repay debt or invest elsewhere in the world. From being one of the world's biggest international borrowers – at least relative to the size of its economy – Malaysia became one of the world's biggest savers.

How did Malaysia manage to pull off this trick? Like other Asian currencies, the Malaysian ringgit collapsed, making imports a lot more expensive for Malaysian consumers but exports a lot cheaper for foreigners. As a result, the economy slowly rebalanced away from growth led by domestic demand towards export-led growth (a polite way of saying that Malaysian workers saw the fruits of their labours heading abroad rather than staying at home). And although the economy collapsed in 1998, it thereafter delivered year after year of rapid economic expansion, having adjusted to the new global economic reality.

Mahathir was also, however, quick to turn economic convention on its head. The Washington Consensus demanded that countries should open their capital markets to international investors. Mahathir argued that this policy had contributed to the crisis. On 1 September 1998, Bank Negara – the Malaysian central bank – released a statement announcing the imposition of capital controls, giving those holding ringgit offshore a month to bring their money back home. Later that day, Mahathir gave an interview to the media where he explained that:

> where the ringgit's value is in an unstable situation, business could not be continued in a way that would be profitable . . . when the ringgit's value is brought down, our income will be reduced . . . we have to fix the ringgit permanently . . . the currency traders . . . make huge profits, while at the same time impoverishing a whole country, regions and peoples.

At the time, the imposition of capital controls led to howls of protest. After all, Mahathir's decision was a direct challenge to the Washington Consensus. And it wasn't long before the Consensus had its say. Some suggested that capital controls were merely a device to provide financial benefits to those Malaysian companies with strong ties to Mahathir.[11] Others noted that both South Korea and Thailand managed to recover in 1998 without using capital controls, thereby suggesting that Mahathir's decision was, at best, irrelevant. Still others simply regarded capital controls as the devil's work.

In reality, the situation was more nuanced. While South Korea and Thailand were showing signs of financial recovery in the summer of 1998, the same couldn't be said about Malaysia.[12] Those who were theologically opposed to capital controls too often forgot that open international capital markets had both advantages and disadvantages: in effect, there was a trade-off between efficient resource allocation – reducing the risk of cronyism by keeping capital markets 'pure' – and heightened vulnerability to financial crises – a reflection of increased dependency on 'hot money' inflows.[13]

Mahathir, however, was less concerned with an academic debate about the pros and cons of capital controls and much more focused on clinging on to power. Suharto's fall earlier in 1998 followed shortly after Indonesia's adoption of a typically brutal IMF programme. For Mahathir, Suharto's demise presented an opportunity to blame Asia's woes on evil forces, both internal and external. The day after Malaysia adopted capital controls, Mahathir sacked Anwar Ibrahim, the Deputy Prime Minister, Minister of Finance and former Mahathir ally.[14] Mahathir saved most of his ire, however, for foreigners, blaming the IMF, suggesting that speculators wanted 'to see blood', warning of the dangers associated with George Soros, the hedge fund manager, and, more generally, suggesting that mysterious foreign forces were conspiring to humiliate Malaysia and other parts of the Islamic world. He stuck to this theme through the remainder of his time in charge:

> There is a feeling of hopelessness among the Muslim countries and their people. They feel that they can do nothing right. They believe that things can only get worse. The Muslims will forever be oppressed and dominated by the Europeans and the Jews . . . But is it true that we should do and can do nothing for ourselves? Is it true that 1.3 billion people can exert no power to save themselves from the humiliation and oppression inflicted upon them by a much smaller enemy?
>
> It cannot be that there is no other way. 1.3 billion Muslims cannot be defeated by a few million Jews . . . We are actually very strong. 1.3 billion people cannot be simply wiped out. The Europeans killed 6 million Jews out of 12 million. But today the Jews rule this world by proxy. They get others to fight and die for them . . .

... We are up against a people who think. They survived 2,000 years of pogroms not by hitting back, but by thinking. They invented and successfully promoted Socialism, Communism, human rights and democracy so that persecuting them would appear to be wrong, so they may enjoy equal rights with others. With these they have now gained control of the most powerful countries and they, this tiny community, have become a world power. We cannot fight them through brawn alone. We must use our brains also.[15]

On a charitable interpretation, it might just be possible to argue that Mahathir was demonstrating secret admiration for the Jewish people, suggesting that, to fight them, Muslims would also have to use their brains. That, however, seems a bit of a stretch. At the very least, he was surely invoking age-old anti-Jewish prejudice to explain why Malaysia, alongside other Islamic nations, had been so vulnerable economically. And his 2003 comments were hardly the first time he had claimed some kind of Jewish conspiracy against his country.

Dismissing claims of crony capitalism, Mahathir survived – and thrived – by blaming others, however unreasonably, for Malaysia's predicament. Unlike Suharto – whose decision to accept an IMF programme may have contributed to his downfall – Mahathir was able to argue that he was defending Malaysia against evil foreign forces. His use of capital controls – which led to a typically fraught debate among academic economists – was not so much an attempt to fix Malaysia's financial problems but, instead, a deliberate decision to portray Malaysia as an innocent victim of an international conspiracy. It may not have been either fair or reasonable, but it worked. He managed to avoid domestic upheaval – preventing the majority Malays and minority Chinese from fighting each other – by aiming the nation's ire at the rest of the world.

Korea: Democracy and Self-Sacrifice

Unlike either Indonesia or Malaysia, Korea was already a reasonably wealthy country at the onset of the Asian crisis. It had a properly developed – if relatively new – democracy.[16] Its incomes per capita averaged around $13,000 a year, higher than in either Portugal or Greece. Yet, for all its success, it was nevertheless unable to avoid the perils of the crisis. Korea, too, had become dependent on capital inflows from abroad: its current account deficit exceeded 4 per cent of GDP in 1996. And, like the other two nations, there was a whiff of corruption in the air: the connections between government and the *chaebol* (translated literally as 'wealth clan' or 'wealth faction'), Korea's large industrial conglomerates, were seen by many as yet another example of Asian crony capitalism.

As with Indonesia and Malaysia, the crisis proved far worse than anyone expected. At the end of 1997, for example, the IMF thought the Korean economy would expand by around 1–2 per cent in 1998, a hopelessly optimistic view: the outcome was a decline of 5.7 per cent.[17] The Korean government was quick to accept an IMF programme and willing to deliver reform. Like the others, it swiftly ended its dependence on inflows of foreign capital and, in 1998, delivered an enormous balance of payments current account surplus, thanks to a collapse in domestic demand that dramatically reduced Korean spending on imports. A year later, however, the Korean economy was expanding rapidly: by the end of 1999, the level of Korean economic activity was already significantly higher than it had been before the crisis. Indeed, it was as if the crisis had never happened.

During the crisis, something remarkable occurred: Koreans showed their willingness to accept potentially painful reform through a spirit of self-sacrifice. Perhaps they recognized they had been living on borrowed time. Maybe they were willing to accept the advice from their democratically elected leaders, a welcome novelty after so many decades of autocratic decree. Possibly they were afraid of losing their seat at the rich man's table having only just joined the OECD. Whatever the explanation, the sacrifice was heartfelt and hugely symbolic. Koreans gave up their wedding rings, their medals, their trophies in an effort to bail their economy out by the sale of gold to foreigners.

It may not have made a great deal of economic difference but the symbolism was nothing short of extraordinary. And it wasn't just individuals. Some of Korea's biggest companies, including Hyundai and Samsung, helped to coordinate the effort, while the notoriously belligerent unions restrained industrial unrest. Rather than blaming each other or, indeed, mysterious foreign forces, Koreans recognized their collective vulnerability. They put differences to one side and opted for national unity. For Koreans, the process came naturally. As the hardest working nation in the OECD, with one of the most extraordinary economic success stories in the second half of the twentieth century, and with an unfriendly northern neighbour, Koreans accepted the need for personal sacrifice in exchange for the common good. In the UK, it would have been called the Dunkirk spirit.

Underneath all this was, perhaps, a fundamental distinction between Korea and other industrialized economies. Despite Korea's heady economic progress in the decades leading up to the financial crisis, Seoul had kept public spending firmly under control. At a mere 15 per cent of national income in 1997, public spending in Korea was between one-quarter and one-half of the amount spent by other OECD nations as a share of their own economies. Spending on social benefits was particularly low: the Korean government spent a total of less than 4 per cent of GDP on pensions, incapacity benefit, health, family support, unemployment and housing. By contrast, in 1995 the US spent 16 per cent of national income on similar benefits, with the UK at 20 per cent, Spain at 21 per cent, Italy at 24 per cent, Germany at 28 per cent, France at 29 per cent and Sweden at a whopping 32 per cent.[18]

Koreans thus had no choice other than to take personal responsibility for their nation's economic collapse. The idea of personal sacrifice came easily to them: there was no obvious sense of entitlement and, hence, the reduction in living standards that was an inevitable consequence of the crisis was accepted with little argument.

ADJUSTING TO A NEW REALITY

My three Asian vignettes only scratch the surface of the extraordinary adjustment that took place in the region during the crisis. A hotel in Singapore that now charges around US$400 per night was, shortly after the crisis, offering rooms at a nightly rate of a mere $25: the willingness to let otherwise empty rooms at remarkably low rates was a typical reaction to Asia's sudden – and, for many, unexpected – impoverishment. In Hong Kong, employees were called into management offices not so much to be let go – even though some redundancies were inevitable – but more commonly to be asked (or, more likely, told) to accept a pay cut of 15 or 20 per cent. The new reality sank in very quickly. International creditors had walked away and, with Asia now in stormy economic and financial waters, it was time to batten down the hatches.

It is near enough impossible to imagine Western nations so meekly accepting such a sudden loss in living standards. Yet, in Asia's case, the willingness to tolerate such losses also provided the springboard for the subsequent recovery. Asia had been living beyond its means. By moving rapidly from balance of payments deficits to surpluses, it was able to repay some of its existing debts and, importantly, reduce its dependency on foreign creditors. By offering antidotes to crony capitalism – Korea, for example, introduced financial reforms to guard against unhealthy nepotism – it was able to convince the world that it was clearing up the mess left in its own backyard. And by cutting wages even as exchange rates tumbled, it was able to secure an improvement in competitiveness that allowed export sectors to flourish.

Yet Asian people still needed a narrative to explain what had gone wrong. That narrative, as we've seen, varied from country to country. For Indonesians, the crisis provided an opportunity to overthrow the existing political order: Suharto may not have caused the crisis but he proved to be a sitting duck thanks to his many abuses of power in earlier decades. In Malaysia, the shrewd Mahathir Mohamad was quick to deflect blame for the crisis onto mysterious foreign forces: his was a classic populist's response, where facts were ignored and a fictitious – at times, unsavoury – narrative was developed to explain why Malaysia had suffered so much. His use of capital controls was no more than a modern-day equivalent of a medieval siege mentality. As for Korea, it had only just joined the world's industrial elite and was hardly going to throw away its newly enfranchised status through the pursuit of some kind of populist short-term policy.

For the West, there is, as yet, no narrative. The political debate for the most part still assumes that recovery lies just around the corner. Those in favour of austerity believe that by adopting a frugal fiscal policy and, thus, keeping interest rates low, the private sector will eventually gain the confidence to consume and invest again, thereby delivering a recovery in economic activity. Those in favour of further stimulus believe that, with the helping hand of the authorities, economies can be nurtured back to life. So far, however, both arguments have been wrong: levels of activity remain well below earlier expectations and the entitlements that we think we can so easily afford are becoming increasingly unaffordable.

As reality sinks in, we are threatened with economic dystopia. The nineteenth-century Gold Standard experiment demonstrates all too clearly that an unwillingness to confront the difficult choices that stem from monetary and economic failure only serves to incubate the rise of populist – and protectionist – politics. Asia's experience in the late twentieth century shows that recovery may ultimately require hard work and considerable self-sacrifice. Even then, the risk of an abuse of political power cannot be ruled out.

CHAPTER NINE

DYSTOPIA

At the end of the twentieth century, it seemed as though markets had emerged triumphant. Whether thanks to Adam Smith with his invisible hand or to Friedrich Hayek with his hatred of central planning,[1] proponents of free markets had won the argument. They knew that a happy and prosperous society depended on the decisions of millions of individuals whose actions were 'coordinated' through the miracle that is the price mechanism. Rapid global growth was a direct result of the spread of market forces around the world. Those who resisted this process would ultimately lose out. Deregulation and privatization spread like wildfire, such was our collective faith in the wisdom of markets. The Soviet model had failed. The Asian model, so it seemed, was also in the process of failing.

Yet we became overconfident. We began to extrapolate economic gains into the future. We began to believe that economies free of excessive government interference could happily expand, over the years delivering higher incomes for all. We were so confident in continued economic progress that we could be educated yesterday, consume today, retire tomorrow, have excellent health care the next day and create a better life for our children while, at the same time, saving very little. Capital markets would take care of everything. Returns would always be high enough to allow us to fulfil our whims: sacrifice was unnecessary. We could borrow from others – foreigners, our children – and invest their money wisely for our collective benefit. And, if we were lucky enough to have some savings, we could invest them all over the world, with returns sufficiently high to guarantee both our own financial futures and the financial futures of those who benefited from our generosity. We hadn't just mastered our economies. We had mastered time itself.

We double, triple, even quadruple counted the benefits of economic success, safe in the assumption that nothing could go wrong. We knew how to avoid a Japan-style stagnation; Argentina was regarded as a peculiar irrelevance, a genetic mutation that wasn't relevant for the rest of us. And we had, surely, learnt the lesson from the 1930s. Never again would there be deflation, depression or stagnation.

Yet we have ended up with colossal failure, so much so that no longer do we trust either capital markets or, for that matter, each other. We don't trust our banks, our politicians, our foreign neighbours, our central banks or even, in at least one case, our comedians. Societies have become increasingly polarized. There are haves and have-nots. There are generational strains. There is growing mistrust between creditors and debtors. These schisms make macroeconomic success all the less likely because, ultimately, they undermine the functioning of markets upon which macroeconomic success ultimately depends.

How can nations escape from the stagnation trap? Asia's experience following the 1997–8 crisis offers only limited clues. At the time, the options were (1) Take the pain up front; (2) Accept you can't live beyond your means; (3) Implement orthodox austerity

Dystopia

medicine (Korea); (4) Blame others (Malaysia); (5) Protect yourself from speculators (Malaysia); (6) Have a revolution and overthrow the ruling elite (Indonesia). In each case, terrible distress was followed by sustained economic recovery. Yet none of the Asian economies had created a Western 'entitlement culture'. Nor had their policy-makers claimed, in the style of King Canute, to be able to control the economic tides.[2]

BACK TO THE FUTURE: THE LESSONS FROM MEDIEVAL WARFARE

In the West, however, we spend money and create entitlements as if we are in control of all our tomorrows. These are hardly new failings. They have a pedigree extending back over many centuries. While, today, the focus is mostly on health care, pensions and other social commitments, for much of human history nations have traditionally focused on another area of entitlement, namely warfare.[3] Kings, queens, nobles, aristocracy, parliamentarians and unelected officials have, over thousands of years, been devoted to this peculiarly toxic area of public spending. Even in the light of severe economic setback, nations have typically maintained a commitment to the pursuit of military conflict. Whereas, today, we have to work out how to fund social expenditures, for most of human history the biggest challenge in public finances was paying for war. Whatever the economic circumstance, war was a full-time commitment, both physically and financially.

Rather than considering whether war was affordable, policy-makers had to resolve a more challenging fiscal issue, namely how war should be funded regardless of economic circumstance. Such was the situation in the fourteenth century when England and France engaged in a series of conflicts that, collectively, became known as the Hundred Years War. Crécy, Poitiers and Agincourt represented early victories for the English before, from their point of view, it all went horribly wrong. It was, in hindsight, a really silly conflict between England and France that created heroes and villains, victories and defeats, extraordinarily high levels of stupidity on both sides yet an overwhelming commitment to public spending on military exploits of one form or another.

In the early stages of this conflict, the ability to engage in warfare suffered a severe setback, the medieval equivalent of a major financial meltdown. In 1347, the Black Death, a noxious mix of bubonic, septicaemic and pulmonary plague, spread by fleas living on black rats or travelling through the air, arrived in Europe. The first symptom of the Black Death was the appearance of a bubo – a boil – in either the armpit or the groin, followed by internal bleeding that led to bruising on the skin. After a few days of terrible pain and suffering, the unlucky victim would drop dead.

The Black Death probably arrived in Europe via the Silk Road, the trading route that connected China to modern-day Turkey and Syria. It didn't help that corpses of plague victims were catapulted into castles during sieges, a sure way of spreading disease with unseemly haste. The Black Death travelled across Europe at tremendous speed and, by the end of 1348, had arrived in England. Thanks to poor sanitation and overcrowding, townsfolk were affected far more than those living in the countryside. More importantly – at least from an economic point of view – the Black Death targeted the young and healthy far more than the elderly and infirm. The population of working age in England was decimated: the number of fatalities thanks to the Black Death is estimated to have been between 1.4 and 2 million – which effectively meant that the population dropped by between one-third and one-half. This was the mother of all pandemics. It was also a huge economic shock, which, in turn, required some form of political response.

Because the Black Death had a particular liking for the young and healthy, English – and European – demographics were turned upside down. Feudal systems worked via a constant supply of cheap labour. Serfs did all the hard back-breaking work while their lords and masters lived off the spoils. Thanks to the Black Death, however, there was an inevitable shortage of workers. Their price began to rise and, as a consequence, the incentive to move around in search of the highest bidder – and, thus, to escape from the bondage of the feudal system – increased. It was a fourteenth-century version of population ageing.

The response from the feudal leaders was predictably draconian. They had no interest in the laws of economics, instead insisting on preserving the status quo. In 1351, Edward III imposed the Statute of Labourers. This new law made work compulsory for anyone under the age of 60, kept wages at pre-Black Death levels and prevented people from moving to take advantage of higher income elsewhere. It was slavery by statute. Put another way, it was an early form of austerity.

Despite the onset of the Black Death, the English nobility saw no reason to sacrifice their fighting ways to help the national economy (if, indeed, such a concept even existed in those days). At first, Edward III (who reigned from 1327 to his death in 1377) borrowed from foreign creditors to fund his war effort. In 1339, however, he was forced to suspend payment on the nation's debts, turning him into an early subprime customer. His actions promptly led to bank failures in Florence.

In 1377, under the auspices of Richard II, a poll tax was imposed on clergy and commoners. When that didn't raise enough money, in 1379 a second poll tax was conjured up. Not surprisingly, there was massive tax evasion. By that stage, town populations were shrinking not so much because of the Black Death but, instead, because wide-scale tax avoidance led to a class of tax-avoiding 'zombies', people who existed in reality but not in the official records. Populations appeared to be decimated, but only on a 'virtual' basis.

The Plantagenet equivalents of men with baseball bats were sent in to resolve the situation. In turn, this led to the first spark of rebellion. In 1381, the people of Brentwood, Essex, simply refused to pay. Before long, the revolt had spread to Kent. Wat Tyler emerged as the leader of the Kentish rebels, while Jack Straw found himself heading the uprising in Essex. The rebels marched on London, which erupted into an orgy of extreme violence: rioting, looting, arson and beheading (the then Archbishop of Canterbury – admittedly a fairly nasty piece of work – was one of the unlucky ones to be decapitated).

For a while, it seemed as though anything could happen. Yet the rebels – many of whom were wealthy individuals, either landowners or skilled artisans, so hardly in the grip of serfdom – suffered a collective failure of imagination. Richard II – Machiavellian long before Machiavelli – was regarded naively by many of the rebels as an innocent young man who was simply being proffered bad advice: after all, he was only 14 years old at the time. John of Gaunt, the effective leader of the country since the death of Edward III and a main object of the rebels' ire, was – conveniently – nowhere to be seen. Somehow the rebels seemed to think that if Richard could be separated from his advisers, he could be turned into a good and just king. They were hopelessly wrong.

At Smithfield Market, Wat Tyler – suffering from a touch too much bravado – rode ahead of his rebels to meet Richard II and his entourage, at which point he was duly hacked to death. The reforms supposedly agreed by Richard II – including amnesties for many of the rebels – were swiftly put into reverse. To show who was boss, Richard sent his henchmen to hunt down the rebels one by one. Most of them lost their heads.

The debate over what, precisely, the revolt achieved continues to this day. Given the paucity of historical evidence and the obvious biases of contemporary observers who regarded any act of rebellion as the devil's work – perhaps fearing for their own lives – that's hardly surprising. However, given that similar rebellions in other parts of Europe occurred at roughly the same time, it's just about possible to argue that the Peasants' Revolt and associated uprisings hastened the end of feudalism.

The period between the outbreak of the Black Death – an economic shock with big political consequences – and the Peasants' Revolt contains important lessons for today. The Black Death was beyond the comprehension of policy-makers. They had no real idea of what had gone wrong or how to adjust to a new, and more difficult, world. Theories abounded. It was the wrath of God. It was the fault of lepers. The water had been poisoned by Jews. Thanks to this last ludicrous claim, pogroms against Jews were launched all over Europe, with tens of thousands murdered as a result.

Because the Black Death's implications were so poorly understood, governments continued with programmes that, in the cold light of day, were no longer affordable. The Hundred Years War was the equivalent of pouring money down the drain yet both the English and the French happily continued with it, placing honour ahead of the interests of taxpayers and international creditors. As the Black Death took hold, ignorance of its causes and consequences led inevitably to witless regulation, notably in England with the Statute of Labourers. More generally, the existing political systems were unable easily to adjust to a new, and poorly understood, economic reality.

Today, governments have excessive debt, just as England had in the fourteenth century. They are committed to spending programmes they can ill afford, in the same way that England and France were committed to military conflict in the fourteenth century. Default – a policy adopted by Edward III – is now a topic of conversation within polite society, thanks to Greece's inability to repay its creditors. Austerity imposes costs on countries not dissimilar to the impact of the Statute of Labourers: innocent people are victimized merely as a consequence of their place of birth. The rioters in Athens, Madrid and Barcelona are no more than modern-day incarnations of Wat Tyler, Jack Straw and the other 1381 rebels. Tax avoidance has become an industry in itself. Regulation is rapidly spreading, so much so that it is in danger of taking on a life of its own with no regard for the longer-term consequences. Economic stagnation, meanwhile, appears to be as poorly understood as the Black Death, with all manner of 'cures' on offer, none of which appears to work very well.

In the absence of growth, and with persistent increase in government borrowing, the numbers simply don't add up. Stuck in this miserable world, how will Western democracies cope?

GLOBALIZATION IN REVERSE

As with the Asian crisis, politicians need a narrative. They need to explain why they are unable to deliver the economic progress we have come to expect. One obvious narrative is to blame foreign forces for domestic difficulties. It is an approach with a rich history: the Smoot-Hawley Tariff Act of 1930, Argentina's self-imposed economic and financial exile in the 1940s and Mahathir Mohamad's accusations regarding the actions of evil speculators.

The eurozone crisis provides a modern-day update on this process. The Germans blame Greece for mismanaging its economy. The Greeks blame the Germans for imposing a level of austerity that, by the end of 2012, had resulted in economic collapse on a par with the worst-affected nations during the Great Depression. The British blame the eurozone collectively for its own failure to recover: many now think the UK might be better off outside the European Union altogether.

Given the lessons from the 1930s, it's difficult – although certainly not impossible – to imagine a return to wide-scale conventional trade protectionism, even if sabre-rattling between the US and China continues apace. Indeed, negotiations over a Trans-Pacific Partnership and the possibility of a transatlantic trade deal mean that we may yet see a more open trading environment. Nevertheless, with China not involved in the TPP and with the UK's membership of the EU in doubt, it's not difficult to imagine the fragmentation of current trading arrangements. The various regional trade blocs could, themselves, become more protectionist, supporting free trade within their respective blocs but not with other blocs. Within the European Union, the Common Agricultural Policy already offers a discouraging precedent.

But it is surely in the financial field that protectionism is most likely to make its mark. Banks short of funding, and in some cases supported by taxpayers, will increasingly be under pressure to lend more 'at home' – in effect, the home of their chief regulator – and less elsewhere. If a shortage of credit is regarded as a key reason behind domestic economic weakness, then diverting available credit to domestic opportunities and away from opportunities abroad might appear to be acting in the national self-interest.

While such a move might be politically expedient in the short term, it would only look after the interests of taxpayers at the expense of shareholders (including future pensioners) and surely would be inconsistent with the need for banks to maximize their returns by investing all over the world. The result would be the return of a home bias to banking, which, in turn, would seriously reduce cross-border capital flows. It would also leave bank share prices that much weaker, threatening the creation of zombie institutions continuously dependent on taxpayer support and unable easily to raise capital in financial markets. Those companies would, in turn, look for other ways of making money, including riskier, but ineffectively regulated, areas of financial endeavour.

A home bias would also make life much more difficult for those countries acutely dependent on foreign funding to make ends meet. This is most obviously the case within the eurozone where, although there is no explicit currency risk, lingering fears of an eventual break-up have contributed to huge variations in borrowing costs. An unlucky resident living in Brennero faces a significantly higher cost of borrowing than his more fortunate counterpart in Brenner even though they live just a few metres away from each other in the same town: Brenner/Brennero just happens to sit on the border between Austria, which enjoys low interest rates, and Italy, which suffers from high interest rates.

And if savings stay at home, what happens? Perhaps they sit under the creditor's mattress, a reflection of growing – and self-fulfilling – risk aversion. If so, demand will weaken and stagnation will become a semi-permanent feature of the economic landscape. Perhaps they will be invested in domestic ventures with lower rates of return than those available abroad, leading to bigger shortfalls for pension funds and insurance companies. Inefficient domestic companies that should have gone to the wall years ago will be given a new lease of life, locking in mediocrity for the long term.

A home bias would also, surely, be the death knell for the eurozone. All successful monetary unions depend on the free flow of capital within their constituent parts, whether as a result of market forces or thanks to government transfers. A home bias within the eurozone would remove, at a stroke, the benefits of the single market and likely condemn the southern nations to decades of grinding economic adjustment. That, surely, would be politically unsustainable.

In time, and making up for lost ground, maybe money will be recycled into risky ventures in hitherto untapped parts of the world economy. Following the first oil shock in 1973, the money earned by Arab nations eventually found its way via the US banking system to Latin America. Yet Latin America was unable to deal with the scale of capital inflows. Poorly invested, they eventually paved the way to the Latin American debt crisis between 1982 and 1984. Hunting for yield is all very well but, without a proper understanding of the associated risk, unsustainable financial bubbles too often become an unfortunate way of life.

MISTRUST OF GOVERNMENT

Ultimately, governments are faced with tough decisions where the costs are felt now but the benefits appear only much later. Should people contribute more to their pensions? Should retirement age go up? How much should people pay for health care? In democracies, the tyranny of the electoral cycle discourages reform where the pay-off appears only over the long term. The easiest thing to do is to procrastinate, to hope that a later administration can clear up the mess that has been left by years of inaction. Yet this approach is ultimately doomed to failure. Even if today's voters are happy for decisions to be postponed or are content to remain blissfully unaware of the need for such decisions, other stakeholders still have the capacity to make life difficult for governments unable to get a grip on the long-term outlook for public finances. Most obviously, creditors can walk away. We know from Asia's experience in 1997–8 and from the eurozone crisis that creditors are, ultimately, a fickle bunch, prepared to give regimes the benefit of the doubt during the good times but more than happy to remove their support during the bad times, inevitably making the bad times even worse.

No government wants to be faced with the prospect of not being able to pay the bills. To avoid default, governments will manoeuvre themselves to the front of the credit queue, pushing other possibly more worthwhile projects to one side in a bid to remain solvent. Acts of financial repression will become increasingly frequent. Our savings will increasingly be diverted to government interests, whether or not those interests really deliver a good rate of return for society.

Admittedly, if companies themselves are hoarding cash – as the largest were in the years following the onset of the financial crisis – it might make good sense for governments to borrow more. In a world of deficient demand, extra government borrowing can offset extra private sector saving. Yet the policy has clear limits, as Japan's two lost decades clearly demonstrate.

It is all too easy to end up locked into a situation where funds are siphoned off to the government – using quantitative easing, for example, to protect the value of government bonds and, therefore, to insulate governments from market discipline – thereby diverting funds away from the rest of the economy. If, for example, the government is able to borrow more only because credit to small and medium-sized companies is rationed, the entrepreneurial spark that ultimately leads to higher growth will be extinguished. At that point, the economy ends up caught in a Japanese-style low growth, low interest rate trap.

This is a fundamentally different issue from the 1930s. The entitlements we take for granted today simply didn't exist back then. The social security, health care and pension entitlements that have become a way of life were no more than figments of the imagination of those with reforming zeal. It was possible for government to increase borrowing significantly in the short term without calling into question its long-term fiscal health because, in those days, there was no such thing as an entitlement culture. Those who advocate vast fiscal stimulus today based on a 'New Deal' mentality are ignoring the impact of such stimulus on the long-run budgetary arithmetic and, thus, on the need for the government to 'repress' the financial system in a bid to raise the relevant funds.

Admittedly, a strong 1930s-style recovery would turn things around: but, in the face of binding long-term fiscal constraints, the chance of it happening is considerably less. Yet governments continue to engage in wishful thinking. Unfortunately, the longer they spend assuming recovery lies just around the corner, the lower the level of trust in their capabilities is likely to be. That, in turn, is likely to lead to even more caution within the private sector, leading to sustained economic weakness and, in time, making the fiscal arithmetic even worse.

MISTRUST OF MONEY

The conventional view is that inflation – let alone hyperinflation – is unlikely in a world of ongoing stagnation. The standard cyclical argument is simply that a country faced with deficient demand will have plenty of spare capacity and, hence, is unlikely to be able to generate conditions that might put upward pressure on prices. Even if the economy has entered into an extended period of stagnation, inflation will still be unlikely, particularly if the stagnation partly results from a banking crisis that chokes off the effect of the central bank's printing press on the broader economy: Japan's two lost decades provide the perfect example of such conditions.

Yet, even in the most extreme recessionary circumstances, it is still possible to generate higher inflation. Roosevelt, after all, managed to do so between 1933 and 1936, fulfilling the pledge made in his May 1933 fireside chat, even though the US economy was, by then, but a shadow of its former self. Roosevelt's inflation was, of course, completely intentional. It is also possible, however, to end up with unintentional inflation. Few, for example, thought inflation was likely to accelerate at the end of the 1960s and certainly policymakers themselves didn't plan an inflationary pick-up, yet that is exactly what transpired: across the developed world, two decades of price stability were followed by the inflationary upheavals of the 1970s.

Could inflation return in current conditions? It seems unlikely. Even as central banks have attempted to reinvigorate economies through quantitative easing, inflation has mostly remained relatively well-behaved. Where it has picked up – most obviously in the UK following sterling's devaluation at the end of 2008 – it has been of a very unusual kind: prices have risen but wages have not followed suit. The wage–price spirals of the 1970s have proved near enough impossible to replicate.

There is, however, one way in which inflation could eventually take off in such an aggressive fashion that it might ultimately lead to hyperinflation. If government debt continues to increase thanks to persistently large budget deficits, and if the government's creditors eventually walk away – fearing, perhaps, they'll never be repaid – then the government is faced with a funding crisis. There are then four possible options: negotiate loans from 'official' creditors (including foreign governments or the IMF), leading to a temporary loss of sovereignty; default, in the process shutting the nation off from international capital markets; austerity, which might be politically impossible to deliver; or inflation, a neat way for government to fund its spending commitments by robbing savers of their money.

Even if the government hasn't decided on the best course of action, it's just possible that the public's fear of inflation will be enough to generate rapidly rising prices. Imagine, for example, that inflationary expectations rise even as the central bank is determined to keep interest rates close to zero in a bid to trigger a rise in economic activity. In effect, the public fears the government will eventually have no choice other than to create inflation to make the fiscal numbers add up. In those circumstances, it makes sense for the public to get rid of its cash more quickly. As a result, spending rises. If output is unable to respond quickly to this increase in demand – perhaps because a sustained period of economic stagnation has undermined the supply potential of the economy – either prices will rise or imports will pick up. The rise in imports will merely serve to put downward pressure on the exchange rate, increasing the price of imports and, hence, adding further to domestic price pressures. An additional increase in inflation will only persuade the public to part with their cash even more quickly. Before long, money will have lost its value. Money, after all, is only worth something if the public trust it. If that trust disappears, money becomes worthless.

How might this mechanism – however unlikely – be triggered in practice? The most plausible route would surely be an initial loss of faith in the currency not so much from the public at large but, instead, from foreign creditors – reserve managers, sovereign wealth funds and the like. They, after all, are most vulnerable to what I labelled in chapter 6 the 'democratic deficit'. Unlike the 1930s, when a government's creditors were almost entirely home-grown (and where, if international credit was available, it came from other governments, not from the private sector), creditors today come from all over the world. The mismatch between the interests of creditors and voters is, therefore, considerable. Governments, as representatives of their voters, are strongly incentivized to defraud their international creditors if the alternative is to damage the interests of voters.

In normal circumstances, government bond yields might rise in the event of creditors heading elsewhere, creating a powerful incentive for governments to behave themselves fiscally. With quantitative easing and other forms of financial repression, however, it's more plausible to argue instead that the currency would collapse, raising import prices. At that point, the public might then make the connection between an unsustainable domestic fiscal position and a lack of monetary control, triggering the beginnings of an inflationary surge associated with a loss of confidence over the value of money.

THE 'STATELY HOME' EFFECT

The democratic deficit raises an important question for creditors. If they don't want to keep their money at home but, equally, are not keen on buying foreign government bonds – fearing the effects of inflation, devaluation or default – what should they invest in? The answer, surely, is for creditors to buy real assets unlikely to be heavily affected by the behaviour of myopic governments. Put another way, if the West wants to live beyond its means, it will have to allow foreigners to 'cherry-pick' the best Western assets to enable a few more years of extravagance.

Western nations are facing the same economic problems that befell the British nobility in the nineteenth century. Fully expecting to continue living in the manner to which they had become accustomed, they gradually discovered being lords of the manor wasn't quite so much fun after all. Their ambitions were undone by industrial urbanization, a process that, in time, led to the emergence of an educated middle class, a widening voter franchise – thanks to the three nineteenth-century Reform Acts that, altogether, increased the voting public from 366,000 in 1831 to 8 million in 1885 – and a significant reduction in available cheap rural labour to run the landed gentry's stately homes.

Blenheim Palace offers a good example of the difficulties facing the nineteenth-century upper classes. Completed in the 1720s, the Palace was a gift from the nation to John Churchill, the 1st Duke of Marlborough, in recognition of his military achievements. It later became something of a millstone for the Marlboroughs. The financial foolishness of George Spencer-Churchill, the 5th Duke, certainly didn't help: a one-man Greece, his spendthrift ways put the family on the verge of bankruptcy by the mid-nineteenth century. As their finances became ever more precarious, the Marlboroughs had no choice other than to sell off the family silver. Even this, however, didn't bring in enough money. The estate's finances were stabilized only when Charles, the 9th Duke, married Consuelo Vanderbilt, the American railroad heiress. That they hated each other was neither here nor there: he got the Vanderbilts' money and she could now call herself a Duchess.

The Marlboroughs still live in Blenheim, but their lives aren't as grand as the ones their nineteenth-century ancestors enjoyed. The house and grounds are open to the public, the Blenheim miniature railway transports visitors through the grounds, the butterfly collection is oddly appealing, people happily lose themselves in the maze and, on occasion, even the 11th Duke's private apartments are open for inspection by the public (for an extra fee). The Marlboroughs are hardly impoverished but, unlike their eighteenth-century and early nineteenth-century ancestors, they have no choice other than to manage what is, in effect, an extraordinarily up-market theme park, only made possible by the Vanderbilt millions.

Today, Western nations are facing the same dilemmas that confronted the 9th Duke at the end of the nineteenth century. Heading for bankruptcy, what can they do to entice foreign money to their shores? If government bonds are no longer to be treated with confidence, other options will come to the fore. Modern-day Vanderbilts – hailing from China, Russia and Saudi Arabia rather than the US – will buy the best properties in the most cosmopolitan parts of the Western world, forcing up London and Manhattan house prices in particular and, via a trickle-down effect, making it near enough impossible for marginal first-time buyers to gain a foot on the property ladder: major international cities will become the ghettos of the wealthy. Companies, and their bespoke technologies, will slowly fall under foreign ownership, turning the US and the UK into nations of worker bees where the profits of their endeavours head overseas. And, with uncertainty about the implications of continuous money printing, commodity prices will rise even as Western currencies fall in value, reducing real incomes.

Such are the costs of trying to keep a country's creditors happy. If they no longer trust governments and the myopic taxpayers who vote for those governments, the creditors will 'asset strip' Western nations, leaving generations to come without the assets – including real estate and companies – that nurtured and sustained previous generations. It is hardly an appealing prospect. It's what happens when you continuously try to live beyond your means.

EUROZONE CRISIS AND THE PARADOX OF GLOBALIZATION

Successful and legitimate globalization requires nation-states to put their differences to one side and work together for the common good. It can be done in other ways – most obviously through conquest and empire building – but, in the modern world, cooperation is generally regarded as preferable to coercion.

The eurozone offered a blueprint for such a move. Parts of Europe may have been temporarily united in the past – thanks to the Romans, Charlemagne, Napoleon and Hitler, among others – but such unity was hardly reached on a voluntary basis. The eurozone was different. Each of the member states had signed up to the single currency on a voluntary basis and each knew what the club rules were. With the establishment of the so-called Single Market in 1992 – designed to free up product, labour and capital markets within the European Union – a single currency seemed to be the natural next step. It would only work, however, if all countries within it recognized their mutual dependency and stuck by the house rules.

The financial crisis showed that, despite their common membership of a single currency, countries would always default to national self-interest in hard times. Yet the pursuit of national self-interest – whether by governments or by the millions of creditors and debtors responsible for the flow of capital across borders – demonstrated that the single currency was a far from complete political project. Faced with a battle between the interests of northern European creditors and those of the southern European debtors in the wake of the financial crisis, the blame game took over.

In the absence of a well-defined fiscal union built on democratic principles, the risk of eventual eurozone break-up is considerable. It's not so much that the project was, in itself, a bad idea but rather that it currently lacks the political glue to hold it together in the wake of extreme economic shocks. No one questions the survival of the

US, and those that question the survival of the UK do so for historical and political reasons and not for its inability to cope with economic shocks. The eurozone, however, is a different kettle of fish altogether. Following the financial crisis, continuous squabbles between creditor and debtor nations are in danger of becoming a way of life. The debtor nations have no easy way of stabilizing their fiscal positions even though the creditors demand action, involving near enough continuous austerity for years to come. The debtors, however, are caught in a trap created not just by their own extravagance but also by the excessive generosity of their creditors in times past.

The political imbalance is clear: it's not obvious that creditors should be able to dictate to debtors when, in effect, they are the other side of the same coin. The crisis is as much about the foolishness of the creditors as it is about the stupidity of the debtors. In the first few years of the euro's life, Germany ended up saving much more than it invested domestically. Those savings had to find a home somewhere else in the world. With the abolition of currency risk, German financial institutions funnelled the nation's savings into the European periphery. In hindsight, it might have been better had the money been invested at home. Instead, German savers found themselves indirectly exposed to southern European economic upheaval.

It's not the first time that creditors have attempted to dictate terms to debtors. In 1931, on the brink of the Great Depression, France treated Austria as only a creditor could treat a debtor, offering financial help to Vienna conditional on Austria sticking to the terms of the Treaty of St Germain, imposed upon Austria after the First World War. Austria, however, decided to enter a customs union with Germany. In retaliation, the French ended their financial assistance and one of Vienna's major banks, Creditanstalt, promptly went bust, providing the catalyst for the global financial upheavals that followed. France itself ended up a major loser from the ensuing conflagration, sticking to the Gold Standard even as others left and discovering that its creditor status offered no protection whatsoever: it ended up with one of the most prolonged depressions of any country in the industrialized world.

The danger is obvious. In the absence of a major reacceleration in economic growth from the eurozone's southern nations, their fiscal arithmetic will continue to deteriorate. Austerity will lock in persistent sluggishness, leave resources unemployed and lead to ongoing competitive losses – unless, that is, wages and prices fall dramatically, a result that was beyond the UK's capabilities in the 1920s. Yet, if northern Europe is only prepared to provide help conditional on further austerity, it's clear that something will eventually have to give. Workers and the unemployed in southern Europe are in danger of becoming the twenty-first century equivalents of the peasants who eventually revolted in 1381, rising up against the financial oppression imposed on them from elsewhere.

A eurozone collapse, however, would not only be a problem for the eurozone. It would surely also demonstrate to investors who have taken full advantage of the trend towards globalization that, in the absence of functioning cross-border political institutions, globalization can all too easily go into reverse. Put another way, our economic and financial ambitions have moved considerably ahead of our current political arrangements: without further political reform, globalization could suddenly find itself in reverse gear. The associated unwinding of cross-border asset holdings could then have a catastrophic effect on the global economy.

THE RETURN OF POLITICAL EXTREMISM

No growth, a loss of trust, a culture of blame, an unequal burden of austerity: it's hardly the most tempting of cocktails. This is a dystopian world of economic and financial failure. It threatens political instability on the grandest of scales. We may no longer be engaged in twentieth-century debates about the relative benefits of the free market versus central planning. Marxist-Leninist dogma has, thankfully, disappeared from view. But we are in danger of letting a culture of blame and mistrust develop. We cannot understand why we have to make sacrifices so we search, instead, for sacrificial lambs. It's a convenient approach, absolving ourselves from blame even as we construct a narrative to blame others. Yet if we all follow the same approach, it won't be long before the politics of hate makes a comeback.

Indeed, it may already be with us. In Greece, it's called Chrysi Avgi but, to the English-speaking world, it's known as the Golden Dawn Party. Its emblem is a thinly disguised swastika. Many of its supporters are skinheads. It is setting up a blood bank for Greeks alone.[4] It is on the extreme right of the political spectrum. It is firmly anti-immigrant. In parts of Athens, its vigilantes have replaced the police as the – unofficial – source of law enforcement, if that's the right term. It vehemently opposes the austerity being imposed on Greece by its foreign creditors. And, in 2012, it enjoyed the support of 14 per cent of Greek voters, a dramatic increase compared with earlier years.

Economic setback breeds political extremism. When the cake isn't big enough, when there aren't enough slices to go round, anger quickly takes over. Political movements that normally wouldn't see the light of day suddenly become mainstream. Think of bloody revolution in eighteenth-century France, anti-Chinese legislation in late nineteenth-century America, anti-Semitism in nineteenth-century Germany and the rise of fascism and Soviet communism in the 1920s and 1930s. Each of these toxic developments was rooted in economic setback. Stagnation not only creates the melancholy state but also serves as an incubator for what might loosely be termed 'supremacist' political movements that thrive on the ridiculous idea that their followers are somehow better than others, in the process invoking hatred towards minorities of whatever race, colour or creed. Stagnation may not be as bad, economically, as depression but, by imposing year after year of austerity, the risk of political turmoil only increases.

At the end of the nineteenth century, the rise of nationalism was, in part, a reaction both to the oppression of empire and of financial failure.[5] The re-emergence of nationalism in the twenty-first century would likely be a reaction to the anonymity – and perceived failure – of globalization. Global capital markets and autonomous nation-states do not sit happily side by side. We may have reached the limits of what globalization can achieve, partly because we're not sure we can easily live with its effects. Yet the return of nationalism will only damage our long-term prospects. Short of workers and facing economic stagnation, we are no longer capable of making good the promises we've made to ourselves. If we are to have any hope of salvaging something for our economic futures, it must come from our increased engagement with the rest of the world. A retreat back to the nationalist, protectionist and racist world of the first half of the twentieth century, whether driven by rivalries within continents or between continents, would only take us down a path towards economic, financial and political oblivion.

Yet disengagement can be seen everywhere. While mainstream politicians in southern Europe pander to the interests of foreign creditors, political extremism is, behind their backs, on the rise. With the UK recognizing that the eurozone may eventually have to move to a fully integrated fiscal policy, so those on the Conservative right spot an opportunity for the UK to escape the the EU's 'shackles'. As global growth slows, so regional tensions are on the rise: China's decision not to send a delegation to the IMF/World Bank meetings in Tokyo in 2012 may have been no more than posturing, but it only emphasized the fragility of political relationships within the region, relationships that will only sour if global growth ends up a lot weaker. And, throughout the Western world, the anti-immigration lobby becomes ever more vociferous, even as many Western nations are running out of workers. The lessons from the late nineteenth century cannot be ignored: persistent stagnation, accompanied by the creation of both winners and losers, will only serve to foster the nationalism and racism that, a hundred years ago, took the world into agonizing conflict.

CHAPTER TEN

AVOIDING DYSTOPIA

How can expectations best be managed when economic life begins to disappoint? What sort of narrative should politicians, business leaders, bankers, trade unions, public servants, newspaper editors, religious leaders and all the rest adopt in the light of economic setback? Should they claim that 'we are all in this together', as George Osborne, the British Chancellor of the Exchequer, once famously argued, even though his own circumstances were hardly humble? Should they choose, instead, to blame others – and to suggest that those others should pick up the bill – for persistent economic disappointment?

When society faces systemic weaknesses, it's all too easy to blame others for one's own plight. Our confidence in economic progress, our insistence that it is somehow a natural state, makes it more likely for us to argue that, when things go wrong, it must result from some kind of human error or, worse, some sort of unpleasant conspiracy: when our illusions are finally shattered, it must be somebody else's fault. The desire to identify scapegoats is precisely the kind of thing that gnaws at the fabric of society. It creates an atmosphere of mistrust in which markets can no longer function successfully. Playing the blame game may be politically attractive but it does little to create conditions under which society's wounds can be healed.

I make no great claims about the proposals outlined in this final chapter. There is no magic wand. It is foolish to pretend that our economic difficulties can be solved with a bit of extra quantitative easing or an extra dose of government spending. Our problems are much more deep-rooted than that: we've lived beyond our means, we've made too many promises to ourselves and, as those promises are broken, so trust is going to be in increasingly short supply. Still, things can be done to make the process of adjustment easier. Here are my suggestions.

DEALING WITH SPACE: RESOLVING THE INTERNATIONAL/ DOMESTIC CONFLICT

With voters in country A and country A's creditors in country B, there is an obvious conflict of interest. The eurozone crisis has unmasked the problem in extreme fashion but the imbalance of savings and investment between the eurozone's member states is hardly unique: similar imbalances exist at the global level. Both Germany and China are nations where savings considerably outstrip investment and both Spain and the US are nations where investment considerably outstrips savings (or, in Spain's case, did so up until the point when its creditors walked away and its economy collapsed).

For the most part, the saving nations hold the trump cards. This reflects what might accurately be labelled a 'moral inconsistency' with regard to balance of payments positions. For every current account surplus, there has to be an offsetting current account deficit. Yet nations that save tend to treat nations that borrow with disdain, as if they are morally inferior.

It's a deeply entrenched view: the scorecard of the European Commission's Macroeconomic Imbalance Procedure (MIP) triggers an alert when a nation-state has a current account deficit of more than 4 per cent of national income or a surplus of more than 6 per cent of national income over a period of at least three years.[1] This is clearly an inconsistent position. For every surplus, there has to be a deficit: they should surely be treated equivalently. Worse, if the surplus country is big and the deficit country small, the deficit will inevitably be very large as a share of the small country's GDP even if the equivalent surplus is small as a share of the large country's GDP. Germany, by far the biggest economy in the eurozone, saves massively, inevitably forcing other, smaller economies to borrow even more massively, at least when measured as a share of their national income.

This is hardly a new problem. John Maynard Keynes highlighted the difficulty in what became known as the Keynes Plan, published as a UK government White Paper in the midst of the Second World War:

> We need a system possessed of an internal stabilising mechanism, by which pressure is exercised on any country whose balance of payments with the rest of the world is departing from equilibrium *in either direction*, so as to prevent movements which must create for its neighbours an equal but opposite want of balance.[2]

The lack of symmetry leads too often to saving nations accumulating excessive levels of foreign assets, which, in turn, triggers the creation of financial bubbles in the deficit countries: it was a problem for Asia in the 1990s, for the US before the onset of the subprime crisis and for those nations in the eurozone that suddenly found themselves awash with inflows thanks to the creation of the single currency and, hence, the removal of currency risk. In all three examples, it all ended in tears.

It's now abundantly clear, however, that deficit countries facing economic collapse can end up in a position where they are unable to repay their creditors. The result is default, inflation, devaluation or some combination of all three. In other words, the risk associated with imbalances lies not only with the debtor nations, which may be forced into painful austerity, but also with those creditor nations that may not be able to get their money back.

One way to deal with this problem is simply to restrict the scale of cross-border capital flows with the reimposition of capital controls. That, however, would prevent capital from flowing to those parts of the world producing the highest returns, leaving poorer nations particularly vulnerable. Another would be to impose a Tobin tax – in effect, a way of throwing sand into the works of speculative financial bets – on foreign exchange transactions. The likely result would be the creation of offshore foreign exchange hubs and the shift of financial business from London and New York to newly emerging centres in Asia and the Middle East.[3] Imbalances would still exist, but they would simply be channelled through centres able to distance themselves from national – or even international – regulation.

A better option, perhaps, is to encourage creditors to think twice before they send their savings abroad, to make them realize early on that, in the event of a debtor meltdown, they too will have to take losses. The simplest way to do this would be to drop the idea that creditors are somehow morally superior. They should, instead, be regarded as architects of ultimate failure and be penalized accordingly. But how?

Ratings agencies could be forced to pass judgement on not only those who issue debt but also those who acquire it. The eurozone crisis provides a good example. The inability of Greece to keep its creditors happy is a problem not only for Greece but also for its creditors: if Greece cannot repay, its creditors lose out. It wouldn't be so difficult, then, to require ratings agencies not only to rate the vulnerabilities of borrowers but also, too, the vulnerabilities of lenders. After all, a major eurozone meltdown would leave Germany in serious trouble in exactly the same way that France ended up in deep difficulty in 1931 following the failure of Creditanstalt. Those who lent too much would see their ratings downgraded. In Germany's case, this could apply either to its financial institutions, who were far too willing to recycle hard-earned German savings to southern Europe during the good times, or to the government in Berlin for failing to understand the full implications of exporting savings to the rest of the world rather than investing them at home: after all, should German financial institutions end up with losses thanks to their exposure to southern European nations, German taxpayers might have no other choice than to pick up the pieces.

DEALING WITH DEBT: THE EUROZONE CRISIS

As I write, the Spanish unemployment rate has reached 25 per cent of the workforce, a massive increase relative to the rate before the financial crisis of 9 per cent, a number that was already far too high. Spain's labour market is in Great Depression territory, even if its economy as a whole has yet to stage a 1930s-style collapse. The social contract between the regions and the centre is in danger of being torn up: Madrid is under pressure from Brussels to deliver painful reforms but the regions are in no mood to bow to Madrid's demand for further austerity, in some cases thinking that a better deal might be negotiated by talking to Brussels directly. As people take the streets and violence erupts, the bond of trust that has held Spain together following General Franco's death is under serious threat.

Spain's problems might appear to be internally generated, reflecting a battle between the semi-autonomous regions and the centre but, in reality, they are no more than a symptom of deep-rooted problems across the eurozone as a whole. The euro won't survive unless these problems are addressed. Forget the legal and political objections: the euro is in danger of collapsing under the weight of its internal inconsistencies.

How should monetary unions ideally work? Labour should be able to move to where the jobs are. Capital should be able to move to where the labour is cheap. A strong federal fiscal authority would both encourage such mobility and stand ready to offer support in the event that factors of production temporarily became immobile. In the absence of exchange rate adjustment, creditors would understand that debtors might occasionally default: as a result, their willingness to lend would be constrained by the possibility of eventual monetary loss. And debtors would endeavour to make sure that capital inflows were spent wisely.

None of this is easy. Yet my 'perfect world' provides clues as to how the eurozone might operate successfully. Spanish workers would migrate to northern Europe, exploring opportunities in labour markets where vacancies are more plentiful. German capital would head to southern Europe, creating jobs for those workers who stayed at home. A central fiscal authority would pursue a regional policy based on 'contingent redistribution' – in effect, offering succour to those in temporary difficulty, funded via centrally collected taxes. It would also, at the very least, fund infrastructure projects that linked the various parts of the union together to create a binding economic and financial community: these would be the eurozone's *grands projets*.

To achieve any of this, however, is near enough impossible given the position the eurozone finds itself in today. It is not so much that there is a lack of will – although sympathy for the plight of others is in worryingly short supply. Rather, the eurozone finds itself in a paradoxical position in which any near-term monetary support from the European Central Bank that eases pressure on interest rates and capital flight reduces the urgency for reforms ultimately required to make the eurozone work. The eurozone is so far over the cliff that climbing back up again will take a Herculean effort, yet that effort only seems to be made during periods of financial crisis.

There is, however, a way to make the eurozone work if – and it is a big 'if' – the politics allow. The member states need to recognize that monetary unions succeed only if they are accompanied by fiscal unions. In the absence of a binding fiscal agreement, the eurozone will fail: better, therefore, for leaders to spell out their vision of such an agreement sooner rather than later.

The challenge is obvious. Can a fiscal union be created that is politically acceptable and, at the same time, sufficiently credible to allow southern European nations access to capital markets on reasonable terms?

One potential compromise is the creation of what I'd call a 'fiscal club', an attempt to preserve fiscal autonomy while, at the same time, providing democratically acceptable safeguards in the event of subsequent fiscal weakness. A club member unable to access capital markets would automatically receive support from other club members without having to pay an excessively painful interest rate. However, during the ensuing bailout, it would lose its fiscal autonomy: the good men and women of Brussels would take over its finance ministry, thereby establishing a contingent principle of 'no European taxation without European representation'.[4] After all, the last thing Europeans need is a series of coffee parties to rival the Boston Tea Party.

That might seem harsh. However, club members would also enjoy significant benefits. Knowing that members would be bailed out, even at the cost of a temporary loss of sovereignty, would surely attract otherwise sceptical investors to come back in their droves, thus lowering government borrowing costs and making bond markets more liquid: default risk would be dramatically lower thanks to the bailout arrangement.

Might an arrangement along these lines be politically acceptable? One way to find out would be to put the proposal to a vote according to a strict timetable – either parliamentary or through referenda – for all countries considering membership. The choice would be clear. Those countries prepared to sign up to the club rules would enjoy the benefits of lower interest rates at the cost of contingent loss of sovereignty. Those choosing to opt out would retain their sovereignty but would never, ever, be bailed out by others: default risk would, therefore, be much greater and the cost of borrowing would, thus, be permanently higher.

It's a shame that such a scheme was not established at the outset. It might well have prevented the current crisis from ever happening. It would, after all, have provided a guarantee that debtors would automatically be bailed out by creditors, so long as they had signed up to the club rules. Moreover, it would have made creditors think twice before lending to countries that, having opted out, had shown that their sovereign interests trumped the interests of their creditors.

Still, that's not how things turned out. While my scheme has advantages, there is one obvious drawback: countries in Southern Europe have excessive debts that no amount of austerity will be sufficient to deal with. To preserve the single currency, some of those debts will have to be written off. With floating currencies, the process would have been easy. Those with excessive debts would have devalued. Foreign creditors would have lost out – one reason why, before the advent of the single currency, Germans used to demand a significant risk premium for lending to countries in Southern Europe. With fixed currencies, the answer, surely, is to allow an orderly default or, more prosaically, a debt restructuring. One possibility would be to take lessons from the 1980s Savings and Loan crisis in the US, where bad debts were ultimately bundled up into the Resolution Trust Corporation. Admittedly, the establishment of a eurozone 'bad bank' would leave eurozone taxpayers to pick up the bill. That, however, would be small price to pay if, as a result, nations within the single currency were then able to thrive: far better to have orderly losses than a catastrophic collapse.

DEALING WITH DEBT: COUNTRIES WITH FLOATING EXCHANGE RATES

The great advantage of an independent monetary policy is the ability to delay until tomorrow what might otherwise be necessary today. It's easy enough, for example, to see that the US, the UK and Japan – all of which have ropey fiscal positions, at least judged by post-war standards – have been under no real pressure to deliver austerity with the savage urgency required of nations in southern Europe. Their borrowing costs have remained low even as their government debt has headed into the stratosphere.

In the short term, that's good news. It reduces the risk of a 1930s austerity death spiral. Yet it comes at a price. Should higher interest rates be indefinitely postponed, governments can live with high debts into perpetuity. Even if the debt stock is high, the cost of servicing that debt will forever be low. Why act to reduce government borrowing if there is no real cost to inaction?

This looks suspiciously like the public sector equivalent of those households who, in the early years of the twenty-first century, borrowed more and more just because interest rates were unusually low. Unfortunately for those households, there was no access to a printing press. They couldn't simply absolve themselves of blame by printing a few more dollars or pounds. Governments, however, don't have that constraint.

Could governments forever enjoy this free lunch? Could governments painlessly deal with their debts in this way, forever postponing the day of reckoning thanks to the miracle of the printing press? It seems implausible. And, indeed, it is.

There's no need to invoke the madness of the Weimar Republic in the early 1920s or modern-day Zimbabwe to realize that things will eventually go wrong. Who ends up carrying the can, however, is not immediately obvious, partly because relations with the rest of the world differ. Japan is a net creditor, having built up a vast array of foreign assets thanks to its persistently high level of domestic savings relative to its domestic investment. For years, the US and the UK have run current account deficits, implying exactly the opposite. For the US, it helps to have the world's reserve currency, allowing easy access to the world's capital markets: its deficit has been persistently higher than the UK's.

Japan's position is remarkable for the simple reason that savings are high enough not only to fund a huge level of government debt but also to acquire an extraordinary range of foreign assets. Those assets are important: they are the lifeline for future Japanese governments that wish to avoid bankruptcy. As the Japanese population ages, so its holdings of foreign capital will have to be sold off to allow Japanese retirees to enjoy their dotage. The capital outflows of old will reverse. The resulting inflows will be spent on imports. Japan will then be running a persistent current account deficit. The government, meanwhile, will be able to tax the returning capital, most obviously through increases in Japan's VAT rate. Put another way, Japan has built up a stockpile of assets that, one way or the other, will be converted into future tax revenue.

The US and the UK also have large holdings of foreign assets. Their liabilities to foreigners are, however, larger still. In the short run, this is not as big an issue as it might initially seem: returns on US assets held abroad (mostly factories and the like) are much higher than payments on liabilities to foreigners (which, for the most part, are low-yielding Treasuries and other assorted bits of paper). Imagine, however, that foreign investors slowly begin to diversify out of Treasuries: after all, as their own capital markets develop, they won't forever remain naive patsies happy to provide the US with funds virtually for free. In a world of high US government debt, what then would happen?

In a normal world, Treasury yields would rise and the dollar might fall. In a world in which the central bank is effectively bailing out the government, Treasury yields would not have to increase at all. The full force of the adjustment would be taken by a falling dollar. This would leave foreign creditors worse off – their US assets would now be measured in devalued dollars – and future US consumers worse off – the cost of imports would rise, pushing domestic prices up relative to domestic wages. It is, then, another version of the generational divide. Failing to deal with debt allows the current generation to consume well but only by diminishing the claims of future generations on the world's scarce resources.

There's more. If governments know that they will forever be bailed out by central banks, their claims on limited resources will be ring-fenced. Central banks can attempt to get around this by buying an ever wider range of assets to encourage a flow of credit to the private sector too – in September 2012, for example, the Federal Reserve announced ongoing purchases of mortgage-backed securities – but this, surely, compounds the problem: if interest rates on an ever increasing amount of debt are determined by the central bank, capital markets become totally redundant. They may not have always worked well in the past but their complete removal surely opens the way for a huge misallocation of capital: absent a functioning price mechanism, it's difficult to see how investment decisions can be made on an informed basis, leading, in turn, to a much lower growth rate of GDP in the future.

So there can be no doubt that high levels of government debt have to be tackled, even in a world where central banks are free to print money. The costs may not be so immediate – in contrast to the Greek and Spanish experience – but high and growing levels of government debt eat away at the fabric of economic progress: one way or the other, they squeeze out the market.

The answer, unfortunately, is a lasting commitment to austerity. That commitment, however, needs to be credible. Blindly pursuing tax increases and spending cuts in each and every year makes little sense. Monetary freedom allows flexibility denied to those nations in southern Europe faced with an ongoing threat of economic implosion. Yet monetary freedom is not an excuse for inaction.

One option would be to commit to a medium-term debt reduction strategy making use of economic 'circuit breakers'. In other words, the government would announce a process that would automatically reduce the deficit year by year with an automatic suspension in years of economic contraction. This is hardly a new idea: the Gramm-Rudman-Hollings Act in the US did exactly the same thing during the late 1980s and early 1990s. However, it allows countries to escape from the 'tyranny of austerity' associated with periods of outright recession while, at the same time, indicating to sceptical investors that any fiscal 'slippage' would be contingent on the onset of temporary periods of unusually weak economic activity. Ideally, the process of deficit reduction would receive all-party support and become legally binding. For good measure, it might even be possible to build in an unusually rapid pace of fiscal consolidation during periods of rapid economic expansion, thus giving the procedure a neat symmetry.

DEALING WITH TIME: ENFRANCHISING THE FUTURE

The Great Reform Acts of the nineteenth century increased dramatically the number of men eligible to vote in British General Elections. Women over 30 with some minimum amount of property got the vote in 1918 and, with the passing of the Representation of the People Act 1928, all women over the age of 21 were granted the vote. More and more voices were heard and government genuinely became a reflection of the wishes of the people, not of the privileged few.

There was, however, a potential problem. The voices being heard were those of the current generation of voters, not those of future generations. Today, the loudest voices of our 'current generation' have come from the mouths of the baby boomers. The boomers' preferences have dominated society's choices since they first reached adulthood in the 1960s and 1970s. In their twenties and thirties, they accepted higher inflation: their mortgages were, in effect, partially written off even as pensioners saw their savings destroyed. Now in their fifties, sixties and seventies, they insist on low inflation, fearing the erosion of their lifetime savings as they head into retirement. The boomers have both had their cake and made sure they could eat it too. Boomers might even be tempted to sell off assets to the highest foreign bidder, allowing them to continue consuming, perhaps without recognizing the consequences for future generations.

One answer would simply be to wait for the selfish generation to expire. By that stage, however, the damage may have been done: their gains will have been the rest of society's losses. Another would be to recognize the futile nature of the large amounts of medical expenditure for those approaching the final curtain, a use of resources for which the returns are, sadly, rather lacking. It seems unlikely, however, that society is yet willing to embrace voluntary euthanasia – let alone the involuntary kind – any time soon, or to become indifferent to death, whatever the age. Another possibility might be to weight adult votes according to the relative size of age cohorts: those cohorts with relatively few people would have their votes artificially 'boosted' compared with other cohorts. Or, taking a leaf out of the world of microfinance, women could be given more votes than men. Women, it seems, are more likely to conserve money than to spend it on beer and gambling: in planning for the future, you'd sooner trust Marge Simpson than her husband.

Admittedly, none of these options is ever likely to see the light of day. I mention them only to emphasize how difficult it is for society to make decisions about the future when its preferences are largely dictated by those whose own futures are necessarily truncated and who might not be sufficiently focused on the kinds of reforms that might secure a better future for younger generations. The social contract between the current generation and future generations, however, is in danger of unravelling at excessive speed. The self-interest of the boomers may eventually become self-defeating. Faced with higher taxes and tuition fees and ever harder work to pay for the boomers' entitlements, the young may simply vote with their feet, heading to other parts of the world where the pressure to subsidize other people's living standards may be lower. A 'youth drain' however, would make the generational arithmetic even more difficult to add up.[5]

To escape from this generational implosion, there needs to be the establishment of a new social contract between the generations. I'm neither a lawyer nor a constitutional expert but, to cope with economic stagnation, there has to be a fair distribution of loss. And one way to do that is to offer constitutional protection to those in danger of being excessively harshly treated. In the same way that the Civil Rights movement in the 1960s led to a landmark US Supreme Court ruling that – finally and belatedly – established that blacks deserved equal treatment, so we need an equivalent 'contract' that looks after the interests of the young, offering them a settlement fair enough to prevent a mass exodus. The most obvious way to offer a social contract is to commit to a period of budget deficit reduction associated with the ring-fencing of expenditure that might benefit younger generations: that means continued support for education, infrastructure and children's health but a serious reduction in public spending elsewhere, including a substantial reduction in, say, defence spending or social benefits. That won't be easy: either services will shrink or, instead, they will have to be paid for privately (indeed, with the spread of new technologies, services that hitherto have been provided out of the public purse could easily be charged for: London's Congestion Charge could not possibly have worked without the technologies that automatically read number plates and charge (and fine) drivers according to their trips into central London). Ultimately, however, it's a choice between benefits today – which will damage our long-term prospects – or investment for tomorrow.

A NEW MONETARY FRAMEWORK

Monetary policy alone cannot solve the Western world's economic ills. Yet there is room for modest reform. Inflation targeting, the backbone of monetary policy throughout much of the Western world, is no longer able to provide the monetary answers. Adherents of inflation targeting gave the impression that monetary policy was somehow merely a job for technicians who could blissfully ignore the day-to-day political fray. That's no longer a tenable position.

As interest rates have dropped near enough to zero and as unconventional policies have, it seems, become increasingly conventional, the separation of monetary church from fiscal state no longer holds. At very low interest rates, it turns out that monetary and fiscal policies are very closely entwined. Central bankers who choose to purchase government bonds in a bid to lower long-term interest rates are changing the nature of the political game. By lowering the cost of government borrowing, they're encouraging governments to borrow more – or, at least, to delay fiscal consolidation – and, hence, increasing the burden on future taxpayers. By reducing both short- and long-term interest rates, they're making life more difficult for already underfunded pension schemes, penalizing savers and, more generally, the culture of saving.

Admittedly, the idea was to kick-start economic recovery but, as I've repeatedly argued throughout this book, it's not obvious that the plan has worked. Where there has been growth, it's been decidedly anaemic. Central bankers have instead ended up making a deal with the fiscal devil. So perhaps it's time to formalize that deal.

Inflation targeting is all very well but nations today desperately need higher levels of activity. Central banks that focus on price stability alone are not in a position to help. Worse, the relationship between growth and inflation has become increasingly peculiar. Since the onset of the financial crisis, the level of economic activity has been disappointingly low yet inflation has either been in line with target or, in the case of the UK, mostly above target. This combination has been a genuine surprise: most economic models suggest that weaker than expected activity should lead to inflationary undershoots. On this occasion, inflation has hardly budged.

From a purely inflation-targeting perspective, it seems as though central bankers are doing the right thing. That, though, surely suggests that inflation targeting is too narrow an ambition. Hitting an inflation target when the economy is on the ropes is a bit like taking pleasure in one's exercise regime even as the cardiologist tells you that you need a heart transplant.

Inflation targeting is neither a necessary nor a sufficient framework for running the economy. It creates an illusion that monetary policy is somehow 'neutral' when monetary decisions are, all the time, creating both winners and losers. Moreover, it suggests that fiscal and monetary policies are entirely separate from one another when, in reality, they are not. It was a convenient illusion to uphold in the 1980s and 1990s, when policy-makers attempted to lance the inflation boil of the 1970s. We now know that it was no more than an illusion. Monetary and fiscal policies are, ultimately, joined at the hip.

Huge budget deficits and ever increasing levels of public debt leave governments extraordinarily vulnerable to the behaviour of sometimes fickle creditors. More than anything, governments need growth to allow their fiscal numbers to add up. After all, it's not so much the amount of borrowing itself that matters but, instead, the amount of borrowing relative to national income. But it is the *value* of national income that matters, not its volume. If the value of national income doesn't rise quickly enough, the best-laid fiscal plans can go horribly wrong. Fiscal uncertainty, in turn, breeds broader economic instability: trust in government falls away, ratings agencies threaten downgrades, borrowing costs rise, default risk goes up, contracts end up null and void and the currency falls. Economic recovery becomes ever less likely.

Far better, then, for central banks to put inflation targeting to one side and, instead, focus on the value of national income. What's needed is not so much an inflation target but, instead, a medium-term commitment to an acceptable growth rate for nominal GDP. It's the relevant measure from the perspective of fiscal policy. It's also the relevant measure for businesses, banks and individuals. Contracts are ultimately honoured in a nominal world, taking into account the value of economic activity, not in a world in which all that matters is the volume of activity.

Imagine an economy with a long-term growth rate of around 2 per cent per annum and a preference for relatively low inflation – again, say 2 per cent per annum. Add the two numbers together and the result is a 4 per cent figure for the growth rate of the value of national income. That is what the central bank should target. If nominal growth is lower than 4 per cent, the central bank should endeavour to push growth higher and not worry too much about whether the reacceleration results in higher activity or, instead, higher inflation. If, alternatively, nominal growth is higher than 4 per cent, the central bank should put its foot on the monetary brakes and not be too concerned as to whether activity or inflation adjusts. If that sounds too precise – which it almost certainly is – the ambition could easily be cast as a range, which provides the central bank with some discretion subject, of course, to congressional or parliamentary oversight.

Admittedly, this may lead to some odd results. *In extremis*, inflation could rise to, say, 20 per cent, with the volume of activity contracting 16 per cent, and yet the central bank would still be hitting its nominal GDP target. This, however, is highly unlikely: it's not how the world works.

Two more realistic examples demonstrate the advantages of nominal GDP targeting.

Imagine, for example, that there's an unexpected fall in import prices, perhaps because of the effects of outsourcing manufacturing production to China or other low-cost producers. Lower import prices will, in time, lead to lower inflation. Under an inflation targeting regime, the central bank should respond by cutting interest rates to lift domestically generated inflation to bring overall inflation back to target. The rise in domestically generated inflation, however, can only be achieved thanks to an excessively low cost of borrowing, which, in time, leads to an increase in dodgy domestic lending practices and an unsustainable housing boom. In this case, the attempt to stabilize inflation leads to undesirable internal imbalances.

Under a nominal GDP targeting regime, the response would be entirely different. Nominal GDP can be measured as the value of output, income or expenditure. Expenditure, in turn, can be broken down into five main subcategories: seen this way, nominal GDP is, in effect, the sum of private consumption, public consumption, investment (including changes in inventories) and exports *minus* imports. If the value of imports falls thanks to, for example, a China effect, nominal GDP goes up: a lower level of imports subtracts less from nominal GDP. The policy implications are, therefore, entirely different. Rather than cutting interest rates, as implied by inflation targeting, there should be a bias towards *raising* interest rates. Had this approach been used in the years running up to the financial crisis, central bankers would have left monetary conditions tighter and the risk of excessive leverage associated with a housing boom would have been much lower.

The second example relates to the post-crisis world. The value of economic activity is, in most countries, now dramatically lower than had been expected pre-crisis. This has left previously written contracts in a parlous state: governments cannot easily repay their creditors, banks are faced with the prospect of ever increasing non-performing loans, households don't know whether they can repay their mortgages and, all the while, trust ebbs away.

A commitment to raising the level of nominal GDP might well help to restore confidence, even if the increase resulted more from higher inflation than a higher volume of activity. The key point is to reduce the fear that contracts will not be honoured. As the fear recedes, and confidence is slowly restored, there's a much better chance of a pick-up in the volume of activity. But to do this requires commitment. It requires the central bank not to become overly exercised in the event that stimulus leads to higher inflation rather than firmer economic activity in the near term. Policy would have to remain loose long after nominal GDP was already on the rise. And the only way to do that in convincing fashion would be for the central bank's mandate to be changed: its job should be to stabilize the rate of growth of nominal activity, not to stabilize the inflation rate.

This simple reform would certainly help matters, but it is hardly an all-encompassing solution. It commits the central bank to supporting a rate of expansion of nominal activity – and thus helps preserve the sanctity of nominal contracts – but leaves the split between output and inflation unclear – and, unlike measures of inflation, nominal GDP estimates are subject to significant revision, one reason why the objective should be seen as a medium-term ambition, not an overly-engineered target. And while it's obvious that a trade-off involving high growth and low inflation is superior to one involving high inflation and low growth, it's less obvious how that happy outcome should be achieved.

That, ultimately, is a choice for society as a whole to make. Ageing populations should, in theory, reduce society's preference for inflation: rapidly rising prices, after all, are the best way to wipe out a lifetime's saving. No politician would push for such an outcome given the voting power of baby boomers. Better, then, to raise nominal GDP by raising the volume of output: in other words, for any increase in demand, there has to be a matching increase in supply. That, however, is more easily delivered through reforms encouraging hard work, innovation, technological advance and so on: it is not something that monetary policy can easily fix. That's up to the rest of us, not the job of the central bank. If we fail to deliver, the result will be higher inflation. Knowing this, the incentive to deliver surely goes up. What matters to society over the long run is not just price stability but also gains in productivity.

IMMOBILE CAPITAL, MOBILE LABOUR

The late twentieth-century version of globalization was made possible only thanks to an extraordinary reduction in financial borders. Whether it was China's vendor financing model – in which China lent cheaply to the US, allowing American companies to rein- vest successfully in the Chinese economy, leaving enough spare cash over to fuel higher levels of US consumer spending – or the spread of German companies into Eastern Europe and Latin America,[6] there was a remarkable change in the allocation of resources globally. Good quality Western capital fused with cheap emerging market labour, allowing the production of goods at lower prices, benefiting consumers all over the world.

The world is much richer thanks to this process. Both the developed and the emerging worlds have ended up significantly better off, although, relative to earlier trends, the emerging nations have proved to be by far the bigger beneficiaries: since 1980, incomes per capita have risen a remarkable fourteen-fold in China and fourfold in India.

Yet, as is now abundantly obvious, capital can also be massively misallocated: global imbalances have ended up distorting capital markets, triggering the US subprime crisis, the failure of British banks and the collapse of economies in southern Europe. The call for more regulation is understandable. The regulators themselves, however, are ill-placed to preserve the international nature of financial markets, answering only to their national or regional parliaments and not to those who might ultimately benefit from the free flow of finance.[7] The inevitable consequence will be a move to national regulation that will only impede cross-border flows: too many economic babies will be thrown out with the regulatory bathwater. Worse, given the deafening demand for more, as opposed to better, regulation, the obvious risk is the re-establishment of a – self-defeating – home bias in financial market activity.[8]

While the result might be greater financial market stability – which, given the innovative nature of financial markets and the remarkable ability of financial market practitioners to dodge regulatory bullets, is not necessarily guaranteed – the danger is also a much lower pace of growth. Faced with regulatory uncertainty, banks are already lending less than they once were, leading to calls for even more regulation for them to lend more, typically at home, regardless of the economic case for doing so. An increased home bias, however, will deny savers the returns that come with the opportunity to invest around the world. By lowering returns, however, many of the challenges facing Western societies – most obviously pension provision – will become even more challenging.

There is, however, a way to deflect the problem. If capital cannot go to where the labour is, let labour go to where the capital is. Think of London or New York, thriving, dynamic cities that owe their strength to their extraordinary cosmopolitan nature. Incomes per capita are high precisely because of their ability to draw on talents from all over the world. Manhattan offers Little Italy, Korea Town and Little Brazil. In recent years, London has become the home of choice for Poles, Hungarians and Czechs. Thanks to François Hollande's 75 per cent income tax rate, it is also becoming a magnet for the French. Without immigrants, after all, there would be no Pret A Manger,[9] no Starbucks and fewer brilliant academic researchers. Immigrants may sometimes be treated with suspicion but more often they have provided the lifeblood for new business opportunities. That means higher levels of GDP per capita, higher tax revenues and reduced pressure on budget deficits. More generally, it means a continued improvement in the allocation of scarce resources. In the absence of either labour or capital mobility, we will all end up poorer: if, then, capital mobility is to be reduced, it makes perfect sense actively to encourage the enhanced mobility of labour both within and between countries.

DEALING WITH THE BANKS

The West's economic problems began long before the onset of the financial crisis. A refusal to accept that our living standards might not increase as rapidly in the future as they had in the past led to many of the decisions that, in turn, made the financial crisis so much worse than it needed to be. Yet the idea that our problems considerably pre-date the crisis is not a widely held view: it is far more convenient to pretend that the whole disaster was the fault of a handful of bankers, a conspiracy of greed that led to the West's economic downfall. Admittedly, there are plenty of greedy bankers out there, but there are also plenty of policy-makers who took their eyes off the ball, who really thought – alongside the bankers – that the good times would roll. Nothing could go wrong, it seemed, because there could no longer be boom and bust.

We were claiming the economic equivalent of immortality. We had tamed the economic cycle, we had unearthed an economic system that promised ever greater riches, and we lived off those promises, believing – foolishly – that we had solved the world's economic problems. When things did go wrong, we were able to seize upon a lengthy cast of pantomime villains to blame. 'Sir' Fred Goodwin and Dick Fuld could always find employment as the Ugly Sisters if they so wished. Their reputations may deservedly be in tatters, but their villainous behaviour has allowed too many of the key issues to disappear under the radar: Goodwin and his ilk are not only villains but also, it seems, remarkably convenient scapegoats. That's worrying, because if we cannot understand the corrosive forces at work, we will never work out how to progress from our economic entropy.

The main lesson for policy-makers, surely, is the need to recognize that the world is an inherently uncertain place which does not respond well to simple macroeconomic rules that, eventually, only lead to distortion and disaster. Whether inflation targeting, deficit targeting, debt targeting or any other brand of 'commitment', these macroeconomic frameworks are only as good as the results they deliver. For the most part, the results have not been good: the frameworks encouraged far too much hubris before the inevitable nemesis. Policy-makers met their mandates yet still ended up in big trouble. In effect, the mandates were excessively simplistic, creating an illusion that economies were perfectly healthy when, in fact, they were not. There are many lessons to be learnt but perhaps the most important is the interaction between individual economies and their international environment: policy-makers like to believe they are in charge of a nation's destiny yet, in truth, there is often little they can do to anticipate and offset forces beyond their control. Any policy commitment must therefore have contingencies built in to allow room to deal with the tales of the unexpected that too often trip up even the most able of policy-makers.

Those who work in financial markets need to recognize that they, too, have to deal not just with risk but also with uncertainty. Their actions may not all be socially useless, but the effects of their actions cannot be known for months, years or even decades. Because of this, it is all too easy for financial investors to walk away with monetary benefits long before any subsequent costs emerge. Lessons need to be taken from the medical profession, where a code of ethics ultimately helps create a bond of trust between patient and professional. Other than the need for a higher level of training – how many pre-crisis bank CEOs really understood the complexities of derivative structures and how many non-executive directors knew enough about what banks were doing? – subsequent retroactive financial punishment may be needed for those found guilty of financial malfeasance, including bonus clawbacks, reduced pension entitlements and fines. And those who misbehave should also be struck off and, in severe cases, be sent to prison. Such an approach would, at the very least, instil greater confidence that financial quacks – as with medical quacks – would slowly be eliminated.

As for the banks themselves, are they too big to fail, too big to save or even too big to manage? Yes and no. The financial crisis ended up with bailouts of some big institutions, costing taxpayers a great deal of money. Other big institutions, however, survived the financial crisis, in the process saving taxpayers a sizeable chunk of money. HSBC's ill-advised acquisition of Household, a major US subprime lender, may not have worked out well for HSBC's shareholders but it certainly saved American taxpayers more than a few dollars.

Meanwhile some of the more spectacular failures – including Northern Rock in the UK and Lehman Brothers in the US – involved relatively small institutions that specialized either in retail or investment banking. Banking crises that threaten to bring economies to their knees can be associated with banks of all sizes and in all areas of financial endeavour: think, for example, of the 10,000 small institutions that failed during the Great Depression. Big isn't always bad.

In truth, banks are faced with a series of potentially inconsistent objectives: a decent return for their shareholders, some of whom are more interested in profit than in risk; the provision of credit on reasonable terms for their borrowers, a competitive interest rate and free banking services to their savers; and a commitment to broad financial stability for the regulators that monitor their operations.

Ahead of the financial crisis, there can be no doubt that banks were under huge pressure from shareholders to deliver higher returns: pension funds, after all, had to meet their future liabilities, which, thanks to population ageing, were getting ever bigger. And shareholders were mostly oblivious of the risks involved. Given banks' social commitments – most obviously the provision of free banking services such as ATMs (in the UK), telephone banking and internet banking – the only way to deliver such high returns was to pursue riskier ventures with higher profits that could then be used to 'subsidize' these social commitments. Riskier ventures, meanwhile, had the support of banks' legions of savers who, for the most part, hoped to earn decent returns safe in the 'knowledge' that bank failures were a thing of the past. After all, given that policy-makers had mastered the economic cycle, what could possibly go wrong?

Banks were thus faced with a series of inconsistent objectives and, in the attempt to meet them all, ended up creating a web of cross-subsidies that hid the true cost of banking services in some areas thanks to excessive risk-taking in other areas.

Untangling this labyrinth won't be easy. Nor will it be necessarily be popular. But it may be the only way to restore confidence in the financial system.

The first step is to prevent banks from pursuing short-run profit at the expense of long-run stability. So-called 'macroprudential rules' are the most obvious solution. Left to their own devices, banks are in danger of chasing ever more risky returns: the CEO who doesn't play ball is at risk of defenestration by his[10] shareholders. A central bank that prevents *all* commercial banks from engaging in an excessively risky venture acts as a 'circuit breaker', stopping the lemming-like behaviour that might otherwise end in tears. One way to do this would be to vary so-called capital adequacy ratios, raising them during the good times and lowering them during the bad times. The ratios could even be shifted on a bank-by-bank basis depending on the 'riskiness' of the activities each bank was engaged in.

The second step is to recognize that international banks cannot easily be regulated by national entities. In the eurozone, the obvious next step is a move towards a banking union, in effect making sure that both regulation and possible bailout of banks should be a cross-border affair. After all, the jurisdiction in which a bank is headquartered is often an accident of history, not a reflection of the willingness of the jurisdiction's taxpayers to offer bailout funds in the light of unanticipated difficulties. Nor does the jurisdiction say anything about the geographical dispersion of a bank's shareholders and bondholders. Globally, where politics dictates that banking union is near enough impossible, national branches of international banks should be treated as subsidiaries, not branches of a global entity: in that way, the potential liability of taxpayers within that nation would necessarily be reduced.

The third step is to stop the cross-subsidization of services. This is a particularly important issue in a world where banks cannot easily deliver profits by borrowing cheaply at short-term interest rates and lending at significantly higher long-term interest rates: quantitative easing has put paid to that particular money-making channel. Instead, banks might charge for basic services – use of ATMs, provision of checking accounts – rather than subsidizing those services via excessive risk-taking in esoteric, poorly understood and risky areas of financial activity. It wouldn't be popular but at least it would make the cost of banking services a lot more transparent: one way or another, ATMs have to be paid for.

SYSTEMIC REALITY: EDUCATION FOR ALL, EDUCATION FOR ECONOMISTS

Yet even with all these reforms, the risk of financial collapse will remain. Systemic financial failures are no different from systemic medical failures: those doctors who prescribed Thalidomide were presumably acting in good faith yet it didn't stop the thousands of terrible tragedies that subsequently followed. Systemic failures in any walk of life are precisely those that few individuals can really be held responsible for. To deal with these kinds of failures, prevention is a much better option than any eventual cure.

We're given plenty of education regarding our physical health (although, sadly, not so much regarding our mental health). The benefits of exercise are emphasized at a young age. Vaccinations are entirely routine. Lots of young people smoke but at least they're fully aware of the risks. Obesity is on the rise, admittedly, but at least people are increasingly aware of the need for a healthy diet, even if they are unable to act upon this advice.

In the financial world, however, there is no education whatsoever. It's a jungle out there and, in the jungle, the fat cats always seem to win. Levelling the playing field will hardly be easy but, at the very least, financial education should be stepped up. People should be able to understand what it means to save for a pension, and the risks that might be involved. They should understand how mortgages work, including the simple distinction between repayment and interest-only mortgages. They should know the fee structures charged by financial intermediaries and be able to shop around for the best deal. And they should have some idea of the safety of the financial institutions that are receiving their money: it wouldn't be difficult for regulators to provide 'health ratings' for banks based on, for example, their loan to deposit ratios or their level of capital (in the same way that all restaurants in New York have to provide a visible hygiene rating). People might then think twice before leaving their lifetime savings with an internet bank that just happened to offer a higher deposit rate than rival institutions. It would be wrong to tell people what to do but there is no reason why they cannot be nudged in the right direction.

As for the economics profession, the dismal science has become a dismal failure. It must do better. Its obsession with precision-engineered mathematical models – partly a consequence of the ability of computers to handle vast reams of often useless data – has made its conclusions both unintelligible to the average policy-maker and hopelessly unable to confront the uncertainties that prevail in the real world. Too many economists thought they had finally solved the world's economic problems. Convinced that their mathematical models contained the answer to life, the universe and everything, they happily disregarded the uncertainties of life, in particular the dangers of systemic collapse.

They also disregarded history. They chose not to recognize the myriad economic failures that have occurred through the ages, believing that those past failures had no relevance for the modern world. So engrained was this perspective that universities no longer bothered with the teaching of economic history: far better to ensure that budding economists could master the mathematics of vector autoregressions and dynamic stochastic general equilibrium models than know anything about the Gold Standard, the Great Depression or the ideas of the great political economists. The claim that economists could solve all problems with their mathematical models has been shown for what it really is: a pretence that, ultimately, has done huge damage.

At the very least, there needs to be a radical overhaul of university teaching, with a much greater emphasis on economic history. And that history should cover not just the obvious episodes – the Great Depression, the inflation of the 1970s – but also those many occasions during which nations tried to live beyond their means, pretending that it would all turn out all right on the night when, in reality, both economic and political disaster threatened. Only by studying these events can economists really claim to have anything useful to say about the challenges we face today and, doubtless, will face tomorrow.

ECONOMIC CHALLENGES FOR OUR GRANDCHILDREN

In 1930, Keynes published a short essay titled 'Economic Possibilities for our Grandchildren'.[11] Even as the world economy was heading into depression, Keynes was confident that, in decades to come, incomes would rise rapidly:

> It is common to hear people say how the epoch of enormous economic progress . . . is over; that the rapid improvement in the standard of life is now going to slow down . . .; that a decline in prosperity is more likely than an improvement . . .
>
> I believe that this is a wildly mistaken interpretation of what is happening to us. We are suffering . . . from the growing-pains of over-rapid changes, from the painfulness of readjustment between one economic period and another . . .

259

> Mankind is solving its economic problem. I would predict that
> the standard of life in progressive countries one hundred years
> hence will be between four and eight times as high as it is today . . .

His hunch was pretty good. Eighty years after he made his long-range forecast, per capita incomes are up four- or fivefold across much of the Western developed world. As Keynes rightly argued, compound arithmetic does wonders for living standards.

So why worry now? The most immediate cause for concern is simply that Western economies have slowed dramatically. At the beginning of the twenty-first century, the growth tap was turned off. Levels of economic activity are way lower than anticipated. Even before the financial crisis, Western economies were slowing. The crisis – both in terms of the depth of recession and pace of recovery – has only made things worse.

Yet we need rapid growth to meet the promises we've made to ourselves – so much so that we've never considered the possibility of persistent economic shortfall. We thought we could govern our futures. We became delusional. We convinced ourselves that capital markets could deliver ever rising prosperity. We thought we could borrow almost without limit, always confident that the future would be better than the past. Not for one moment did we think we would ever succumb to Japanese-style economic stagnation or Argentine-style broken promises. Instead, we basked in an 'optimism bias'.

Our beliefs, it turns out, were false. Rapid economic growth is not guaranteed. Indeed, the more we believed it was guaranteed, the less stable our economic foundations became. Those foundations are now crumbling, not so much through a failure of macroeconomic endeavour but, instead, through a grass-roots breakdown in trust.

Through our pensions, our health care, our high levels of debt, our (fast-waning) belief in financial alchemy and our refusal to accept that this is anything other than a cyclical economic setback, we are persistently trying to consume tomorrow's income today. In the 1930s, most people couldn't dip into the future: capital markets and social security systems weren't sufficiently developed to allow them to do so. Today, people dip into the future without a care in the world. Without persistent economic expansion, however, their aspirations will go unmet. An unseemly fight over the spoils will only make matters worse, threatening political upheaval or worse. Is this really the legacy we want to leave for future generations? I sincerely hope not. It is time to drop the pretence that we're simply living through a cyclical blip. Instead, we urgently need to tackle the structural problems that threaten all our economic futures.

NOTES

INTRODUCTION

1. Source: Office for National Statistics and HSBC estimates.
2. I have deliberately focused on per capita gains: overall increases in GDP can be distorted through demographic change, in the short term most obviously through waves of emigration and immigration. Too often, people fail to make the distinction between per capita and total gains.
3. In 1970, fewer than 45 per cent of women of working age in the UK were in paid work; by 2010, the number had risen to 57 per cent. Over the same period, the participation rate for men dropped from 87 per cent to 70 per cent. A. Benito and P. Bunn, 'Understanding Labour Force Participation in the United Kingdom', *Bank of England Quarterly Bulletin*, 2011 Q1, London.
4. C. Reinhart and K. Rogoff, *This Time Is Different: Eight Centuries of Financial Folly* (Princeton University Press, Princeton, 2009).
5. In the 1930s, those nations that left the Gold Standard were able to recover even as others came face to face with depression.
6. R. J. Gordon, 'Is US Economic Growth Over? Faltering Innovation Confronts the Six Headwinds', National Bureau of Economic Research (NBER) Working Paper No. 18315, Aug. 2012.
7. B. S. Bernanke, 'The Economic Recovery and Economic Policy', Speech at the New York Economic Club, New York, 20 Nov. 2012, at http://www.federalreserve.gov/newsevents/speech/bernanke20121120a.htm (accessed Jan. 2013).
8. See, for example, W. H. Gross, 'On the "Course" to a New Normal', Sept. 2009, at http://www.pimco.com/EN/Insights/Pages/Gross%20Sept%20On%20the%20Course%20to%20a%20New%20Normal.aspx (accessed Jan. 2013).

CHAPTER 1: TAKING PROGRESS FOR GRANTED

1. Source: A. Maddison; all data can be found at the historical statistics section at http://www.ggdc.net/maddison/oriindex.htm.
2. See, for example, A. M. Taylor, 'Three Phases of Argentine Economic Growth', Historical Paper No. 60, NBER Working Paper Series on Historical Factors in Long Run Growth, Oct. 1994.
3. See F. Campante and E. Glaeser, 'Yet Another Tale of Two Cities: Buenos Aires and Chicago', NBER Working Paper No. 15104, June 2009.
4. A privilege that ended when the UK joined the European Economic Community in 1973.
5. *Nixon in China* is an opera by John Adams, the American minimalist composer, but while it has enjoyed critical success, it hasn't kept the cash tills ringing in quite the way achieved by Messrs Rice and Lloyd Webber thanks to *Evita*.
6. F. Sturzenegger and J. Zettelmeyer, *Debt Defaults and Lessons from a Decade of Crises* (MIT Press, Cambridge, MA, 2006).
7. R. Barro and J. Ursúa, 'Stock-Market Crashes and Depressions', NBER Working Paper No. 14760, 2009.
8. Source: *The Economist*.
9. See, for example, A. Aherne, J. Gagnon, J. Haltmaier and S. Kamin, 'Preventing Deflation: Lessons from Japan's Experience in the 1990s', Federal Reserve International Finance Discussion Paper, Washington, DC, 2002.
10. B. S. Bernanke, 'Deflation: Making Sure "It" Doesn't Happen Here', Remarks before the National Economists Club, Washington, DC, 21 Nov. 2002.
11. See M. Fackler, 'Japan's Big-Works Stimulus Is Lesson', *New York Times*, 5 Feb. 2009, at http://www.nytimes.com/2009/02/06/world/asia/06japan.html?pagewanted=all (accessed Jan. 2013).
12. Max Weber, *The Protestant Work Ethic and the Spirit of Capitalism: The Revised 1920 Edition*, trans. and updated by Stephen Kalberg (Oxford University Press, Oxford, 2011).
13. Wolfgang Schäuble, the German Finance Minister in 2011, upset the Greek government when he said, 'We are very well aware of our responsibility for Greece and the Greek people. As I have always said, we can help, but we can't put [money] into a bottomless pit.'
14. David Landes, *The Wealth and Poverty of Nations* (Norton, New York, 1998). The six 'killer apps' are competition, science, democracy, medicine, consumerism and the work ethic. See Niall Ferguson, *Civilisation* (Allen Lane, London, 2011).
15. For a detailed discussion of this issue, see S. King, *Losing Control: The Emerging Threats to Western Prosperity* (Yale University Press, London, 2010).
16. See *Businessweek Online*, 31 Jan. 2000, at http://www.businessweek.com/2000/00_05/b3666002.htm (accessed Jan. 2013).
17. Source: Federal Deposit Insurance Incorporation. The complete list can be found at http://www.fdic.gov/bank/individual/failed/banklist.html (accessed Jan. 2013).
18. Source: S&P Case-Shiller index.

CHAPTER 2: THE PAIN OF STAGNATION

1. See R. Skidelsky and E. Skidelsky, *How Much Is Enough? The Love of Money, and the Case for the Good Life* (Allen Lane, London, 2012).
2. T. Malthus, *An Essay on the Principle of Population*, ed. G. Gilbert (Oxford University Press, Oxford, 1993).

3. *The Economics of Climate Change: The Stern Review* (Cambridge University Press, Cambridge, 2006).
4. A. Smith, *An Inquiry into the Nature and Causes of the Wealth of Nations*, Book 1, ch. 8: 'Of the Wages of Labour'.
5. D. Kahneman, J. L. Knetsch and R. H. Thaler, 'Experimental Tests of the Endowment Effect and the Coase Theorem', *Journal of Political Economy*, 98.6 (1990).
6. Source: Maddison; all data can be found at the historical statistics section at http://www.ggdc.net/maddison/oriindex.htm.
7. O. Wright and K. Rawlinson, 'Jobseekers "Slept Rough" Then Staffed Royal Pageant for Free', *Independent*, 6 June 2012, at http://www.independent.co.uk/news/uk/home-news/jobseekers-slept-rough-then-staffed-royal-pageant-for-free-7818043.html (accessed Jan. 2013).
8. W. Beveridge, *Social Insurance and Allied Services* (HMSO, London, 1942).
9. For the official word on available treatments, see, for example, 'NHS Services and Treatments', at http://www.nhs.uk/chq/Pages/category.aspx?CategoryID=68; Citizens Advice also offers information at http://www.adviceguide.org.uk/england/healthcare_e/healthcare_nhs_healthcare_e/what_health_care_can_i_get_on_the_nhs.htm (both accessed Jan. 2013).
10. 'Public Service Productivity: Health', UK Centre for the Measurement of Government Activity, Office for National Statistics, London, Feb. 2006.
11. See J. Browne and A. Hood, 'A Survey of the UK Benefit System', IFS Briefing Note BN113, Institute for Fiscal Studies, London, Nov. 2012.
12. For details on retirement age – actual and official – within the OECD, latest estimates can be found on the OECD website at http://www.oecd.org/document/47/0,3746,en_2649_33927_39371887_1_1_1_1,00.html (accessed Jan. 2013).
13. See *The 2012 Ageing Report: Economic and Budgetary Projections for the 27 EU Member States (2010–2060)* (European Commission, Brussels, 2012).
14. The survey was conducted by AFL-CIO, the American labour union, and reported in, for example, the *Wall Street Journal*. See http://online.wsj.com/article/SB10001424052702304458604577490842584787190.html (accessed Jan. 2013).
15. Source: OECD Economic Outlook 90 database.
16. S. Freud, *The Future of an Illusion*, trans. J. Underwood and S. Whiteside (Penguin, London, 2004).
17. Banks love dealing in euphemisms. A non-performing loan is, of course, a loan that is unlikely ever to be repaid. Non-performing loans became a huge problem for the Japanese banking system in the 1990s when the underlying rate of economic expansion dropped from over 4 per cent a year in real terms to only 1 per cent a year.
18. 'The 2012 Long-Term Budget Outlook', Congressional Budget Office, Washington, DC, June 2012.
19. Source: OECD, 2006.

CHAPTER 3: FIXING A BROKEN ECONOMY

1. See L. von Mises, *The Causes of the Economic Crisis and Other Essays before and after the Great Depression*, ed. Percy L. Greaves (Ludwig von Mises Institute, Alabama, 2006).
2. J. M. Keynes, *The General Theory of Employment, Interest and Money* (Macmillan, London, 1936).
3. A. C. Pigou, 'The Classical Stationary State', *Economic Journal* (Royal Economic Society, London), 53 (1943).
4. M. Kalecki, 'Professor Pigou on "The Classical Stationary State": A Comment', *Economic Journal*, 54 (1944).

5. M. Friedman and A. Schwartz, *A Monetary History of the United States: 1867–1960* (Princeton University Press, Princeton, 1960).
6. To be fair, this is an oversimplification: our expectations cannot affect the weather but, through confidence effects, they may have a sizeable economic impact, at least in the short term.
7. C. Bean, 'Some Current Issues in UK Monetary Policy', Speech to the Institute of Economic Affairs, Bank of England, London, July 2004.
8. J. Yellen, 'Housing Bubbles and Monetary Policy', Speech to the Fourth Haas Gala, Federal Reserve Bank of San Francisco, San Francisco, 21 Oct. 2005.
9. Frank's words have been widely reported. See, for example, M. Caruso-Cabrera, 'Barney Frank's Conflicting Words on Housing', CNBC, 21 May 2010, at http://www.cnbc.com/id/37276604/Barney_Frank_s_Conflicting_Words_on_Housing (accessed Jan. 2013).

CHAPTER 4: STIMULUS JUNKIES

1. See, for example, Bank for International Settlements, '82nd Annual Report, 1 April 2011–31 March 2012', particularly the box 'US monetary policy response and crisis dynamics: the Great Depression vs the global financial crisis' (p. 41).
2. Source: Abbott Laboratories.
3. 'Opening Remarks by the Governor', Inflation Report press conference, Bank of England, London, Nov. 2009.
4. 'Board of Governors of the Federal Reserve, Monetary Policy Report to the Congress', Washington, DC, July 2010.
5. 'Inflation Report', Bank of England, Aug. 2010.
6. C. Bean, 'Pension Funds and Quantitative Easing', Speech to the National Association of Pension Funds' Local Authority Conference, Bank of England, London, 23 May 2012.
7. Various other schemes have since been concocted to increase the supply of loans to small and medium-sized companies, most obviously the Bank of England's Funding for Lending scheme. See, for example, http://www.bankofengland.co.uk/markets/Pages/FLS/default.aspx (accessed Jan. 2013).
8. The decision in November 2012 to return the interest earned on the Bank of England's QE-related holdings of gilts to the Treasury to reduce its near-term borrowing is a case in point.
9. Source: Reserve Bank of Zimbabwe. The two decimal places are theirs, not mine.
10. Financial repression is hardly new. In the 1950s and 1960s, the US imposed 'regulation Q' on banks, preventing them from paying interest on deposits. This, in turn, significantly lowered the cost of government funding.
11. At the beginning of 2013, an ambiguous set of minutes from the Federal Open Markets Committee, suggesting to some investors that the Federal Reserve might end QE in 2013, led to a sudden large increase in Treasury yields.
12. See, for example, the November 2012 edition of the Bank of England's 'Inflation Report', esp. pp. 30–2.
13. See Bank for International Settlements, 'Group of Governors and Heads of Supervision Endorses Revised Liquidity Standard for Banks', press release, 6 Jan. 2013, at http://www.bis.org/press/p130106.htm (accessed Jan. 2013).
14. The Hong Kong Monetary Authority purchased equities during the 1997–8 Asian crisis, the Bank of Japan has, on occasion, underwritten the Tokyo stock market, and many emerging nations continue to 'manage' their currencies by accumulating foreign exchange reserves. In September 2012, the Federal Reserve announced it would be

purchasing $40 billion of mortgage-backed securities each and every month until and unless there was a meaningful decline in the US unemployment rate.

15. New Zealand kicked the process off at the end of the 1980s. In 2012, both the Federal Reserve and the Bank of Japan finally got around to adopting formal inflation targets, ironically after inflation targeting had failed to prevent the financial crisis.

16. See, for example, P. Krugman, 'It's Baaack! Japan's Slump and the Return of the Liquidity Trap', Brookings Papers on Economic Activity, Washington, DC, 1998, or G. Eggertsson and M. Woodford, 'The Zero Bound on Interest Rate and Optimal Monetary Policy', Brookings Papers on Economic Activity, Washington, DC, 2003.

17. See G. Eggertsson, 'The Deflation Bias and Committing to being Irresponsible', Journal of Money, Credit and Banking, 38 (2006).

18. Ipsos MORI, 'How Britain Voted in 2010', 21 May 2010, at http://www.ipsos-mori.com/researchpublications/researcharchive/poll.aspx?oItemId=2613 (accessed Jan. 2013).

19. J. M. Keynes, The General Theory of Employment, Interest and Money (Macmillan, London, 1935).

20. M. King, Speech given by Governor of the Bank of England at the Civic Centre, Newcastle, 25 Jan. 2011.

21. See my article 'Uneasy Is the Banker Who Wears the Crown', The Times, 27 Feb. 2012.

22. A. Darling, Back from the Brink (Atlantic Books, London, 2011).

23. R. Paul, 'Our Central Bankers Are Intellectually Bankrupt', Financial Times, 2 May 2012.

24. M. Draghi, Introductory statement to the press conference (with Q&A) following the Governing Council meeting of the European Central Bank, Barcelona, 3 May 2012.

25. Although Scottish independence might change all that.

26. See my article 'Rouble Poses Worrying Parallels for Euro Crisis', Financial Times, 9 Aug. 2011.

CHAPTER 5: THE LIMITS TO STIMULUS: LESSONS FROM HISTORY

1. J. M. Keynes, 'The Economy Bill' (Sept. 19, 1931)', in Essays in Persuasion (Norton, New York, 1963).

2. From The Times, 11 Sept. 1931.

3. See, for example, an article by Ed Balls, the Shadow Chancellor of the Exchequer, titled 'Don't Repeat the 30s Folly', Guardian, 18 July 2010, at http://www.guardian.co.uk/commentisfree/2010/jul/18/deficit-cuts-dont-repeat-30s-folly (accessed Jan. 2013).

4. See, for example, B. Eichengreen and O. Jeanne, 'Currency Crisis and Unemployment: Sterling in 1931', in P. Krugman (ed.), Currency Crises (University of Chicago Press, Chicago, 2000).

5. S. Broadberry and P. Howlett, 'The United Kingdom during World War I: Business as Usual?', 18 June 2003, at http://www2.warwick.ac.uk/fac/soc/economics/staff/academic/broadberry/wp/wwipap4.pdf (accessed Jan. 2013).

6. B. S. Bernanke and H. James, 'The Gold Standard, Deflation and Financial Crisis in the Great Depression: An International Comparison', in B. S. Bernanke, Essays on the Great Depression (Princeton University Press, Princeton, 2000).

7. This was a consequence of the Poincaré stabilization, in which France moved rapidly to stamp out post-World War I hyperinflation.

8. See J. M. Keynes, 'The Economic Consequences of Mr Churchill', in Essays in Persuasion (Norton, New York, 1963).

9. In Keynes's case, his dislike of aspects of high finance appears closely connected with his anti-Semitism. Following a meeting with Albert Einstein in 1926, Keynes noted that Einstein 'is – a naughty Jew-boy, covered with ink – that kind of Jew – the kind which

has its head above water, the sweet, tender imps who have not sublimated immortality into compound interest. He was the nicest, and the only talented, person I saw in all Berlin, except perhaps old Fuerstenberg, the banker ... and Kurt Singer, two foot by five, the mystical economist from Hamburg. And he was a Jew; and so was Fuerstenberg and so was Singer. And my dear Melchior is a Jew too. Yet if I lived there, I felt I might turn anti-Semite. For the poor Prussian is too slow and heavy on his legs for the other kind of Jews, the ones who are not imps but serving devils, with small horns, pitch forks and oily tails. It is not agreeable to see civilisation so under the ugly thumbs of its impure Jews who have all the money and the power and the brains.' J. M. Keynes, 'Einstein', in *The Collected Works of John Maynard Keynes*, vol. 28: *Social, Political and Literary Writings* (Macmillan, London, 1982).

10. See B. Macarthur (ed.), *The Penguin Book of Twentieth-Century Speeches* (Penguin, London, 1993).
11. Matthew 21:12.
12. F. D. Roosevelt, 'On the Bank Crisis', Radio address, PBS, 7 May 1933.
13. G. Eggertsson, 'Great Expectations and the End of the Depression', *American Economic Review*, 98.4 (Sept. 2008).
14. See Bernanke and James, *The Gold Standard, Deflation, and Financial Crisis*.
15. P. Krugman, *End This Depression Now!* (Norton, New York, 2012).
16. See J. Yellen, 'A Minsky Meltdown: Lessons for Central Bankers', Board of Governors of the Federal Reserve, Washington, DC, Apr. 2009. Named after Hyman Minsky, a Minsky moment is a situation where, in an over-indebted economy, people are forced to sell good assets to meet the obligations to their creditors, leading to a financial melt-down and a huge increase in the demand for cash.
17. J. M. Keynes, *How to Pay for the War: A Radical Plan for the Chancellor of the Exchequer* (Macmillan, London, 1940).
18. Real per capita GDP rose only 1.3 per cent per annum between 1929 and 1939.
19. Source: Consensus Forecasts, January editions since 2004, (containing forecasts made by a large number of forecasting organisations that are used to compute an average 'consensus' number) compared with inflation outcomes as reported by the US Bureau of Labor Statistics.
20. I took part in the House of Commons debate. Both the Krugman/Layard manifesto and a recording of the debate can be found at http://www.manifestoforeconomicsense.org/ (accessed Jan. 2013).
21. Krugman, *End This Depression Now!*.
22. Source: OECD Economic Outlook 2012.
23. P. Krugman, 'Dubya's Double Dip?', *New York Times*, 2 Aug. 2002, at http://www.nytimes.com/2002/08/02/opinion/dubya-s-double-dip.html (accessed Jan. 2013).

CHAPTER 6: LOSS OF TRUST, LOSS OF GROWTH

1. G. Akerlof, 'The Market for "Lemons": Quality Uncertainty and the Market Mechanism', *Quarterly Journal of Economics*, 84.3 (Aug. 1970): 488–500.
2. J. Wood and P. Berg, 'Rebuilding Trust in Banks', *Gallup Business Journal*, at http://businessjournal.gallup.com/content/148049/rebuilding-trust-banks.aspx#2 (accessed Jan. 2013).
3. B. Stevenson and J. Wolfers, 'Trust in Public Institutions over the Business Cycle', Federal Reserve Bank of San Francisco Working Paper Series 2011-11, San Francisco, Mar. 2011.
4. See Barclays, 'Our History', at http://www.barcap.com/about-barclays-capital/our-firm/our-history.html (accessed Jan. 2013).

5. See Barclays, 'Our Culture', at http://www.barcap.com/about-barclays-capital/our-firm/our-culture.html (accessed Jan. 2013).
6. See Richard Saville, 'Sober Set with Quaker Roots', *Times Higher Education*, 3 May 2002, at http://www.timeshighereducation.co.uk/story.asp?storycode=168809 (accessed Jan. 2013).
7. One of the emails published in the wake of the Libor-fixing scandal – in response to a Barclays employee who had fudged the numbers on behalf of a competitor – said 'Dude. I owe you big time! Come over one day after work and I'm opening a bottle of Bollinger'; see 'Eagle Fried', *The Economist*, 27 June 2012, at http://www.economist.com/blogs/schumpeter/2012/06/barclays%E2%80%99-libor-embarrassment (accessed Jan. 2013).
8. It's important not to get too nostalgic about the wonders of old-fashioned banking: see, for example, D. Lascelles, 'Banking's "Golden Age" is a Myth', *Financial Times*, 25 Oct. 2012, at http://www.ft.com/cms/s/0/e108d200-1c57-11e2-a63b-00144feabdc0.html#axzz2CHB2AXLw (accessed Jan. 2013).
9. For Robert Peston's scoop, see 'Northern Rock Gets Bank Bail Out', 13 Sept. 2007, at http://news.bbc.co.uk/1/hi/business/6994099.stm (accessed Jan. 2013).
10. K. J. Arrow, *The Limits of Organization*, Fels Lectures for 1970–1 (Norton, New York, 1974).
11. Ibid.
12. See National Trust at http://www.nationaltrust.org.uk/about-us/ (accessed Jan. 2013).
13. For details of the involvement of Goldman Sachs in currency swaps to hide the extent of Greek government borrowing, see E. Martinuzzi, 'Goldman Sachs, Greece Didn't Disclose Swap Contract (Update 1)', Bloomberg, 17 Feb. 2010, at http://www.bloomberg.com/apps/news?pid=newsarchive&sid=asBNXSLtlN9E (accessed Jan. 2013).
14. L. Saad, 'Americans Express Historic Negativity toward US Government', Gallup, 26 Sept. 2011, at http://www.gallup.com/poll/149678/americans-express-historic-negativity-toward-government.aspx (accessed Jan. 2013).
15. See J. M. Jones, 'Americans Say Federal Government Wastes over Half of Every Dollar', Gallup, 19 Sept. 2011, at http://www.gallup.com/poll/149543/Americans-Say-Federal-Gov-Wastes-Half-Every-Dollar.aspx (accessed Jan. 2013).
16. Edelman Trust Barometer 2012, Annual Global Study. The Executive Summary is available at http://trust.edelman.com/trust-download/executive-summary/ (accessed Jan. 2013).
17. The relevant clip can be seen at http://www.youtube.com/watch?v=HXibReHW3UA (accessed Jan. 2013).

CHAPTER 7: THREE SCHISMS

1. See, for examples, N. Davies, 'Spain Promises to Spare Needy from Eviction after Suicides', Reuters report, 12 Nov. 2012, at http://uk.reuters.com/article/2012/11/12/uk-spain-evictions-idUKBRE8AB0X620121112 (accessed Jan. 2013).
2. In this respect, he has something in common with the family of George Osborne, the Chancellor of the Exchequer.
3. S. Schama, *Citizens: A Chronicle of the French Revolution* (Knopf, New York, 1989).
4. Specifically, King James II was deposed, the risk of a Catholic monarchy was reduced, William and Mary took the throne and Parliament reigned supreme.
5. R. Wilkinson and K. Pickett, *The Spirit Level: Why Equality Is Better for Everyone* (Allen Lane, London, 2009).
6. See F. Roth, 'Trust and Economic Growth: Conflicting Results between Cross-Sectional and Panel Analysis', Program on the Future of the European Social Model, Göttingen, 2007.

7. 'Economy Rankings', Doing Business Project: Measuring Business Regulations, International Finance Corporation/World Bank, 2012, at http://www.doingbusiness.org/rankings/ (accessed Jan. 2013).
8. 'Trends in the Distribution of Household Income between 1979 and 2007', Congressional Budget Office, Washington, DC, Oct. 2011. Both 1979 and 2007 marked peak years in the economic cycle, enabling a like-for-like comparison to be made.
9. F. Alvaredo, A. Atkinson, T. Piketty and E. Saez, The World Top Incomes Database, at http://g-mond.parisschoolofeconomics.eu/topincomes/#Database (accessed Jan. 2013).
10. 'Country Comparison: Distribution of Family Income – Gini Index', in *CIA World Factbook* (Central Intelligence Agency, Washington, DC, 2012).
11. Sources: US Census Bureau and US Bureau of Economic Analysis.
12. Source: Camelot.
13. If there are complaints, they're typically about 'undeserving winners'. Edward Carroll, a convicted rapist, won almost £5 million on the Lottery in 2009.
14. 'BrandFinance®, Football 50: No trophies but Man United Is Still the Brand Champion', press release, 2012, at http://www.brandfinance.com/images/upload/football_50_2012_press_release.pdf (accessed Jan. 3013).
15. Source: *Sunday Times* Rich List 2011.
16. T. Philippon and A. Reshef, 'Wages and Human Capital in the US Financial Industry: 1909–2006', NBER Working Paper No. 14644, 2009.
17. Although the Glass-Steagall Act, which separated commercial bank activity from the activity of broking firms, was finally repealed in 1999, it had become mostly ineffective over the previous two or three decades, a victim of continuous financial innovation.
18. See 'The Widening Gap Update', The Pew Center on the States, Washington, DC, June 2012.
19. Audit Commission, 'Local Government Pensions in England: An Information Paper', July 2010.

CHAPTER 8: FROM ECONOMIC DISAPPOINTMENT TO POLITICAL INSTABILITY

1. K. Marx, *Capital: Critique of Political Economy*, 1867, Pelican edition 1976, p. 799.
2. In 1817, the sovereign was introduced, valued at 20 shillings: it contained 113 grains of gold.
3. D. Ricardo, 'Evidence on the Resumption of Cash Payments', Testimony before a Committee of Parliament, 1819, in *The Works and Correspondence of David Ricardo*, ed. P. Sraffa, vol. 5: *Speeches and Evidence* (Cambridge University Press, Cambridge, 1952).
4. Senator John H. Reagan, 1890.
5. James Laurence Laughlin, 1886.
6. 'US Business Cycle Expansions and Contractions', National Bureau of Economic Research, Cambridge, MA, 2012.
7. J. Bacon, *The Illustrated Atlas of Jewish Civilization* (André Deutsch, London, 1990).
8. See, for example, A. Liptak, 'Blocking Parts of Arizona Law, Justices Allow Its Centerpiece', *New York Times*, 25 June 2012, at http://www.nytimes.com/2012/06/26/us/supreme-court-rejects-part-of-arizona-immigration-law.html?pagewanted=all (accessed Jan. 2013).
9. See, for example, P. Krugman, 'The Myth of Asia's Miracle', *Foreign Affairs*, 73.6 (Nov.–Dec. 1994): 62.
10. Roger W. Ferguson Jr, 'The Asian Crisis: Lessons to be Learned and Relearned', Remarks before America's Community Bankers, Washington, DC, 4 Mar. 1998.

11. See S. Johnson and T. Mitton, 'Cronyism and Capital Controls: Evidence from Malaysia', NBER Working Paper 8521, Oct. 2001.

12. See E. Kaplan and D. Rodrik, 'Did the Malaysian Capital Controls Work?', John F. Kennedy School of Government, Harvard University, Feb. 2001.

13. For a useful discussion, see B. Eichengreen and D. Leblang, 'Capital Account Liberalization and Growth: Was Mr Mahathir Right?', *International Journal of Finance and Economics*, 8.3 (July 2003): 205–224.

14. Anwar was pro-austerity and, in Mahathir's mind, too closely associated with the IMF. Things got worse for Anwar in the years that followed: jailed for six years in 1999 for corruption, he was then sentenced in 2000 to another nine years in jail for sodomy. He was only cleared of the sodomy charge in 2004, one year after Mahathir had stepped down as Prime Minister.

15. Speech given at the opening of the Tenth Session of the Islamic Summit Conference, Putrajaya, Malaysia, 16 Oct. 2003

16. For much of its history – which effectively started with independence in 1948 – South Korea had been ruled by autocrats who, like Suharto, were not exactly keen on open political debate. Syngman Rhee, Korea's first President, had the leader of the opposition executed in 1952, supposedly on grounds of treason. Thereafter, he happily changed the constitution to maintain his grip on power and, in 1960, won a landslide victory in the presidential election, which, more than anything else, highlighted his ability to rig the outcome to suit his own interests. The protests that followed, however, showed this to be a catastrophic misjudgement on his part and he stepped down shortly after. Attempts thereafter to build democracy failed in the light of a military coup in 1961 led by Park Chung-hee, who, two years later, conveniently turned himself into Korea's next 'civilian' President. His assassination in 1979 saw the return of the military and it wasn't until 1987 and the formation of Korea's Sixth Republic that any real sense of democracy saw the light of day. By that stage, however, Korea was on the fast track to becoming a fully fledged member of the world's industrial elite. Having hosted the Olympics in 1988, it spent the next few years negotiating OECD membership, committing to the removal of capital controls as part of the process. It eventually joined the 'rich nations' club' in 1996, one year before the onset of the Asian crisis. In 1992, meanwhile, Kim Young-sam was elected President, Korea's first non-military leader in 30 years. By the time of the crisis, therefore, Koreans had no need for either revolution or finger-pointing. They'd had more than their fair share of upheavals in earlier decades and could now use the ballot box to remove leaders they were no longer enamoured with. Indeed, Kim Young-sam was voted out of office in 1997, replaced by Kim Dae-jung, even as the IMF was waiting in the wings to offer its own mixture of economic reform, financial assistance and budgetary cod liver oil.

17. The IMF is prone to such errors: it treated Greece in much the same way in 2010, arguing that austerity would have only a modest impact on the Greek economy. The economy then duly collapsed.

18. Source: OECD StatExtracts at http://stats.oecd.org/Index.aspx?datasetcode=SOCX_AGG (accessed Jan. 2013).

CHAPTER 9: DYSTOPIA

1. See F. Hayek, 'The Use of Knowledge in Society', *American Economic Review*, 35.4 (Sept. 1945).

2. Canute never claimed to be able to control the tides: he merely wanted to demonstrate that, as a mere king, he didn't have the powers of God.

3. To be fair, the period between the Congress of Vienna in 1815 and the outbreak of war in 1914 was relatively peaceful.
4. M. Campbell and P. Pangalos, ' "Get Stench out of Greece", Say Far-Right Golden Dawn Party', *Sunday Times*, 28 Oct. 2012, 'preview' at http://www.thesundaytimes.co.uk/sto/news/world_news/Europe/article1156453.ece (accessed Jan. 2013). It would be amusing if the policy were based only on the arguments used by Pureblood wizards in the *Harry Potter* franchise: sadly, it is not.
5. There was, of course, more to it than that: Hegel, the German philosopher, saw national identity as the glue holding society together, particularly given the decline of religion and the aristocracy. And it cut both ways: some groupings wanted to split apart, others – most obviously, individual German and Italian states – wanted to come together.

CHAPTER 10: AVOIDING DYSTOPIA

1. See, for example, 'MIP Scoreboard', at http://ec.europa.eu/economy_finance/economic_governance/macroeconomic_imbalance_procedure/mip_scoreboard/index_en.htm (accessed Jan. 2013).
2. J. K. Horsefield (ed.), *The International Monetary Fund 1945–1965: Twenty Years of International Monetary Cooperation*, vol. 3: *Documents* (International Monetary Fund, Washington, DC, 1969), at http://www.imsreform.org/reserve/pdf/keynesplan.pdf (accessed Jan. 2013).
3. See, for example, Helmut Reisen, 'Tobin Tax: Could It Work?', *OECD Observer*, 231–2 (May 2002), at http://www.oecdobserver.org/news/archivestory.php/aid/664/Tobin_tax:could_it_work__.html (accessed Jan. 2013).
4. Of course, if the offending country refused to play ball, the political ramifications would be enormous.
5. See C. Tiebout, 'A Pure Theory of Local Expenditures', *Journal of Political Economy*, 64.5 (1956): 416–24.
6. Daimler-Benz has operations all over the world.
7. I'm not thinking here of the financial middlemen who hope to receive large bonuses.
8. See A. Haldane, 'The Dog and the Frisbee', Bank of England, 31 Aug. 2012, for a fascinating discussion on the risks associated with excessive regulation.
9. The sandwich chain was created by two British men but it is heavily staffed by immigrant labour.
10. It is a matter of considerable regret that there are very few 'hers'.
11. See J. M. Keynes, *Essays in Persuasion* (Norton, New York, 1963).

BIBLIOGRAPHY

Abbott Laboratories. 'Vicodin (Hydrocodone Bitartrate and Acetaminophen, USP)', Chicago, Sept. 2011

Acemoglu, D. and Robinson, J. *Why Nations Fail: The Origins of Power, Prosperity and Poverty*, Crown, New York, 2012

Ahamad, L. *Lords of Finance*, Random House, New York, 2009

Aherne, A., Gagnon, J., Haltmaier, J. and Kamin, S. 'Preventing Deflation: Lessons from Japan's Experience in the 1990s', Federal Reserve International Finance Discussion Paper, Washington, DC, 2002

Akerlof, G. 'The Market for "Lemons": Quality Uncertainty and the Market Mechanism', *Quarterly Journal of Economics*, 84.3 (Aug. 1970): 488–500

'A Makeshift Budget', *The Times*, 28 Apr. 1931

'An Emergency Budget', *The Times*, 11 Sept. 1931

Arrow. K. J. *The Limits of Organization*, The Fels Lectures on Public Policy Analysis, Norton, New York, 1974

Bacon, J. *The Illustrated Atlas of Jewish Civilization*, André Deutsch, London, 1990

Balls, E. 'Don't Repeat the 30s Folly', *Guardian*, 18 July 2010

Bank for International Settlements. 'The Limits of Monetary Policy', in '82nd Annual Report, 1 April 2011–31 March 2012', Basel, 2012

Barro, R. and Ursúa, J. 'Stock-Market Crashes and Depressions', NBER Working Paper No. 14760, 2009

Bean, C. 'Pension Funds and Quantitative Easing', Speech to the National Association of Pension Funds' Local Authority Conference, Bank of England, London, 23 May 2012

Bean, C. 'Some Current Issues in UK Monetary Policy', Speech to the Institute of Economic Affairs, Bank of England, London, July 2004

Benito, A. and Bunn, P. 'Understanding Labour Force Participation in the United Kingdom', *Bank of England Quarterly Bulletin*, 2011 Q1, London

Bernanke, B. S. 'Deflation: Making Sure "It" Doesn't Happen Here', Remarks before the National Economists Club, Washington, DC, 21 Nov. 2002

Bernanke, B. S. 'The Economic Recovery and Economic Policy', Speech at the New York Economic Club, Board of Governors of the Federal Reserve, 20 Nov. 2012

Bernanke, B. S. *Essays on the Great Depression*, Princeton University Press, Princeton, 2000

Bernanke, N. and James, H. 'The Gold Standard, Deflation and Financial Crisis in the Great Depression: An International Comparison', in B. S. Bernanke, *Essays on the Great Depression*, Princeton University Press, Princeton, 2000

Beveridge, W. *Social Insurance and Allied Services*, HMSO, London, 1942

Blanchard, O. and Leigh, D. 'Growth Forecast Errors and Fiscal Multipliers', IMF Working Paper, Washington, DC, Jan. 2013

Board of Governors of the Federal Reserve. 'Monetary Policy Report to the Congress', Washington, DC, July 2010

Borio, C. 'The Financial Turmoil of 2007–?: A Preliminary Assessment and Some Policy Considerations', Bank for International Settlements Working Paper No. 251, Basel, Mar. 2008

Broadberry, S. and Howlett, P. 'The United Kingdom during World War 1: Business as Usual?', University of Warwick, June 2003

Brown, W. A. 'The World of Sterling and the World of Gold, September 1931 to April 1933', in W. A. Brown, *The International Gold Standard Reinterpreted, 1914–1934*, National Bureau of Economic Research, Cambridge, MA, 1940

Browne, J. and Hood, A. 'A Survey of the UK Benefit System', IFS Briefing Note BN13, Institute of Fiscal Studies, London, Nov. 2012

Bruner, R. F. and Carr, S. D. *The Panic of 1907: Lessons Learned from the Market's Perfect Storm*, Wiley, Hoboken, 2007

Campante, F. and Glaeser, E. 'Yet Another Tale of Two Cities: Buenos Aires and Chicago', NBER Working Paper No. 15104, June 2009

Campbell, C. *Scapegoat: A History of Blaming Other People*, Duckworth Overlook, London, 2011

Coggan, P. *Paper Promises: Money, Debt and the New World Order*, Allen Lane, London, 2011

Congressional Budget Office, 'Trends in the Distribution of Household Income between 1979 and 2007', US Congress, Washington, DC, Oct. 2011

Congressional Budget Office, 'The 2012 Long-Term Budget Outlook', US Congress, Washington, DC, June 2012

Coyle, D. *The Economics of Enough: How to Run the Economy as if the Future Matters*, Princeton University Press, Princeton, 2011

Coyle, D. (ed.). *What's the Use of Economics? Teaching the Dismal Science after the Crisis*, London Publishing Partnership, London, 2012

Cribb, J., Joyce, R. and Phillip, D. *Living Standards, Poverty and Inequality in the UK: 2012*, IFS Commentary C124, Institute for Fiscal Studies, London, June 2012

Darling, A. *Back from the Brink*, Atlantic Books, London, 2011

Davies, N. *Europe: A History*, Oxford University Press, Oxford, 1996

De Tocqueville, A. *The Ancien Régime and the Revolution*, trans. G. Bevan, Penguin, London, 2008

'Dialogue with Dr. Mahathir: Why Malaysia Needs Capital Controls', *Executive Intelligence Review*, 11 Sept. 2008

Dickens, C. *The Works of Charles Dickens*, Golgotha Press, London, 2010

Edelman. 'Executive Summary', Edelman Trust Barometer 2012, London, 2012

Eggertsson, G. B. 'The Deflation Bias and Committing to being Irresponsible', *Journal of Money, Credit and Banking*, 38 (2006)

Eggertsson, G. B. 'Great Expectations and the End of the Depression', *American Economic Review*, 98.4 (2008)

Bibliography

Eggertsson, G. B. and Woodford, M. 'The Zero Bound on Interest Rate and Optimal Monetary Policy', Brookings Papers on Economic Activity, Washington, DC, 2003

Eichengreen, B. 'The British Economy between the Wars', University of California, Berkeley, Apr. 2002

Eichengreen, B. and Jeanne, O. 'Currency Crisis and Unemployment: Sterling in 1931', in P. Krugman (ed.), *Currency Crises*, University of Chicago Press, Chicago, 2000

Eichengreen, B. and Leblang, D. 'Capital Account Liberalisation and Growth: Was Mr Mahathir Right?', *International Journal of Finance and Economics*, 8.3 (2003)

European Commission, *The 2012 Ageing Report: Economic and Budgetary Projections for the 27 EU Member States (2010–2060)*, European Union, Brussels, 2012

Fackler, M. 'Japan's Big-Works Stimulus Is Lesson', *New York Times*, 5 Feb. 2009

Ferguson, N. *The Ascent of Money: A Financial History of the World*, Allen Lane, London, 2008

Ferguson, N. *Civilisation*, Allen Lane, London, 2011

Ferguson, R. W. 'The Asian Crisis: Lessons to be Learned and Relearned', Remarks before America's Community Bankers, Washington, DC, 4 Mar. 1998

Financial Services Authority. 'Rates of Return for FSA Prescribed Projections, Report of PricewaterhouseCooper and Peer Reviewers' Comments', FSA, London, Apr. 2012

Freud, S. *The Future of an Illusion*, trans. J. Underwood and S. Whiteside, Penguin, London, 2004

Friedman, B. *The Moral Consequences of Economic Growth*, Knopf, New York, 2005

Friedman, M. 'The Crime of 1873', *Journal of Political Economy*, 98.6 (Dec. 1990)

Friedman, M. and Schwartz, A. *A Monetary History of the United States: 1867–1960*, Princeton University Press, Princeton, 1960

Fukuyama, F. *The Origins of Political Order*, Farrar, Strauss & Giroux, New York, 2011

Fukuyama, F. *Trust: The Social Virtues and the Creation of Prosperity*, Free Press, New York, 1996

Fukuyama, F. and Marwah, S. 'Dimensions of Development: Comparing East Asia and Latin America', *Journal of Democracy*, 11.4 (Oct. 2000)

Gordon, R. J. 'Is US Economic Growth Over? Faltering Innovation Confronts the Six Headwinds', NBER Working Paper No. 18315, Aug. 2012

Gross, W. 'On the "Course" to a New Normal', PIMCO Investment Outlook, Sept. 2009.

Haldane, A. 'The Dog and the Frisbee', Bank of England, London, 2012

Hayek, F. A. 'The Use of Knowledge in Society', *American Economic Review*, 35.4 (Sept. 1945)

Hibbert, C. *The French Revolution*, Allen Lane, London, 1980

Horsefield, J. K. (ed.). *The International Monetary Fund 1945–1965: Twenty Years of International Monetary Cooperation*, vol. 3: *Documents*, International Monetary Fund, Washington, DC, 1969

Johnson, S. and Mitton, T. 'Cronyism and Capital Controls: Evidence from Malaysia', NBER Working Paper No. 8521, Oct. 2001

Jones, J. 'Americans Say Federal Government Wastes Over Half of Every Dollar', Gallup, 19 Sept. 2011

Kahneman, D. *Thinking Fast and Slow*, Allen Lane, London, 2011

Kahneman, D., Knetsch, J. L. and Thaler, R. H. 'Experimental Tests of the Endowment Effect and the Coase Theorem', *Journal of Political Economy*, 98.6 (1990)

Kalecki, M. 'Professor Pigou on "The Classical Stationary State": A Comment', *Economic Journal* (Royal Economic Society), 54 (1944)

Kaplan, E. and Rodrik, D. 'Did the Malaysian Capital Controls Work?', John F. Kennedy School of Government, Harvard University, Cambridge, MA, Feb. 2001

Keynes, J. M. 'The Economic Consequences of Mr Churchill', in *Essays in Persuasion*, Norton, New York, 1963

Keynes, J. M. 'Economic Possibilities for Our Grandchildren', in *Essays in Persuasion*, Norton, New York, 1963

Keynes, J. M. 'The Economy Bill (Sept. 19, 1931)', in *Essays in Persuasion*, Norton, New York, 1963

Keynes, J. M. 'Einstein', in *The Collected Works of John Maynard Keynes*, vol. 28: *Social, Political and Literary Writings*, Macmillan, London, 1982

Keynes, J. M. *Essays in Persuasion*, Norton, New York, 1963

Keynes, J. M. *The General Theory of Employment, Interest and Money*, Macmillan, London, 1936

Keynes, J. M. *How to Pay for the War: A Radical Plan for the Chancellor of the Exchequer*, Macmillan, London, 1940

King, M. Opening Remarks by the Governor, Inflation Report press conference, Bank of England, London, Nov. 2009

King, M. Speech given by Governor of the Bank of England at the Civic Centre, Newcastle, 25 Jan. 2011

King, S. *Losing Control: The Emerging Threats to Western Prosperity*, Yale University Press, New Haven, 2010

King, S. 'Rouble Poses Worrying Parallels for Euro Crisis', *Financial Times*, 9 Aug. 2011

King, S. 'Uneasy Is the Banker Who Wears the Crown', *The Times*, 27 Feb. 2012

Krugman, P. *End this Depression Now!*, Norton, New York, 2012

Krugman, P. 'It's Baaack! Japan's Slump and the Return of the Liquidity Trap', Brookings Papers on Economic Activity, Washington, DC, 1998

Krugman, P. 'The Myth of Asia's Miracle', *Foreign Affairs*, 73.6 (Nov.–Dec. 1994)

Krugman, P. and Layard, R. 'A Manifesto for Economic Sense', 2012, at http://www.manifestoforeconomicsense.org/ (accessed Jan. 2013)

Leavans, D. H. *Silver Money*, Principia Press, Bloomington, 1939

Lascelles, D. 'Banking's 'Golden Age' Is a Myth', *Financial Times*, 25 Oct. 2012

MacArthur, B. (ed.). *The Penguin Book of Twentieth-Century Speeches*, Penguin, London, 1993

Malthus, T. *An Essay on the Principle of Population*, ed. G. Gilbert, Oxford University Press, Oxford, 1993

Marr, W. *Der sieg des Judenthums über das Germanenthum*, 8th edn, Bern, 1879

Marx, K. *Capital: Critique of Political Economy*, London, 1867, Pelican edition, 1976

McLynn, F. *The Road Not Taken: How Britain Narrowly Missed a Revolution*, Bodley Head, London, 2012

Milanovic, B. *The Haves and the Have-Nots: A Brief and Idiosyncratic History of Global Inequality*, Basic Books, New York, 2011

Minsky, H. P. *Stabilizing an Unstable Economy*, Yale University Press, New Haven, 1986

Morris, I. *Why the West Rules – For Now: The Patterns of History and What They Reveal about the Future*, Farrar, Straus & Giroux, New York, 2010

Morrone, A., Tontoranelli, N. and Ranuzzi, G. 'How Good Is Trust? Measuring Trust and Its Role for the Progress of Societies', OECD Statistics Working Papers, Paris, Mar. 2009

National Bureau of Economic Research. *US Business Cycle Expansions and Contractions*, Cambridge, MA, 2012

OECD. 'An Overview of Growing Income Inequalities in OECD Countries: Main Findings', in *Divided We Stand: Why Inequality Keeps Rising*, OECD, Paris, 2011

OECD, *Pensions Outlook 2012*, OECD, Paris, 2012

Office for National Statistics. 'Public Service Productivity: Health', UK Centre for the Measurement of Government Activity, London, Feb. 2006

Paul, R. 'Our Central Bankers Are Intellectually Bankrupt', *Financial Times*, 2 May 2012

Bibliography

Pew Center. 'The Widening Gap Update', Washington, DC, June 2012

Philippon, T. and Reshef, A. 'Wages and Human Capital in the US Financial Industry: 1909–2006', NBER Working Paper No. 14644, Jan. 2009

Pigou, A. C. 'The Classical Stationary State', *Economic Journal* (Royal Economic Society), 53 (1943)

Pomeranz, K. *The Great Divergence: China, Europe and the Making of the Modern World Economy*, Princeton University Press, Princeton, 2000

Reinhart, C. and Rogoff, K. *This Time Is Different: Eight Centuries of Financial Folly*, Princeton University Press, Princeton, 2009

Reinhart, C, M. and Sbrancia, M. B. 'The Liquidation of Government Debt', NBER Working Paper No. 16893, Mar. 2011

Ricardo, D. 'Evidence on the Resumption of Cash Payments', Testimony before a Committee of Parliament, 1819, in *The Works and Correspondence of David Ricardo*, ed. P. Sraffa, vol. 5, *Speeches and Evidence*, Cambridge University Press, Cambridge, 1952

Roosevelt, F. D. 'On the Bank Crisis', Radio address, PBS, 7 May 1933

Roth, F. 'The Effects of the Financial Crisis on Systemic Trust', CEPS Working Paper No. 316, Centre for European Policy Studies, Brussels, July 2009

Roth, F. 'Trust and Economic Growth: Conflicting Results between Cross-Sectional and Panel Analysis', Program on the Future of the European Social Model, Göttingen, June 2007

Roth, F. 'Who Can Be Trusted after the Financial Crisis?', CEPS Working Paper No. 322, Centre for European Policy Studies, Brussels, Nov. 2009

Saad, L. 'Americans Express Historic Negativity toward US Government', Gallup, Sept. 2011

Saville, R. 'Sober Set with Quaker Roots', *Times Higher Education*, 3 May 2002

Schama, S. *Citizens: A Chronicle of the French Revolution*, Knopf, New York, 1989

Skidelsky, R. and Skidelsky, E. *How Much Is Enough? The Love of Money, and the Case for the Good Life*, Allen Lane, London, 2012

Smith, A. *An Inquiry in the Nature and Causes of the Wealth of Nations*, Penguin, London, 1999

Snyder, T. (ed.). '120 Years of American Education: A Statistical Portrait', US Department of Education, Office of Educational Research and Improvement, Washington, DC, Jan. 1993

Stern, N. *The Economics of Climate Change: The Stern Review.* Cambridge University Press, Cambridge, 2006

Stevenson B. and Wolfers, J. 'Trust in Public Institutions over the Business Cycle', Federal Reserve Bank of San Francisco Working Paper Series, San Francisco, Mar. 2011

Sturzenegger, F. and Zettelmeyer, J. *Debt Defaults and Lessons from a Decade of Crises*, MIT Press, Cambridge, MA, 2006

Taylor, A. M. 'Three Phases of Argentine Economic Growth', Historical Paper No. 60, NBER Working Paper Series on Historical Factors in Long Run Growth, Oct. 1994

Tiebout, C. 'A Pure Theory of Local Expenditures', *Journal of Political Economy*, 64.5 (1956)

von Mises, L. *The Causes of the Economic Crisis and Other Essays before and after the Great Depression*, ed. P. L. Greaves, Ludwig von Mises Institute, Alabama, 2006

Wasserstein, B. *On the Eve: The Jews of Europe before the Second World War*, Profile Books, London, 2012

Weber, Max. *The Protestant Work Ethic and the Spirit of Capitalism: The Revised 1920 Edition*, trans. and updated by Stephen Kalberg, Oxford University Press, Oxford, 2011

Weinberg, D. H. 'US Neighbourhood Income Inequality in the 2005–2009 Period', American Community Survey Reports, United States Census Bureau, Washington, DC, Oct. 2011

Wilkinson, R. and Pickett, K. *The Spirit Level: Why Equality Is Better for Everyone*, Allen Lane, London, 2009

Wood, J. and Berg, P. 'Rebuilding Trust in Banks', *Gallup Business Journal*, at http://business-journal.gallup.com/content/148049/rebuilding-trust-banks.aspx#2 (accessed Jan. 2013)

Yellen, J. 'Housing Bubbles and Monetary Policy', Speech to the Fourth Haas Gala, Federal Reserve Bank of San Francisco, San Francisco, 21 Oct. 2005

Yellen, J. 'A Minsky Meltdown: Lessons for Central Bankers', Board of Governors of the Federal Reserve, Washington, DC, Apr. 2009

Zarnowitz, V. and Moore, G. 'Forecasting Recessions under the Gramm-Rudman-Hollings Law', NBER Working Paper No. 2066, Nov. 1986

INDEX

Index